C.B. MACPHERSON is Professor of Political Science at the University of Toronto.

The legitimate rôle of the state in relation to property and the justification of property institutions of various kinds are matters of increasing concern in the modern world. Political and social theorists, jurists, economists, and historians have taken positions for and against the property institutions upheld in their time by the state, and further debate seems inevitable. This book brings together ten classic statements which set out the main arguments that are now appealed to and places them in historical and critical perspective.

The extracts presented – all substantial – are from Locke, Rousseau, Bentham, Marx, Mill, Green, Veblen, Tawney, Morris Cohen, and Charles Reich. A note by the editor at the head of each extract highlights the argument in it and relates it to the time at which it was written. Professor Macpherson's introductory and concluding essays expose the roots of some common misconceptions of property, identify current changes in the concept of property, and predict future changes. Macpherson argues that a specific change in the concept (which now appears possible) is needed to rescue liberal democracy from its present impasse.

Property is both a valuable text on a crucial topic in political and social theory and a significant contribution to the continuing debate.

Property

Mainstream and Critical Positions

edited, with an introductory
and concluding essay, by

C.B. MACPHERSON

University of Toronto Press

TORONTO BUFFALO

UNIVERSITY OF TORONTO PRESS

Toronto Buffalo London
Printed in Canada
Reprinted 1981, 1983, 1987, 1989, 1992, 2008

Library of Congress Cataloging in Publication Data

Main entry under title:
Property, mainstream and critical positions.

1. Property – Addresses, essays, lectures.
I. Macpherson, Crawford Brough.
HB701.P753 330.1′7 78-2311
ISBN 0-8020-2305-3
ISBN 0-8020-6336-5 pbk.

Preface

No one will doubt that the institution and the concept of property are central to the current debates about capitalism, socialism, and such problems of 'post-industrial' society as the rights of the individual, the corporation, and the state, in relation to natural resource conservation and control of pollution and other side-effects of new technologies. Few will doubt that property is equally central to any analysis of the prospects of liberal democracy. That issue was first raised, in contemporary terms, in 1942, in Joseph Schumpeter's remarkable work, *Capitalism, Socialism and Democracy*. It has not, since then, had all the attention it deserves. I have attempted in this volume to provide a more extensive historical dimension, in the chapters and extracts here reproduced from some of the most important works relating property to politics from the seventeenth century to the twentieth; and to advance the contemporary analysis in an opening and a closing essay.

Department of Political Economy,
University of Toronto
January 1978

C.B. MACPHERSON

Contents

Preface
v

1 / The Meaning of Property
1

2 / JOHN LOCKE
Of Property
15

3 / JEAN-JACQUES ROUSSEAU
The Origin of Inequality
29

4 / JEREMY BENTHAM
Security and Equality of Property
39

5 / KARL MARX
Bourgeois Property and Capitalist Accumulation
59

6 / JOHN STUART MILL
Of Property
75

7/THOMAS HILL GREEN
The Right of the State In Regard to Property
101

8/THORSTEIN VEBLEN
The Natural Right of Investment
119

9/R. H. TAWNEY
Property and Creative Work
133

10 /MORRIS COHEN
Property and Sovereignty
153

11 /CHARLES A. REICH
The New Property
177

12/ Liberal-Democracy and Property
199

PROPERTY

1 / The Meaning of Property

1 / PROBLEMS OF CHANGE

The meaning of property is not constant. The actual institution, and the way people see it, and hence the meaning they give to the word, all change over time. We shall see that they are changing now. The changes are related to changes in the purposes which society or the dominant classes in society expect the institution of property to serve.

When these expectations change, property becomes a controversial subject: there is not only argument about what the institution of property ought to be, there is also dispute about what it is. For when people have different expectations they are apt to see the facts differently. The facts about a man-made institution which creates and maintains certain relations between people - and that is what property is - are never simple. Since the institution is man-made, it is assumed to have been made, and to be kept up, for some purpose: either (or both) to serve some supposed essentially human needs, which would determine (at least the limits of) what the institution is; or to meet the wants of the classes which from time to time have set up the institution or have reshaped it, that is, have made it what it is. In either case, those who see the purpose differently will see the thing differently.

How people see the thing - that is, what concept they have of it - is both effect and cause of what it is at any time. What they see must have some relation (though not necessarily an exact correspondence) to what is actually there; but changes in what is there are due partly to changes in the ideas people have of it. This is simply to say that property is both an institution and a concept and that over time the institution and the concept influence each other.

Before turning to some of the controversial works of leading modern writers it will be helpful to try to take a preliminary general view. Can anything of general validity be said about what property is? Not very much, for the reasons just stated. It is not easy to define a changing and purposeful concept like property. But something more can be said. If we address ourselves to certain difficulties which are peculiar to this concept we may see our way to some firm ground.

One obvious difficulty is that the current common usage of the word 'property' is at variance with the meaning which property has in all legal systems and in all serious treatments of the subject by philosophers, jurists, and political and social theorists. In current common usage, property is *things*; in law and in the writers, property is not things but *rights*, rights in or to things. We shall see that the current common usage is the product of some particular historical circumstances, and that it is already growing obsolete.

Another difficulty is that property, in the works of most modern writers, is usually treated as identical with *private* property, an *exclusive* individual right, my right to exclude you from some use or benefit of something. This usage, like the other, can be seen as the product of a particular set of historical circumstances.

I shall argue that both these usages are misusages. They are of unequal importance. The one is merely a popular misuse of the word: it does not necessarily carry with it a misunderstanding, although it may be taken as a sign of a limited understanding, of what property is. The other one is more serious. It is a genuine misconception, which affects the whole theoretical handling of the concept of property by many modern writers. Both usages can be traced historically to about the same period, the period of the rise of the full capitalist market society. These coincidences give us a clue as to how both usages arose. And when this is followed up we shall be able to see why each is now becoming, or is likely to become, obsolete.

Before investigating the sources of these usages we may state the *prima facie* case that each is a misusage. I shall show (in section 2) that property both in law and in logic means rights, not things; and (in section 3) that the concept of property cannot logically be confined to private property. Then (in section 4) I shall show how the current common misusage arose and why it is now becoming obsolete, and (in section 5) how the more serious misusage arose and why it is likely to become obsolete. Then (in section 6) I shall show why there is always a need for justificatory theories of property, and why they generally include both property in the consumable means of life and property in land and capital and labour.

2 / PROPERTY A RIGHT, NOT A THING

As soon as any society, by custom or convention or law, makes a distinction between property and mere physical possession it has in effect defined property as a right. And even primitive societies make this distinction. This holds both for land or flocks or the produce of the hunt which were held in common, and for such individual property as there was. In both cases, to have a property is to have a right in the sense of an enforceable claim to some use or benefit of something, whether it is a right to a share in some common resource or an individual right in some particular things. What distinguishes property from mere momentary possession is that property is a claim that will be enforced by society or the state, by custom or convention or law.

If there were not this distinction there would be no need for a concept of property: no other concept than mere occupancy or momentary physical possession would be needed. No doubt it is for this reason that philosophers, jurists, and political and social theorists have always treated property as a right, not a thing: a right in the sense of an enforceable claim to some use or benefit of something.

This is not to say that all of the theorists have approved of the set of rights existing in their society. In recognizing that property consists of actual rights (enforceable claims) they do not necessarily endorse the existing rights as morally right. They have, on the contrary, often argued that the existing set of rights (enforceable claims) is not morally right, and that a different set of rights should be installed. In doing so, they are simply arguing that a different set of claims ought to be made enforceable: they are not questioning that property consists of enforceable claims.

Moreover, in saying that serious theorists have always held property to be a right in the sense of an enforceable claim, I do not mean to imply that they have thought, or that anyone now does think, that the right rests on nothing more than the threat of force. On the contrary, the threat of force is invoked only as an instrument that is thought to be necessary to guarantee a right that is held to be basic. The perennial justification of any institution of property is that property ought to be an enforceable claim because property is necessary for the realization of man's fundamental nature, or because it is a natural right. Property is not thought to be a right because it is an enforceable claim: it is an enforceable claim only because and in so far as the prevailing ethical theory holds that it is a necessary human right.

With these qualifications then – that to see property as a right does not imply approving of any particular system of property as morally right, and that to define the actual right as an enforceable claim does not imply that force justifies the right – we may re-assert our original point: the concept of property is, historically and logically, a concept of rights in the sense of enforceable claims. For reasons we shall see (in section 4), popular usage has departed from this concept in the last few centuries; we shall also see that this departure appears to be temporary.

We may notice here one logical implication of the definition of property as an enforceable claim: namely, that property is a political relation between persons. That property is *political* is evident. The idea of an enforceable claim implies that there be some body to enforce it. The only body that is extensive enough to enforce it is a whole organized society itself or its specialized organization, the state; and in modern (i.e., post-feudal) societies the enforcing body has always been the state, *the* political institution of the modern age. So property is a political phenomenon. That property is a political *relation* between persons is equally evident. For any given system of property is a system of rights of each person in relation to other persons. This is clearest in the case of modern private property, which is my right to exclude you from something, but it is equally true of any form of common property, which is the right of each individual not to be excluded from something.

3 / COMMON PROPERTY, PRIVATE PROPERTY, STATE PROPERTY

The definition of property as an enforceable claim *of a person* to some use or benefit of something is often taken to rule out the idea of *common* property. But a little analysis will show that it does not.

Society or the state may declare that some things – for example, common lands, public parks, city streets, highways – are for common use. The right to use them is then a property of individuals, in that each member of the society has an enforceable claim to use them. It need not be an unlimited claim. The state may, for instance, have to ration the use of public lands, or it may limit the kinds of uses anyone may make of the streets or of common waters (just as it now limits the uses anyone may make of his private property), but the right to use the common things, however limited, is a right of individuals.

This point needs some emphasis, for it can easily be lost sight of. The fact that we need some such term as 'common property,' to distinguish such rights from the exclusive individual rights which are private property, may easily lead to our thinking that such common rights are not individual rights. But they are. They are the property of individuals, not of the state. The state indeed creates and enforces the right which each individual has in the things the state declares to be for common use. But so does the state create and enforce the exclusive rights which are private property. In neither case does the fact that the state creates the right make the right the property of the state. In both cases what is created is a right of individuals. The state *creates* the rights, the individuals *have* the rights. Common property is created by the guarantee to each individual that he will not be excluded from the use or benefit of something; private property is created by the guarantee that an individual can exclude others from the use or benefit of something. Both kinds of property, being guarantees to individual persons, are individual rights.

In the case of private property the right may, of course, be held by an artificial person, that is, by a corporation or an unincorporated grouping created or recognized by the state as having the same (or similar) property rights as a natural individual. The property which such a group has is the right to the use and benefit, and the right to exclude non-members from the use and benefit, of the things to which the group has a legal title. Corporate property is thus an extension of individual private property.

Both the kinds of property we have noticed so far are thus, directly or by extension, individual rights. Both are rights of distinct natural or artificial persons. We have now to notice that there is another kind of property which appears not to be an individual right at all. This may be called 'state property': it consists of rights which the state has not only created but has kept for itself or has taken over from private individuals or corporations. The right to use the airwaves for radio and television communication, for instance, may be retained wholly or partially by the state, as it is in countries with publicly owned and operated broadcasting systems. Again, various enterprises, e.g., railways and airlines, are in many countries owned by the state. The rights which the state holds and exercises in respect of these things, the rights which comprise the state's property in these things, are akin to private property rights, for they consist of the right to the use and benefit, and the right to exclude others from the use and benefit, of something. In effect, the state itself is taking and exercising the powers of a corporation: it is acting as an artificial person.

Now state property, as just described, does not give the individual citizen a direct right to use, nor a right not to be excluded from, the assets held by the state acting as a corporation. Air France and British Railways are not freely available to all the citizens of those countries; a state-owned railway is apt to be as jealous of its property as is a privately owned one. State property, then, is not common property as we have defined it: state property is not an individual right not to be excluded. It is a corporate right to exclude. As a corporate right to exclude others it fits the definition of (corporate) private property.

It may seem paradoxical to call it a kind of private property, for by definition it is the property of the whole state. The paradox disappears when we notice that the state, in any modern society, is not the whole body of citizens but a smaller body of persons who have been authorized (whether by the whole body of citizens or not) to command the citizens. Although Idealist philosophers, in order to emphasize their belief that every state ought to be (or that the good or true state is) a community of all the citizens, may define the state as a community of all, political realists have always seen that the state is in fact the persons who are acknowledged by the citizens to have the right to command them. This was more obviously true of the state before the rise of democracy – Louis XIV could say, not unrealistically, 'l'état, c'est moi' – but it is just as true of democratic states: the body of persons that is authorized by the citizens in a democracy is not the whole body of citizens. It acts in their name, but it is not they. And *it* is the body that holds the rights called state property. When the state is seen in this way, it becomes perfectly intelligible that the state can have a corporate right to exclude others, including citizens, from the use or benefit of something, in just the same way as it permits a private owner to do.

State property, then, is to be classed as corporate property, which is exclusive property, and not as common property, which is non-exclusive property. State property is an exclusive right of an artificial person.

Two points emerge from this analysis of the three kinds of property. One is that all three kinds – common, private, and state property – are rights of persons, either natural individuals or artificial persons. The other is that common property, rather than being ruled out by the very concept of property as rights (enforceable claims) of persons, turns out to be the most unadulterated kind of property. For common property is always a right of the natural individual person, whereas the other two kinds of property are not always so: private property may be a right of either a natural or an artificial person, and state property is always a right of an artificial person.

In the light of this analysis it is apparent that the concept of property as enforceable claims of persons to some use or benefit of something cannot logically be confined to exclusive private property.

Having now seen, in this and the preceding section, that property is rights, not things, and that property cannot logically be confined to private property, we are ready to enquire how these two misconceptions arose, and how transient they are likely to be.

4 / THE MISCONCEPTION OF PROPERTY AS THINGS

In current ordinary language, property generally means things. We commonly refer to a house, a plot of land, a shop, as a property. We advertise 'Properties for Sale' and 'Properties to Let.' What the advertisement describes as being for sale or for rent is the building and the land it stands on. But in fact what is offered, and what constitutes the property, is the legal title, the enforceable exclusive right, to or in the tangible thing. This is more obvious in the case of a lease, where the right is to the use of the thing for a limited period and on certain conditions, than in the case of an outright sale, but in both cases what is transferred is an enforceable exclusive right.

Yet we still speak of property as the thing itself. How did this current usage begin, and how long is it likely to last? It began late in the seventeenth century, and it is not likely to outlast the twentieth.

In ordinary English usage, at least through the seventeenth century, it was well understood that property was a right in something. Indeed, in the seventeenth century, the word property was often used, as a matter of course, in a sense that seems to us extraordinarily wide: men were said to have a property not only in land and goods and in claims on revenue from leases, mortgages, patents, monopolies, and so on, but also a property in their lives and liberties. It would take us too far afield to try to trace the source of that very wide use of the term, but clearly that wide sense is only intelligible while property *per se* is taken to be a right not a thing.

And there were good reasons then for treating property as the right not the thing. In the first place, the great bulk of property was then property in land, and a man's property in a piece of land was generally limited to certain uses of it and was often not freely disposable. Different people might have different rights in the same piece of land, and by law or manorial custom many of those rights were not fully disposable by the current owner of them either by sale or bequest. The property he had was obviously some right in the land, not the land itself. And in the second place, another substantial segment of property consisted of those rights to a revenue which were provided by such things as corporate charters, monopolies granted by the state, tax-farming rights, and the incumbency of various political and ecclesiastical offices. Clearly here too the property was the right, not any specific material thing.

The change in common usage, to treating property as the things themselves, came with the spread of the full capitalist market economy from the seventeenth century on, and the replacement of the old limited rights in land and other valuable things by virtually unlimited rights. As rights in land became more absolute, and parcels of land became more freely marketable commodities, it became natural to think of the land itself as the property. And as aggregations of commercial and industrial capital, operating in increasingly free markets and themselves freely marketable, overtook in bulk the older kinds of moveable wealth based on charters and monopolies, the capital itself, whether in money or in the form of actual plant, could easily be thought of as the property. The more freely and pervasively the market operated, the more this was so. It appeared to be the things themselves, not just rights in them, that were exchanged in the market. In fact the difference was not that things rather than rights in things were exchanged, but that previously unsaleable rights in things were now saleable; or, to put it differently, that limited and not always saleable rights *in* things were being replaced by virtually unlimited and saleable rights *to* things.

As property became increasingly saleable absolute rights to things, the distinction between the right and the thing was easily blurred. It was the more easily blurred because, with these changes, the state became more and more an engine for guaranteeing the full right of the individual to the disposal as well as use of things. The state's protection of the right could be so much taken for granted that one did not have to look behind the thing to the right. The thing itself became, in common parlance, the property.

This usage, as we have seen, is still with us today. But meanwhile, from about the beginning of the twentieth century the preponderant nature of property has been changing again, and property is again beginning to be seen as a right to something: now, more often than not, a right to a revenue rather than a right to a specific material thing.

The twentieth century change is twofold. First, the rise of the corporation as the dominant form of business enterprise has meant that the dominant form of property is the expectation of revenue. The market value of a modern corporation consists not of its plant and stocks of materials but of its presumed ability to produce a revenue for itself and its shareholders by its organization of skills and its manipulation of the market. Its value as a property is its ability to produce a revenue. The property its shareholders have is the right to a revenue from that ability.

Secondly, even in the countries most devoted to the idea of free enterprise and the free market, a sharply increasing proportion of the individual's and the corporation's rights to any revenue at all depends on their relation to the government. When the right to practise a trade or profession depends on state-authorized licensing bodies and on judicial interpretations of their powers; when the right to engage in various kinds of enterprise depends on legislative enactments and administrative and judicial rulings; when the right to a pension or social security payments and the like depends on similar rulings; and when the earnings of a corporation depend more on what it can get, both by way of government contracts and by way of legislation favourable to its own line and scale of business, than on the free play of the market: then the old idea of property as things becomes increasingly unrealistic.

Property for the most part becomes, and is increasingly seen to become, a right – a somewhat uncertain right that has constantly to be re-asserted. It is the right to an income.

We may conclude, from this sketch of the changing content of private property, that the notion of property as things is on its way out and that it is being superseded by the notion of property as a right to an income. But this will still leave the more basic misconception, that property means exclusive private property: all the examples of new kinds of property we have noticed are examples of private property; in all of them, property is seen as the right of an individual or a corporation to an income for his or its exclusive benefit.

5 / THE MISCONCEPTION OF PROPERTY AS PRIVATE PROPERTY

This misconception may, as we have just seen, be left intact with the disappearance of the more superficial misconception that property is things. But it too may be on its way out, for pressures on it are developing. It will probably take longer to disappear: not because, as one might think at first glance, it has a longer history, but because it is more needed by a market society.

Although concern about private (i.e., exclusive) property goes back to the earliest theory, the identification of property with private property does not go back much farther than the seventeenth century. It is true that from the beginning – and argument about property is as old as political theory itself – the argument was mainly about private property. This is not surprising, since it is only the existence of private property that makes property a contentious moral issue. In any case, the earliest extant theorizing about property was done in societies which did have private property. But those societies were also familiar with common property. So, while the argument was mainly about private property, the theorists did not equate it with property. Aristotle could talk about two systems of property, one where all things were held in common and one where all things were held privately, and about mixed systems where land was common but produce was private and where produce was common but land was private: all these he saw as systems of property.

From then on, whether the debate was about the relative merits of private versus common property, or about how private property could be justified or what limits should be put on it, it was private property that bulked largest in the debate. It was attacked by Plato as incompatible with the good life for the ruling class; defended by Aristotle as essential for the full use of human faculties and as making for a more efficient use of resources; denigrated by earliest Christianity; defended by St Augustine as a punishment and partial remedy for original sin; attacked by some heretical movements in mediaeval (and Reformation) Europe; justified by St Thomas Aquinas as in accordance with natural law, and by later mediaeval and Reformation writers by the doctrine of stewardship. In all that early controversy, stretching down through the sixteenth century, what was chiefly in question was an exclusive, though a limited or conditional, individual right in land and goods.

But in that early period the theorists, and the law, were not unacquainted with the idea of common property. Common property was, by one writer or another, advocated as an ideal, attributed to the primitive condition of mankind, held to be suitable only to man before the Fall, and recognized as existing alongside private property in such forms as public parks, temples, markets, streets, and common lands. Indeed, Jean Bodin, the first of the great early modern political theorists, in making a strong case at the end of the sixteenth century for modern private property, argued that in any state there must also be some common property, without which there could be no sense of community and hence no viable state; part of his case for private property was that without it there could be no appreciation of common property.

It is only when we enter the modern world of the full capitalist market society, in the seventeenth century, that the idea of common property drops virtually out of sight. From then on, 'common property' has come to seem a contradiction in terms.

That it has done so can be seen as a reflection of the changing facts. From the sixteenth and seventeenth centuries on, more and more of the land and resources in settled countries was becoming private property, and private property was becoming an individual right unlimited in amount, unconditional on the performance of social functions, and freely transferable, as it substantially remains to the present day.

Modern private property is indeed subject to certain limits on the uses to which one can put it: the law commonly forbids using one's land or buildings to create a nuisance, using any of one's goods to endanger lives, and so on. But the modern right, in comparison with the feudal right which preceded it, may be called an absolute right in two senses: it is a right to dispose of, or alienate, as well as to use; and it is a right which is not conditional on the owner's performance of any social function.

This of course was exactly the kind of property right needed to let the capitalist market economy operate. If the market was to operate fully and freely, if it was to do the whole job of allocating labour and resources among possible uses, then all labour and resources had to become, or be convertible into, this kind of property. As the capitalist market economy found its feet and grew, it was expected to, and did, take on most of this work of allocation. As it did so, it was natural that the very concept of property should be reduced to that of *private* property – an exclusive, alienable, 'absolute' individual or corporate right in things.

Now, however, the facts are changing again. Even in the most capitalist countries, the market is no longer expected to do the whole work of allocation. The society as a whole, or the most influential sections of it, operating through the instrumentality of the welfare state and the warfare state – in any case, the regulatory state – is doing more and more of the work of allocation. Property as exclusive, alienable, 'absolute' individual or corporate rights in things therefore becomes less necessary.

This does not mean that this kind of property is any less desired by the corporations and individuals who still have it in any quantity. But it does mean that as this kind of property becomes less demonstrably necessary to the work of allocation, it becomes harder to defend this kind as the very essence of property. Again, no one would suggest that the removal or reduction of the necessity of this kind of property would by itself result in the disappearance or weakening of this as the very image of property: positive social pressures would also be required.

Positive social pressures against this image of property are now developing, as a fairly direct result of the unpleasant straits to which the operation of the market has brought the most advanced societies. The most striking of these pressures comes from the growing public consciousness of the menaces of air and water pollution. Air and water, which hitherto had scarcely been regarded as property at all, are now being thought of as common property – a right to clean air and water is coming to be regarded as a property from which nobody should be excluded.

So the identification of property with exclusive private property, which we have seen has no standing in logic, is coming to have less standing in fact. It is no longer as much needed, and no longer as welcomed, as it was in the earlier days of the capitalist market society. I return to this point in the final essay of this volume.

6 / THE NEED FOR JUSTIFICATORY THEORIES

We may conclude this part of our analysis by emphasizing a point that was implicit in what was said at the very beginning about property being a controversial subject. Property is controversial, I have said, because it subserves some more general purposes of a whole society, or the dominant classes of a society, and these purposes change over time: as they change, controversy springs up about what the institution of property is doing and what it ought to be doing.

The most general point is that the institution – any institution – of property is always thought to need justification by some more basic human or social purpose. The reason for this is implicit in two facts we have already seen about the nature of property: first, that property is a right in the sense of an enforceable claim; second, that while its enforceability is what makes it a *legal* right, the enforceability itself depends on a society's belief that it is a *moral* right. Property is not thought to be a right because it is an enforceable claim: it is an enforceable claim because it is thought to be a human right. This is simply another way of saying that any institution of property requires a justifying theory. The legal right must be grounded in a public belief that it is morally right. Property has always to be justified by something more basic; if it is not so justified, it does not for long remain an enforceable claim. If it is not justified, it does not remain property.

We shall see, in the extracts presented in this volume, a variety of such justifications. But attention may be drawn here to a general characteristic of the justifications: they are apt to shift from one level of property, that is, property in the consumable means of life, to another level, namely, property in the means of producing the means of life.

The ultimate justification of any institution of property, of any variety of the property right, has always been the individual right to life - not merely to continued existence once born, but to a fully human life: a 'good' life, as idealist philosophers from Plato to T.H. Green would have it, or at least what materialist philosophers like Hobbes could summarize as 'commodious living.' This means, obviously, a right to a flow of the consumable things needed to maintain such a life. But serious thinkers soon saw that rights in what was needed to *produce* the means of life were even more important.

No doubt, the right to things needed to maintain life is in one sense the most basic: without a property in one's daily bread no other kind of property would be of any use. Yet the other kinds - the property in land and capital especially - are more important in another way: they carry with them, when they are held in quantities larger than an individual can work by himself, a power to control in some measure the lives of others. So property in land and capital stands in rather more need of justification than does simple property in the consumable means of life. And property in labour itself (labour being, in addition to land and capital, the other means of producing the means of life) is, as we shall see, deeply involved in the justification of any of the other kinds of property. For these reasons, theories of property, though they may start from a justification of property in things for consumption, have concerned themselves mainly with justifying (or attacking) property in land and capital and labour.

Some of the theorists slid from one justification to the other, without apparently recognizing how different the two needed to be. Locke was the prime offender in this respect, as will be apparent to the careful reader of his chapter 'Of Property.' His influence was so considerable that the illogic of his position had still to be pointed out, in the twentieth century, by Morris Cohen (in our chapter 10) though earlier writers, from Rousseau on, had made the point that property is power and so is at the heart of the political question.

The extracts which follow have been chosen to display the main justifications and some of the leading critiques of the modern institution of property. They illustrate also the point made at the beginning of this introductory essay, that justification (or criticism) goes hand in hand with definition. To formulate, or merely to accept, a particular concept of property is to justify or criticize a given institution of property. The extracts illustrate, too, that property is always a political phenomenon. Whether or not we go as far as Locke and Rousseau (and many others, for instance Hume) in saying that property is what makes political society necessary, we may grant that the protection and regulation of some variety of property is central to the purposes of every modern state. A system of property rights is an instrument by which a society seeks to realize the purposes of its members, or some of the purposes of some of its members. But any system of property is apt to change by its own momentum, bringing about effects other than were intended. As it does so, it needs to be re-defined if its intended purposes are to be served. Attempts at such re-definition can be seen in several of our extracts. The last two extracts are especially relevant to the problem of late twentieth-century liberal democracy, arguing as they do from two different points of view that the survival of the most important values of liberal-democratic society now requires a re-definition of the concept of property.

Our extracts are mostly from nineteenth and twentieth century writers, but we begin with two earlier though recognizably modern ones. The first extract is from John Locke, because he, at the end of the seventeenth century, set out for the first time the case for an individual right of unlimited appropriation. His case remained the standby of those who shaped the thinking of the ruling class in England, from the Whig Revolution for a century or more, and of those who made and consolidated the French and American Revolutions in the eighteenth century. His justification of property was thus in effect written into, or at least was implied in, the constitutions of the first great modern capitalist nation-states.

Our other pre-nineteenth century theorist is Rousseau, who launched the first far-reaching critique of property in the means of others' labour, and explored its ramifying effects on man and society. Rousseau's influence is by no means spent today. The reappearance of his ideas in the justifying theories of some of the newly independent underdeveloped countries of Africa is very noticeable, and not least important in this revival is his idea of the relation between property and the state.

The importance of the later theorists whose work is reproduced in this volume is generally self-evident. They deepened the original analyses, introduced new justifications and critiques as called for by changes in the intellectual climate and in the institution of property itself, and in doing so contributed to further changes in the intellectual climate. The nearer they are to our own day the more obvious their relevance to our own problems.

2 / JOHN LOCKE

Locke was the first to make a case for property *of unlimited amount* as a *natural* right of the individual, prior to governments and overriding them. Many others had made a general case for limited government: Locke's great innovation was to justify it as necessary to protect unlimited property. Since men formed themselves into civil societies in order to protect their individual properties, no civil society could conceivably wish to take away any part of any man's property except in so far as necessary to protect property as an institution (that is, by such taxation as was necessary to maintain law and government); and governments, whose rightful powers were only those delegated to them by the whole civil society, could therefore never have the right to interfere with anyone's property beyond what was required to protect property.

What made his case for unlimited property so persuasive was that it seemed to be based simply on an equal natural right to one's own labour and to the means of labour, a right which is ethically pretty acceptable. And in spite of its strained logic (see the analysis in my *Political Theory of Possessive Individualism*, chapter V) his case soon became a standard one.

Reprinted here is chapter V of Locke's *Second Treatise of Government*. It is taken, with the permission of the publisher, from Locke's *Two Treatises of Government: A Critical Edition with an Introduction and Apparatus Criticus* by Peter Laslett (Cambridge University Press, revised edition, 1964). This is the definitive edition of the *Treatises*, incorporating all the revisions and additions made to the first printing (1689) by Locke before his death (1704). Laslett's extensive editorial notes are omitted here but should be consulted by students interested in placing Locke in relation to his contemporaries and predecessors.

Of Property

25. Whether we consider natural *Reason*, which tells us, that Men, being once born, have a right to their Preservation, and consequently to Meat and Drink, and such other things, as Nature affords for their Subsistence: Or *Revelation*, which gives us an account of those Grants God made of the World to *Adam*, and to *Noah*, and his Sons, 'tis very clear, that God, as King *David* says, *Psal.* CXV. xvj. *has given the Earth to the Children of Men*, given it to Mankind in common. But this being supposed, it seems to some a very great difficulty, how any one should ever come to have a *Property* in any thing: I will not content my self to answer, That if it be difficult to make out *Property*, upon a supposition, that God gave the World to *Adam* and his Posterity in common; it is impossible that any Man, but one universal Monarch, should have any *Property*, upon a supposition, that God gave the World to *Adam*, and his Heirs in Succession, exclusive of all the rest of his Posterity. But I shall endeavour to shew, how Men might come to have a *property* in several parts of that which God gave to Mankind in common, and that without any express Compact of all the Commoners.

26. God, who hath given the World to Men in common, hath also given them reason to make use of it to the best advantage of Life, and convenience. The Earth, and all that is therein, is given to Men for the Support and Comfort of their being. And though all the Fruits it naturally produces, and Beasts it feeds, belong to Mankind in common, as they are produced by the spontaneous hand of Nature; and no body has originally a private Dominion, exclusive of the rest of Mankind, in any of them, as they are thus in their natural state: yet being given for the use of Men, there must of necessity be a means *to appropriate* them some way or other before they can be of any use, or at all beneficial to any particular Man. The Fruit, or Venison, which nourishes the

wild *Indian*, who knows no Inclosure, and is still a Tenant in common, must be his, and so his, *i.e.* a part of him, that another can no longer have any right to it, before it can do him any good for the support of his Life.

27. Though the Earth, and all inferior Creatures be common to all Men, yet every Man has a *Property* in his own *Person.* This no Body has any Right to but himself. The *Labour* of his Body, and the *Work* of his Hands, we may say, are properly his. Whatsoever then he removes out of the State that Nature hath provided, and left it in, he hath mixed his *Labour* with, and joyned to it something that is his own, and thereby makes it his *Property.* It being by him removed from the common state Nature placed it in, it hath by this *labour* something annexed to it, that excludes the common right of other Men. For this *Labour* being the unquestionable Property of the Labourer, no Man but he can have a right to what that is once joyned to, at least where there is enough, and as good left in common for others.

28. He that is nourished by the Acorns he pickt up under an Oak, or the Apples he gathered from the Trees in the Wood, has certainly appropriated them to himself. No Body can deny but the nourishment is his. I ask then, When did they begin to be his? When he digested? Or when he eat? Or when he boiled? Or when he brought them home? Or when he pickt them up? And 'tis plain, if the first gathering made them not his, nothing else could. That *labour* put a distinction between them and common. That added something to them more than Nature, the common Mother of all, had done; and so they became his private right. And will any one say he had no right to those Acorns or Apples he thus appropriated, because he had not the consent of all Mankind to make them his? Was it a Robbery thus to assume to himself what belonged to all in Common? If such a consent as that was necessary, Man had starved, notwithstanding the Plenty God had given him. We see in *Commons*, which remain so by Compact, that 'tis the taking any part of what is common, and removing it out of the state Nature leaves it in, which *begins the Property*; without which the Common is of no use. And the taking of this or that part, does not depend on the express consent of all the Commoners. Thus the Grass my Horse has bit; the Turfs my Servant has cut; and the Ore I have digg'd in any place where I have a right to them in common with others, become my *Property*, without the assignation or consent of any body. The *labour* that was mine, removing them out of that common state they were in, hath *fixed* my *Property* in them.

29. By making an explicit consent of every Commoner, necessary to any ones appropriating to himself any part of what is given in common, Children or Servants could not cut the Meat which their Father or Master had provided for them in common, without assigning to every one his peculiar part. Though the Water running in the Fountain be every ones, yet who can doubt, but that

in the Pitcher is his only who drew it out? His *labour* hath taken it out of the hands of Nature, where it was common, and belong'd equally to all her Children, and *hath* thereby *appropriated* it to himself.

30. Thus this Law of reason makes the Deer, that *Indian's* who hath killed it; 'tis allowed to be his goods who hath bestowed his labour upon it, though before, it was the common right of every one. And amongst those who are counted the Civiliz'd part of Mankind, who have made and multiplied positive Laws to determine Property, this original Law of Nature for the *beginning of Property*, in what was before common, still takes place; and by vertue thereof, what Fish any one catches in the Ocean, that great and still remaining Common of Mankind; or what Ambergriese any one takes up here, is *by* the *Labour* that removes it out of that common state Nature left it in, *made* his *Property* who takes that pains about it. And even amongst us the Hare that any one is Hunting, is thought his who pursues her during the Chase. For being a Beast that is still looked upon as common, and no Man's private Possession; whoever has imploy'd so much *labour* about any of that kind, as to find and pursue her, has thereby removed her from the state of Nature, wherein she was common, and hath *begun a Property*.

31. It will perhaps be objected to this, That if gathering the Acorns, or other Fruits of the Earth, *&c.* makes a right to them, then any one may *ingross* as much as he will. To which I Answer, Not so. The same Law of Nature, that does by this means give us Property, does also *bound* that *Property* too. *God has given us all things richly*, I Tim. vi. 17. is the Voice of Reason confirmed by Inspiration. But how far has he given it us? *To enjoy*. As much as any one can make use of to any advantage of life before it spoils; so much he may by his labour fix a Property in. Whatever is beyond this, is more than his share, and belongs to others. Nothing was made by God for Man to spoil or destroy. And thus considering the plenty of natural Provisions there was a long time in the World, and the few spenders, and to how small a part of that provision the industry of one Man could extend it self, and ingross it to the prejudice of others; especially keeping within the *bounds*, set by reason of what might serve for his *use*; there could be then little room for Quarrels or Contentions about Property so establish'd.

32. But the *chief matter of Property* being now not the Fruits of the Earth, and the Beasts that subsist on it, but the *Earth it self*; as that which takes in and carries with it all the rest: I think it is plain, that *Property* in that too is acquired as the former. *As much Land* as a Man Tills, Plants, Improves, Cultivates, and can use the Product of, so much is his *Property*. He by his Labour does, as it were, inclose it from the Common. Nor will it invalidate his right to say, Every body else has an equal Title to it; and therefore he cannot appropriate, he cannot inclose, without the Consent of all his Fellow-Commoners, all Mankind. God, when he gave the World in common to all Mankind,

commanded Man also to labour, and the penury of his Condition required it of him. God and his Reason commanded him to subdue the Earth, *i.e.* improve it for the benefit of Life, and therein lay out something upon it that was his own, his labour. He that in Obedience to this Command of God, subdued, tilled and sowed any part of it, thereby annexed to it something that was his *Property*, which another had no Title to, nor could without injury take from him.

33. Nor was this *appropriation* of any parcel of *Land*, by improving it, any prejudice to any other Man, since there was still enough, and as good left; and more than the yet unprovided could use. So that in effect, there was never the less left for others because of his inclosure for himself. For he that leaves as much as another can make use of, does as good as take nothing at all. No Body could think himself injur'd by the drinking of another Man, though he took a good Draught, who had a whole River of the same Water left him to quench his thirst. And the Case of Land and Water, where there is enough of both, is perfectly the same.

34. God gave the World to Men in Common; but since he gave it them for their benefit, and the greatest Conveniencies of Life they were capable to draw from it, it cannot be supposed he meant it should always remain common and uncultivated. He gave it to the use of the Industrious and Rational, (and *Labour* was to be *his Title* to it;) not to the Fancy or Covetousness of the Quarrelsom and Contentious. He that had as good left for his Improvement, as was already taken up, needed not complain, ought not to meddle with what was already improved by another's Labour: If he did, 'tis plain he desired the benefit of another's Pains, which he had no right to, and not the Ground which God had given him in common with others to labour on, and whereof there was as good left, as that already possessed, and more than he knew what to do with, or his Industry could reach to.

35. 'Tis true, in *Land* that is *common* in *England*, or any other Country, where there is Plenty of People under Government, who have Money and Commerce, no one can inclose or appropriate any part, without the consent of all his Fellow-Commoners: Because this is left common by Compact, *i.e.* by the Law of the Land, which is not to be violated. And though it be Common, in respect of some Men, it is not so to all Mankind; but is the joint property of this Country, or this Parish. Besides, the remainder, after such inclosure, would not be as good to the rest of the Commoners as the whole was, when they could all make use of the whole: whereas in the beginning and first peopling of the great Common of the World, it was quite otherwise. The Law Man was under, was rather for *appropriating*. God Commanded, and his Wants forced him to *labour*. That was his *Property* which could not be taken from him where-ever he had fixed it. And hence subduing or cultivating the Earth, and having Dominion, we see are joyned together. The one gave Title to the other. So that God, by commanding to subdue, gave Authority so far to *appropriate*.

And the Condition of Humane Life, which requires Labour and Materials to work on, necessarily introduces *private Possessions*.

36. The measure of Property, Nature has well set, by the Extent of Mens *Labour, and the Conveniency of Life*: No Mans Labour could subdue, or appropriate all: nor could his Enjoyment consume more than a small part; so that it was impossible for any Man, this way, to intrench upon the right of another, or acquire, to himself, a Property, to the Prejudice of his Neighbour, who would still have room, for as good, and as large a Possession (after the other had taken out his) as before it was appropriated. This *measure* did confine every Man's *Possession*, to a very moderate Proportion, and such as he might appropriate to himself, without Injury to any Body in the first Ages of the World, when Men were more in danger to be lost, by wandering from their Company, in the then vast Wilderness of the Earth, than to be straitned for want of room to plant in. And the same *measure* may be allowed still, without prejudice to any Body, as full as the World seems. For supposing a Man, or Family, in the state they were, at first peopling of the World by the Children of *Adam*, or *Noah*; let him plant in some in-land, vacant places of *America*, we shall find that the *Possessions* he could make himself upon the *measures* we have given, would not be very large, nor, even to this day, prejudice the rest of Mankind, or give them reason to complain, or think themselves injured by this Man's Incroachment, though the Race of Men have now spread themselves to all the corners of the World, and do infinitely exceed the small number [which] was at the beginning. Nay, the extent of *Ground* is of so little value, *without labour*, that I have heard it affirmed, that in *Spain* it self, a Man may be permitted to plough, sow, and reap, without being disturbed, upon Land he has no other Title to, but only his making use of it. But, on the contrary, the Inhabitants think themselves beholden to him, who, by his Industry on neglected, and consequently waste Land, has increased the stock of Corn, which they wanted. But be this as it will, which I lay no stress on; This I dare boldly affirm, That the same *Rule of Propriety*, (*viz.*) that every Man should have as much as he could make use of, would hold still in the World, without straitning any body, since there is Land enough in the World to suffice double the Inhabitants had not the *Invention of Money*, and the tacit Agreement of Men to put a value on it, introduced (by Consent) larger Possessions, and a Right to them; which, how it has done, I shall, by and by, shew more at large.

37. This is certain, That in the beginning, before the desire of having more than Men needed, had altered the intrinsick value of things, which depends only on their usefulness to the Life of Man; or [Men] had *agreed, that a little piece of yellow Metal*, which would keep without wasting or decay, should be worth a great piece of Flesh, or a whole heap of Corn; though Men had a Right to appropriate, by their Labour, each one to himself, as much of the things of Nature, as he could use: Yet this could not be much, nor to the

Prejudice of others, where the same plenty was still left, to those who would use the same Industry. To which let me add, that he who appropriates land to himself by his labour, does not lessen but increase the common stock of mankind. For the provisions serving to the support of humane life, produced by one acre of inclosed and cultivated land, are (to speak much within compasse) ten times more, than those, which are yeilded by an acre of Land, of an equal richnesse, lyeing wast in common. And therefor he, that incloses Land and has a greater plenty of the conveniencys of life from ten acres, than he could have from an hundred left to Nature, may truly be said, to give ninety acres to Mankind. For his labour now supplys him with provisions out of ten acres, which were but the product of an hundred lying in common. I have here rated the improved land very low in making its product but as ten to one, when it is much nearer an hundred to one. For I aske whether in the wild woods and uncultivated wast of America left to Nature, without any improvement, tillage or husbandry, a thousand acres will yeild the needy and wretched inhabitants as many conveniencies of life as ten acres of equally fertile land doe in Devonshire where they are well cultivated?

Before the Appropriation of Land, he who gathered as much of the wild Fruit, killed, caught, or tamed, as many of the Beasts as he could; he that so employed his Pains about any of the spontaneous Products of Nature, as any way to alter them, from the state which Nature put them in, *by* placing any of his *Labour* on them, did thereby *acquire a Propriety in them*: But if they perished, in his Possession, without their due use; if the Fruits rotted, or the Venison putrified, before he could spend it, he offended against the common Law of Nature, and was liable to be punished; he invaded his Neighbour's share, for he had *no Right, farther than his Use* called for any of them, and they might serve to afford him Conveniencies of Life.

38. The same *measures* governed the *Possession of Land* too: Whatsoever he tilled and reaped, laid up and made use of, before it spoiled, that was his peculiar Right; whatsoever he enclosed, and could feed, and make use of, the Cattle and Product was also his. But if either the Grass of his Inclosure rotted on the Ground, or the Fruit of his planting perished without gathering, and laying up, this part of the Earth, notwithstanding his Inclosure, was still to be looked on as Waste, and might be the Possession of any other. Thus, at the beginning, *Cain* might take as much Ground as he could till, and make it his own Land, and yet leave enough to *Abel*'s Sheep to feed on; a few Acres would serve for both their Possessions. But as Families increased, and Industry inlarged their Stocks, their *Possessions inlarged* with the need of them; but yet it was commonly *without any fixed property in the ground* they made use of, till they incorporated, settled themselves together, and built Cities, and then, by consent, they came in time, to set out the *bounds of their distinct Territories*, and agree on limits between them and their Neighbours, and by Laws

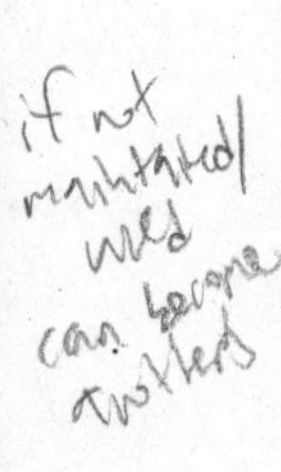

within themselves, settled the *Properties* of those of the same Society. For we see, that in that part of the World which was first inhabited, and therefore like to be best peopled, even as low down as *Abraham*'s time, they wandred with their Flocks, and their Herds, which was their substance, freely up and down; and this *Abraham* did, in a Country where he was a Stranger. Whence it is plain, that at least, a great part of the *Land lay in common*; that the Inhabitants valued it not, nor claimed Property in any more than they made use of. But when there was not room enough in the same place, for their Herds to feed together, they, by consent, as *Abraham* and *Lot* did, *Gen.* xiii. 5. separated and inlarged their pasture, where it best liked them. And for the same Reason *Esau* went from his Father, and his Brother, and planted in *Mount Seir*, Gen. xxxvi. 6.

39. And thus, without supposing any private Dominion, and property in *Adam*, over all the World, exclusive of all other Men, which can no way be proved, nor any ones Property be made out from it; but supposing the *World* given as it was to the Children of Men *in common*, we see how *labour* could make Men distinct titles to several parcels of it, for their private uses; wherein there could be no doubt of Right, no room for quarrel.

40. Nor is it so strange, as perhaps before consideration it may appear, that the *Property of labour* should be able to over-ballance the Community of Land. For 'tis *Labour* indeed that *puts the difference of value* on every thing; and let any one consider, what the difference is between an Acre of Land planted with Tobacco, or Sugar, sown with Wheat or Barley; and an Acre of the same Land lying in common, without any Husbandry upon it, and he will find, that the improvement of *labour makes* the far greater part of *the value.* I think it will be but a very modest Computation to say, that of the *Products* of the Earth useful to the Life of Man $\frac{9}{10}$ are the *effects of labour*: nay, if we will rightly estimate things as they come to our use, and cast up the several Expences about them, what in them is purely owing to *Nature*, and what to *labour*, we shall find, that in most of them $\frac{99}{100}$ are wholly to be put on the account of *labour.*

41. There cannot be a clearer demonstration of any thing, than several Nations of the *Americans* are of this, who are rich in Land, and poor in all the Comforts of Life; whom Nature having furnished as liberally as any other people, with the materials of Plenty, *i.e.* a fruitful Soil, apt to produce in abundance, what might serve for food, rayment, and delight; yet for want of improving it by labour, have not one hundreth part of the Conveniencies we enjoy: And a King of a large and fruitful Territory there feeds, lodges, and is clad worse than a day Labourer in *England.*

42. To make this a little clearer, let us but trace some of the ordinary provisions of Life, through their several progresses, before they come to our use, and see how much they receive of their *value from Humane Industry.* Bread, Wine and Cloth, are things of daily use, and great plenty, yet notwith-

standing, Acorns, Water, and Leaves, or Skins, must be our Bread, Drink and Clothing, did not *labour* furnish us with these more useful Commodities. For whatever *Bread* is more worth than Acorns, *Wine* than Water, and *Cloth* or *Silk* than Leaves, Skins, or Moss, that is wholly *owing to labour* and industry. The one of these being the Food and Rayment which unassisted Nature furnishes us with; the other provisions which our industry and pains prepare for us, which how much they exceed the other in value, when any one hath computed, he will then see, how much *labour makes the far greatest part of the value* of things, we enjoy in this World: And the ground which produces the materials, is scarce to be reckon'd in, as any, or at most, but a very small, part of it; So little, that even amongst us, Land that is left wholly to Nature, that hath no improvement of Pasturage, Tillage, or Planting, is called, as indeed it is, *wast*; and we shall find the benefit of it amount to little more than nothing. This shews, how much numbers of men are to be preferd to largenesse of dominions, and that the increase of lands and the right imploying of them is the great art of government. And that Prince who shall be so wise and godlike as by established laws of liberty to secure protection and incouragement to the honest industry of Mankind against the oppression of power and narrownesse of Party will quickly be too hard for his neighbours. But this bye the bye. To return to the argument in hand.

43. An Acre of Land that bears here Twenty Bushels of Wheat, and another in *America*, which, with the same Husbandry, would do the like, are, without doubt, of the same natural, intrinsick Value. But yet the Benefit Mankind receives from the one, in a Year, is worth 5 *l.* and from the other possibly not worth a Penny, if all the Profit an *Indian* received from it were to be valued, and sold here; at least, I may truly say, not $\frac{1}{1000}$. 'Tis *Labour* then which *puts the greatest part of Value upon Land*, without which it would scarcely be worth any thing: 'tis to that we owe the greatest part of all its useful Products: for all that the Straw, Bran, Bread, of that Acre of Wheat, is more worth than the Product of an Acre of as good Land, which lies wast, is all the Effect of Labour. For 'tis not barely the Plough-man's Pains, the Reaper's and Thresher's Toil, and the Bakers Sweat, is to be counted into the *Bread* we eat; the Labour of those who broke the Oxen, who digged and wrought the Iron and Stones, who felled and framed the Timber imployed about the Plough, Mill, Oven, or any other Utensils, which are a vast Number, requisite to this Corn, from its being seed to be sown to its being made Bread, must all be *charged on* the account of *Labour*, and received as an effect of that: Nature and the Earth furnished only the almost worthless Materials, as in themselves. 'Twould be a strange *Catalogue of things, that Industry provided and made use of, about every Loaf of Bread*, before it came to our use, if we could trace them; Iron, Wood, Leather, Bark, Timber, Stone, Bricks, Coals, Lime, Cloth, Dying-Drugs, Pitch, Tar, Masts, Ropes, and all the Materials made use of in the Ship, that

brought any of the Commodities made use of by any of the Workmen, to any part of the Work, all which, 'twould be almost impossible, at least too long, to reckon up.

44. From all which it is evident, that though the things of Nature are given in common, yet Man (by being Master of himself, and *Proprietor of his own Person*, and the Actions or *Labour* of it) had still in himself *the great Foundation of Property*; and that which made up the great part of what he applyed to the Support or Comfort of his being, when Invention and Arts had improved the conveniencies of Life, was perfectly his own, and did not belong in common to others.

45. Thus *Labour*, in the Beginning, *gave a Right of Property*, where-ever any one was pleased to imploy it, upon what was common, which remained, a long while, the far greater part, and is yet more than Mankind makes use of. Men, at first, for the most part, contented themselves with what un-assisted Nature offered to their Necessities: and though afterwards, in some parts of the World, (where the Increase of People and Stock, with the *Use of Money*) had made Land scarce, and so of some Value, the several *Communities* settled the Bounds of their distinct Territories, and by Laws within themselves, regulated the Properties of the private Men of their Society, and so, *by Compact* and Agreement, *settled the Property* which Labour and Industry began; and the Leagues that have been made between several States and Kingdoms, either expressly or tacitly disowning all Claim and Right to the Land in the others Possession, have, by common Consent, given up their Pretences to their natural common Right, which originally they had to those Countries, and so have, by *positive agreement, settled a Property* amongst themselves, in distinct Parts and parcels of the Earth: yet there are still *great Tracts of Ground* to be found, which (the Inhabitants thereof not having joyned with the rest of Mankind, in the consent of the Use of their common Money) *lie waste*, and are more than the People, who dwell on it, do, or can make use of, and so still lie in common. Tho' this can scarce happen amongst that part of Mankind, that have consented to the Use of Money.

46. The greatest part of *things really useful* to the Life of Man, and such as the necessity of subsisting made the first Commoners of the World look after, as it doth the *Americans* now, *are* generally things *of short duration*; such as, if they are not consumed by use, will decay and perish of themselves: Gold, Silver, and Diamonds, are things, that Fancy or Agreement hath put the Value on, more then real Use, and the necessary Support of Life. Now of those good things which Nature hath provided in common, every one had a Right (as hath been said) to as much as he could use, and had a Property in all that he could affect with his Labour: all that his Industry could extend to, to alter from the State Nature had put it in, was his. He that *gathered* a Hundred Bushels of Acorns or Apples, had thereby a *Property* in them; they were his Goods as

soon as gathered. He was only to look that he used them before they spoiled; else he took more then his share, and robb'd others. And indeed it was a foolish thing, as well as dishonest, to hoard up more than he could make use of. If he gave away a part to any body else, so that it perished not uselesly in his Possession, these he also made use of. And if he also bartered away Plumbs that would have rotted in a Week, for Nuts that would last good for his eating a whole Year, he did no injury; he wasted not the common Stock; destroyed no part of the portion of Goods that belonged to others, so long as nothing perished uselesly in his hands. Again, if he would give his Nuts for a piece of Metal, pleased with its colour; or exchange his Sheep for Shells, or Wool for a sparkling Pebble or a Diamond, and keep those by him all his Life, he invaded not the Right of others, he might heap up as much of these durable things as he pleased; the *exceeding of the bounds of his* just *Property* not lying in the largeness of his Possession, but the perishing of any thing uselesly in it.

47. And thus *came in the use of Money*, some lasting thing that Men might keep without spoiling, and that by mutual consent Men would take in exchange for the truly useful, but perishable Supports of Life.

48. And as different degrees of Industry were apt to give Men Possessions in different Proportions, so this *Invention of Money* gave them the opportunity to continue and enlarge them. For supposing an Island, separate from all possible Commerce with the rest of the World, wherein there were but a hundred Families, but there were Sheep, Horses and Cows, with other useful Animals, wholsome Fruits, and Land enough for Corn for a hundred thousand times as many, but nothing in the Island, either because of its Commonness, or Perishableness, fit to supply the place of *Money*: What reason could any one have there to enlarge his Possessions beyond the use of his Family, and a plentiful supply to its Consumption, either in what their own Industry produced, or they could barter for like perishable, useful Commodities, with others? Where there is not something both lasting and scarce, and so valuable to be hoarded up, there Men will not be apt to enlarge their *Possessions of Land*, were it never so rich, never so free for them to take. For I ask, What would a Man value Ten Thousand, or an Hundred Thousand Acres of excellent *Land*, ready cultivated, and well stocked too with Cattle, in the middle of the in-land Parts of America, where he had no hopes of Commerce with other Parts of the World, to draw *Money* to him by the Sale of the Product? It would not be worth the inclosing, and we should see him give up again to the wild Common of Nature, whatever was more than would supply the Conveniencies of Life to be had there for him and his Family.

49. Thus in the beginning all the World was *America*, and more so than that is now; for no such thing as *Money* was any where known. Find out something that hath the *Use and Value of Money* amongst his Neighbours, you shall see the same Man will begin presently to *enlarge* his *Possessions.*

50. But since Gold and Silver, being little useful to the Life of Man in proportion to Food, Rayment, and Carriage, has its *value* only from the consent of Men, whereof Labour yet makes, in great part, *the measure*, it is plain, that Men have agreed to disproportionate and unequal Possession of the Earth, they having by a tacit and voluntary consent found out a way, how a man may fairly possess more land than he himself can use the product of, by receiving in exchange for the overplus, Gold and Silver, which may be hoarded up without injury to any one, these metalls not spoileing or decaying in the hands of the possessor. This partage of things, in an inequality of private possessions, men have made practicable out of the bounds of Societie, and without compact, only by putting a value on gold and silver and tacitly agreeing in the use of Money. For in Governments the Laws regulate the right of property, and the possession of land is determined by positive constitutions.

51. And thus, I think, it is very easie to conceive without any difficulty, *how Labour could at first begin a title of Property* in the common things of Nature, and how the spending it upon our uses bounded it. So that there could then be no reason of quarrelling about Title, nor any doubt about the largeness of Possession it gave. Right and conveniency went together; for as a Man had a Right to all he could imploy his Labour upon, so he had no temptation to labour for more than he could make use of. This left no room for Controversie about the Title, nor for Incroachment on the Right of others; what Portion a Man carved to himself, was easily seen; and it was useless as well as dishonest to carve himself too much, or take more than he needed.

3 / JEAN-JACQUES ROUSSEAU

Rousseau, like Locke, started from natural right, but took it to a very different conclusion. Property of the limited amount that a man could work on by himself was a sacred right: the unlimited property that Locke had justified and that was now the rule in modern Western societies was totally unjustified because it deprived most men of any property at all and so contradicted the natural right. Existing governments, in upholding the unlimited right, were thus fundamentally unjust.

Rousseau's case has profoundly influenced most subsequent critics of the established view, right down to our time: its echoes in some of the Third World countries are particularly noticeable.

The strength of his case lies in his evolutionary view of human nature and hence of natural right. He showed persuasively how men must have changed over the aeons from a near-animal condition through savagery and barbarism to civilization as their skills and wants had increased. Their original nature, on which alone a genuine natural right could be based, had been perverted by the growth of artificial wants: the turning point was the introduction of unequal private property, which enslaved some men to others. Locke's natural right, being deduced from this later nature of man, was not a true natural right. Whatever one may think of Rousseau's particular version of evolutionary change, the very concept of such change undermined the structure Locke had built on his unhistorical postulate of an unchanging human nature, and exposed his confusion in reading back into an original natural condition of mankind the later apparatus of money, markets, trade for profit, and wage-labour.

This extract comprises a substantial portion of the Second Part of Rousseau's *Discourse on the Origin and Foundations of Inequality* (his Second Discourse, of 1755) in the English translation by Roger D. and Judith R. Masters. It is reprinted, by permission of the publishers, from *The First and Second Discourses of Rousseau*, edited by Roger D. Masters (New York: St Martin's Press, 1964).

The Origin of Inequality

The first person who, having fenced off a plot of ground, took it into his head to say *this is mine* and found people simple enough to believe him, was the true founder of civil society. What crimes, wars, murders, what miseries and horrors would the human race have been spared by someone who, uprooting the stakes or filling in the ditch, had shouted to his fellow-men: Beware of listening to this impostor; you are lost if you forget that the fruits belong to all and the earth to no one! But it is very likely that by then things had already come to the point where they could no longer remain as they were. For this idea of property, depending on many prior ideas which could only have arisen successively, was not conceived all at once in the human mind. It was necessary to make much progress, to acquire much industry and enlightenment, and to transmit and augment them from age to age, before arriving at this last stage of the state of nature. ...

As long as men were content with their rustic huts, as long as they were limited to sewing their clothing of skins with thorns or fish bones, adorning themselves with feathers and shells, painting their bodies with various colors, perfecting or embellishing their bows and arrows, carving with sharp stones a few fishing canoes or a few crude musical instruments; in a word, as long as they applied themselves only to tasks that a single person could do and to arts that did not require the cooperation of several hands, they lived free, healthy, good, and happy insofar as they could be according to their nature, and they continued to enjoy among themselves the sweetness of independent intercourse. But from the moment one man needed the help of another, as soon as they observed that it was useful for a single person to have provisions for two, equality disappeared, property was introduced, labor became necessary; and vast forests were changed into smiling fields which had to be watered with the sweat of men, and in which slavery and misery were soon seen to germinate and grow with the crops.

Metallurgy and agriculture were the two arts whose invention produced this great revolution. For the poet it is gold and silver, but for the philosopher it is iron and wheat which have civilized men and ruined the human race. Accordingly, both of these were unknown to the savages of America, who therefore have always remained savage; other peoples even seem to have remained barbarous as long as they practiced one of these arts without the other. And perhaps one of the best reasons why Europe has been, if not earlier, at least more constantly and better civilized than the other parts of the world is that it is at the same time the most abundant in iron and the most fertile in wheat. It is very difficult to guess how men came to know and use iron; for it is not credible that by themselves the thought of drawing the raw material from the mine and giving it the necessary preparations to fuse it before they knew what would result. From another point of view, it is even harder to attribute this discovery to some accidental fire, because mines are formed only in arid spots, stripped of both trees and plants; so that one would say that nature had taken precautions to hide this deadly secret from us. There only remains, therefore, the extraordinary circumstance of some volcano which, by throwing up metallic materials in fusion, would have given observers the idea of imitating this operation of nature. Even so, it is necessary to suppose in them much courage and foresight to undertake such difficult labor and to envisage so far in advance the advantages they could gain from it: all of which hardly suits minds that are not already more trained than theirs must have been.

With regard to agriculture, its principle was known long before its practice was established, and it is hardly possible that men, constantly occupied with obtaining their subsistence from trees and plants, did not rather promptly have an idea of the ways used by nature to grow plants. But their industry probably turned in that direction only very late, either because trees, which along with hunting and fishing provided their food, did not have need of their care; or for want of knowing how to use wheat; or for want of implements to cultivate it; or for want of foresight concerning future need; or, finally, for want of means to prevent others from appropriating the fruit of their labor. Once they became industrious, it is credible that, with sharp stones and pointed sticks, they began by cultivating a few vegetables or roots around their huts long before they knew how to prepare wheat and had the implements necessary for large-scale cultivation. Besides, to devote oneself to that occupation and seed the land, one must be resolved to lose something at first in order to gain a great deal later: a precaution very far from the turn of mind of savage man, who, as I have said, has great difficulty thinking in the morning of his needs for the evening.

The invention of the other arts was therefore necessary to force the human race to apply itself to that of agriculture. As soon as some men were needed to smelt and forge iron, other men were needed to feed them. The more the number of workers was multiplied, the fewer hands were engaged in furnishing the common subsistence, without there being fewer mouths to consume it; and since some needed foodstuffs in exchange for their iron, the others finally found the secret of using iron in order to multiply foodstuffs. From this arose husbandry and agriculture on the one hand, and on the other the art of working metals and multiplying their uses.

From the cultivation of land, its division necessarily followed; and from property once recognized, the first rules of justice. For in order to give everyone what is his, it is necessary that everyone can have something; moreover, as men began to look to the future and as they all saw themselves with some goods to lose, there was not one of them who did not have to fear reprisals against himself for wrongs he might do to another. This origin is all the more natural as it is impossible to conceive of the idea of property arising from anything except manual labor; because one can not see what man can add, other than his own labor, in order to appropriate things he has not made. It is labor alone which, giving the cultivator a right to the product of the land he has tilled, gives him a right to the soil as a consequence, at least until the harvest, and thus from year to year; which, creating continuous possession, is easily transformed into property. When the ancients, says Grotius, gave Ceres the epithet of legislatrix, and gave the name of Thesmaphories to a festival celebrated in her honor, they thereby made it clear that the division of lands produced a new kind of right: that is, the right of property, different from the one which results from natural law.

Things in this state could have remained equal if talents had been equal, and if, for example, the use of iron and the consumption of foodstuffs had always been exactly balanced. But this proportion, which nothing maintained, was soon broken; the stronger did more work; the cleverer turned his to better advantage; the more ingenious found ways to shorten his labor; the farmer had greater need of iron or the blacksmith greater need of wheat; and working equally, the one earned a great deal while the other barely had enough to live. Thus does natural inequality imperceptibly manifest itself along with contrived inequality; and thus do the differences among men, developed by those of circumstances, become more perceptible, more permanent in their effects, and begin to have a proportionate influence over the fate of individuals.

Things having reached this point it is easy to imagine the rest. I shall not stop to describe the successive invention of the other arts, the progress of languages, the testing and use of talents, the inequality of fortunes, the use or abuse of wealth, nor all the details that follow these, and that everyone can easily fill in. I shall simply limit myself to casting a glance at the human race placed in this new order of things.

Behold all our faculties developed, memory and imagination in play, vanity aroused, reason rendered active, and the mind having almost reached the limit of the perfection of which it is susceptible. Behold all the natural qualities put into action, the rank and fate of each man established, not only upon the quantity of goods and the power to serve or harm, but also upon the mind, beauty, strength, or skill, upon merit or talents. And these qualities being the only ones which could attract consideration, it was soon necessary to have them or affect them; for one's own advantage, it was necessary to appear to be other than what one in fact was. To be and to seem to be became two altogether different things; and from this distinction came conspicuous ostentation, deceptive cunning, and all the vices that follow from them. From another point of view, having formerly been free and independent, behold man, due to a multitude of new needs, subjected so to speak to all of nature and especially to his fellowmen, whose slave he becomes in a sense even in becoming their master; rich, he needs their services; poor, he needs their help; and mediocrity cannot enable him to do without them. He must therefore incessantly seek to interest them in his fate, and to make them find their own profit, in fact or in appearance, in working for his. This makes him deceitful and sly with some, imperious and harsh with others, and makes it necessary for him to abuse all those whom he needs when he cannot make them fear him and does not find his interest in serving them usefully. Finally, consuming ambition, the fervor to raise one's relative fortune less out of true need than in order to place oneself above others, inspires in all men a base inclination to harm each other, a secret jealousy all the more dangerous because, in order to strike its blow in greater safety, it often assumes the mask of benevolence: in a word, competition and rivalry on one hand, opposition of interest on the other; and always the hidden desire to profit at the expense of others. All these evils are the first effect of property and the inseparable consequence of nascent inequality.

Before representative signs of wealth had been invented, it could hardly consist of anything except land and livestock, the only real goods men can possess. Now when inheritances had increased in number and extent to the point of covering the entire earth and of all bordering on each other, some of them could no longer be enlarged except at the expense of others; and the supernumeraries, whom weakness or indolence had prevented from acquiring an inheritance in their turn, having become poor without having lost anything – because while everything around them changed they alone had not changed at all – were obliged to receive or steal their subsistence from the hand of the rich; and from that began to arise, according to the diverse characters of the rich and the poor, domination and servitude or violence and rapine. The rich, for their part, had scarcely known the pleasure of domination when they soon disdained all others, and using their old slaves to subdue new ones, they thought only of subjugating and enslaving their neighbors: like those famished wolves which, having once tasted human flesh, refuse all other food and thenceforth want only to devour men.

Thus, as the most powerful or most miserable made of their force or their needs a sort of right to the goods of others, equivalent according to them to the right of property, the destruction of equality was followed by the most frightful disorder; thus the usurpations of the rich, the brigandage of the poor, the unbridled passions of all, stifling natural pity and the as yet weak voice of justice, made man avaricious, ambitious, and evil. Between the right of the stronger and the right of the first occupant there arose a perpetual conflict which ended only in fights and murders. Nascent society gave way to the most horrible state of war: the human race, debased and desolated, no longer able to turn back or renounce the unhappy acquisitions it had made, and working only toward its shame by abusing the faculties that honor it, brought itself to the brink of its ruin.

> Attonitus novitate mali, divesque, miserque,
> Effugere optat opes, et quae modo voverat, odit.*

It is not possible that men should not at last have reflected upon such a miserable situation and upon the calamities overwhelming them. The rich above all must have soon felt how disadvantageous to them was a perpetual war in which they alone paid all the costs, and in which the risk of life was common to all while the risk of goods was theirs alone. Moreover, whatever pretext they might give for their usurpations, they were well aware that these were established only on a precarious and abusive right, and that having been acquired only by force, force could take them away without their having grounds for complaint. Even those enriched by industry alone could hardly base their property upon better titles. In vain might they say: But I built this wall; I earned this field by my labor. Who gave you its dimensions, they might be answered, and by virtue of what do you presume to be paid at our expense for work we did not impose on you? Do you not know that a multitude of your brethren die or suffer from need of what you have in excess, and that you needed express and unanimous consent of the human race to appropriate for yourself anything from common subsistence that exceeded your own? Destitute of valid reasons to justify himself and of sufficient forces to defend himself; easily crushing an individual, but himself crushed by groups of bandits; alone against all, and unable because of mutual jealousies to unite with his equals against enemies united by the common hope of plunder, the rich, pressed by necessity, finally conceived the most deliberate project that ever

* [Both rich and poor, shocked at their new-found ills,
Would fly from wealth and lose what they had sought.
Ovid, *Metamorphoses* XI, 127]

entered the human mind. It was to use in his favor the very forces of those who attacked him, to make his defenders out of his adversaries, inspire them with other maxims, and give them other institutions which were as favorable to him as natural right was adverse.

To this end, after having shown his neighbors the horror of a situation that made them all take up arms against one another, that made their possessions as burdensome as their needs, and in which no one found security in either poverty or wealth, he easily invented specious reasons to lead them to his goal. 'Let us unite,' he says to them, 'to protect the weak from oppression, restrain the ambitious, and secure for everyone the possession of what belongs to him. Let us institute regulations of justice and peace to which all are obliged to conform, which make an exception of no one, and which compensate in some way for the caprices of fortune by equally subjecting the powerful and the weak to mutual duties. In a word, instead of turning our forces against ourselves, let us gather them into one supreme power which governs us according to wise laws, protects and defends all the members of the association, repulses common enemies, and maintains us in an eternal concord.'

Far less than the equivalent of this discourse was necessary to win over crude, easily seduced men, who in addition had too many disputes to straighten out among themselves to be able to do without arbiters, and too much avarice and ambition to be able to do without masters for long. All ran to meet their chains thinking they secured their freedom, for although they had enough reason to feel the advantages of a political establishment, they did not have enough experience to forsee its dangers. Those most capable of anticipating the abuses were precisely those who counted on profiting from them; and even the wise saw the necessity of resolving to sacrifice one part of their freedom for the preservation of the other, just as a wounded man has his arm cut off to save the rest of his body.

Such was, or must have been, the origin of society and laws, which gave new fetters to the weak and new forces to the rich, destroyed natural freedom for all time, established forever the law of property and inequality, changed a clever usurpation into an irrevocable right, and for the profit of a few ambitious men henceforth subjected the whole human race to work, servitude, and misery. It is easily seen how the establishment of a single society made that of all the others indispensable, and how, to stand up to the united forces, it was necessary to unite in turn. Societies, multiplying or spreading rapidly, soon covered the entire surface of the earth; and it was no longer possible to find a single corner in the universe where one could free oneself from the yoke and withdraw one's head from the sword, often ill-guided, that every man saw perpetually hanging over his head. Civil right having thus become the common rule of citizens, the law of nature no longer operated except between the various societies, where, under the name law of nations, it was tempered by some tacit conventions in order to make intercourse possible and to take the place of natural commiseration which, losing between one society and another nearly all the force it had between one man and another, no longer dwells in any but a few great cosmopolitan souls, who surmount the imaginary barriers that separate peoples and who, following the example of the sovereign Being who created them, include the whole human race in their benevolence.

The bodies politic, thus remaining in the state of nature with relation to each other, soon experienced the inconveniences that had forced individuals to leave it; and among these great bodies that state became even more fatal than it had previously been among the individuals of whom they were composed. Hence arose the national wars, battles, murders, and reprisals which make nature tremble and shock reason, and all those horrible prejudices which rank the honor of shedding human blood among the virtues. The most decent men learned to consider it one of their duties to murder their fellow-men; at length men were seen to massacre each other by the thousands without knowing why; more murders were committed on a single day of fighting and more horrors in the capture of a single city than were committed in the state of nature during whole centuries over the entire face of the earth. Such are the first effects one glimpses of the division of the human race into different societies. Let us return to their institution.

I know that many have attributed other origins to political societies, such as conquests by the more powerful, or union of the weak; and the choice among these causes is indifferent to what I want to establish. However, the one I have just presented appears to me the most natural for the following reasons. 1. In the first case, the right of conquest, as it is not a right, could not have founded any other, since the conqueror and the conquered peoples always remain toward each other in a state of war, unless the nation, given back its complete freedom, should voluntarily choose its conqueror as its chief. Until then, whatever capitulations may have been made, as they have been founded only upon violence and are consequently null by that very fact, following this hypothesis there can be neither true society nor body politic, nor any other law than that of the stronger. 2. These words *strong* and *weak* are equivocal in the second case; for, in the interval between the establishment of the right of property or of the first occupant and that of political governments, the meaning of these terms is better expressed by the terms *poor* and *rich*, since before the laws a man did not, in fact, have any other means of subjecting his equals than by attacking their goods or by giving them some of his. 3. The poor having nothing to lose except their freedom, it would have been great folly for them to give away voluntarily the sole good remaining to them, gaining nothing in the exchange; on the contrary, the rich being so to speak vulnerable in every part of their goods, it was much easier to harm them; they consequently had more precautions to take in order to protect themselves from harm; and finally it is reasonable to believe that a thing was invented by those to whom it is useful rather than by those whom it wrongs.

4 / JEREMY BENTHAM

With Bentham, whose influence was immense in the nineteenth century, we come to a new justification of modern unequal property. Bentham discarded the natural rights case which, after Rousseau had shown how it could be turned against modern property, was quite unreliable. Bentham rested everything – the property right and the rights of governments – on the principle of 'utility' or the greatest happiness of the greatest number, happiness measured by the excess of pleasure over pain.

That principle, Bentham argued, absolutely required the institution of unequal property. The argument, as set out in this extract, has been at least as persuasive, in Bentham's time and ever since, as Locke's was in his time. The fallacies in it, which are many (see my *Life and Times of Liberal Democracy*, chapter II), were (and are) unnoticed by those who have found in it an apparently solid case, resting on the sort of cost/benefit analysis which is now so fashionable.

This extract comprises chapters II–V, VI (part), VII–IX, XI (part), and XII, of Bentham's *Principles of the Civil Code*, which was first published (in French) in 1802 and in English in 1830. It appears in the Bowring edition of Bentham's *Works*, vol. I, 1843. The best edition is that contained in Bentham's *The Theory of Legislation*, edited by C.K. Ogden (London: Kegan Paul, 1931), which is a reprint of the Hildreth 1864 translation, which is the text used here. One footnoted reference has been omitted.

Security and Equality of Property

CHAPTER II
Ends of Civil Law

In the distribution of rights and obligations, the legislator, as we have said, should have for his end the happiness of society. Investigating more distinctly in what that happiness consists, we shall find four subordinate ends:-

Subsistence.
Abundance.
Equality.
Security.

The more perfect enjoyment is in all these respects, the greater is the sum of social happiness: and especially of that happiness which depends upon the laws.

We may hence conclude that all the functions of law may be referred to these four heads: - To provide subsistence; to produce abundance; to favour equality; to maintain security.

This division has not all the exactness which might be desired. The limits which separate these objects are not always easy to be determined. They approach each other at different points, and mingle together. But it is enough to justify this division, that it is the most complete we can make; and that, in fact, we are generally called to consider each of the objects which it contains, separately and distinct from all the others.

Subsistence, for example, is included in abundance; still it is very necessary to consider it separately; because the laws ought to do many things for subsistence which they ought not to attempt for the sake of abundance.

Security admits as many distinctions as there are kinds of actions which may be hostile to it: It relates to the person, the honour, to property, to condition. Acts injurious to security, branded by prohibition of law, receive the quality of offences.

Of these objects of the law, security is the only one which necessarily embraces the future. Subsistence, abundance, equality, may be considered in relation to a single moment of present time; but security implies a given extension of future time in respect to all that good which it embraces. Security, then, is the pre-eminent object.

I have mentioned equality as one of the objects of law. In an arrangement designed to give to all men the greatest possible sum of good, there is no reason why the law should seek to give more to one individual than to another. There are abundance of reasons why it should not; for the advantages acquired on one side, never can be an equivalent for the disadvantages felt upon the other. The pleasure is exclusively for the party favoured; the pain for all who do not share the favour.

Equality may be promoted either by protecting it where it exists, or by seeking to produce it. In this latter case, the greatest caution is necessary; for a single error may overturn social order.*

Some persons may be astonished to find that *Liberty* is not ranked among the principal objects of law. But a clear idea of liberty will lead us to regard it as a branch of security. Personal liberty is security against a certain kind of injuries which affect the person. As to what is called *political liberty*, it is another branch of security, - security against injustice from the ministers of government. What concerns this object belongs not to civil, but to constitutional law.

CHAPTER III
Relations between these Ends

These four objects of law are very distinct in idea, but they are much less so in practice. The same law may advance several of them; because they are often united. That law, for example, which favours security, favours, at the same time, subsistence and abundance.

But there are circumstances in which it is impossible to unite these objects. It will sometimes happen that a measure suggested by one of these principles will be condemned by another. Equality, for example, might require a distribution of property which would be incompatible with security.

* Equality may be considered in relation to all the advantages which depend upon laws. Political equality is an equality of political rights; civil equality is an equality of civil rights. When used by itself, the word is commonly understood to refer to the distribution of property. It is so used in this treatise.

When this contradiction exists between two of these ends, it is necessary to find some means of deciding the pre-eminence; otherwise these principles, instead of guiding us in our researches, will only serve to augment the confusion.

At the first glance we see subsistence and security arising together to the same level; abundance and equality are manifestly of inferior importance. In fact, without security, equality could not last a day; without subsistence, abundance could not exist at all. The two first objects are life itself; the two latter, the ornaments of life.

In legislation, the most important object is security. Though no laws were made directly for subsistence, it might easily be imagined that no one would neglect it. But unless laws are made directly for security, it would be quite useless to make them for subsistence. You may order production; you may command cultivation; and you will have done nothing. But assure to the cultivator the fruits of his industry, and perhaps in that alone you will have done enough.

Security, as we have said, has many branches; and some branches of it must yield to others. For example, liberty, which is a branch of security, ought to yield to a consideration of the general security, since laws cannot be made except at the expense of liberty.

We cannot arrive at the greatest good, except by the sacrifice of some subordinate good. All the difficulty consists in distinguishing that object which, according to the occasion, merits pre-eminence. For each, in its turn, demands it; and a very complicated calculation is sometimes necessary to avoid being deceived as to the preference due to one or the other.

Equality ought not to be favoured except in the cases in which it does not interfere with security; in which it does not thwart the expectations which the law itself has produced, in which it does not derange the order already established.

If all property were equally divided, at fixed periods, the sure and certain consequence would be, that presently there would be no property to divide. All would shortly be destroyed. Those whom it was intended to favour, would not suffer less from the division than those at whose expense it was made. If the lot of the industrious was not better than the lot of the idle, there would be no longer any motives for industry.

To lay down as a principle that all men ought to enjoy a perfect *equality of rights*, would be, by a necessary connection of consequences, to render all legislation impossible. The laws are constantly establishing inequalities, since they cannot give rights to one without imposing obligations upon another. To say that all men – that is, all human beings – have equal rights, is to say that there is no such thing as subordination. The son then has the same rights with his father; he has the same right to govern and punish his father that his father has to govern and punish him. He has as many rights in the house of his father as the father himself. The maniac has the same right to shut up others that others have to shut up him. The idiot has the same right to govern his family that his family have to govern him. All this is fully implied in the absolute equality of rights. It means this, or else it means nothing. I know very well that those who maintain this doctrine of the equality of rights, not being themselves either fools or idiots, have no intention of establishing this absolute equality. They have, in their own minds, restrictions, modifications, explanations. But if they themselves cannot speak in an intelligible manner, will the ignorant and excited multitude understand them better than they understand themselves?

CHAPTER IV
Laws relatively to Subsistence

What can the law do for subsistence? Nothing directly. All it can do is to create *motives*, that is, punishments or rewards, by the force of which men may be led to provide subsistence for themselves. But nature herself has created these motives, and has given them a sufficient energy. Before the idea of laws existed, *needs* and *enjoyments* had done in that respect all that the best concerted laws could do. Need, armed with pains of all kinds, even death itself, commanded labour, excited courage, inspired foresight, developed all the faculties of man. Enjoyment, the inseparable companion of every need satisfied, formed an inexhaustible fund of rewards for those who surmounted obstacles and fulfilled the end of nature. The force of the physical sanction being sufficient, the employment of the political sanction would be superfluous.

Besides, the motives which depend on laws are more or less precarious in their operation. It is a consequence of the imperfection of the laws themselves; or of the difficulty of proving the facts in order to apply punishment or reward. The hope of impunity conceals itself at the bottom of the heart during all the intermediate steps which it is necessary to take before arriving at the enforcement of the law. But the natural effects, which may be regarded as nature's punishments and rewards, scarcely admit of any uncertainty. There is no evasion, no delay, no favour. Experience announces the event, and experience confirms it. Each day strengthens the lesson of the day before; and the uniformity of this process leaves no room for doubt. What could be added by direct laws to the constant and irresistible power of these natural motives?

But the laws provide for subsistence indirectly, by protecting men while they labour, and by making them sure of the fruits of their labour. *Security* for the labourer, *security* for the fruits of labour; such is the benefit of laws; and it is an inestimable benefit.

CHAPTER V
Laws relatively to Abundance

Shall laws be made directing individuals not to confine themselves to mere subsistence, but to seek abundance? No! That would be a very superfluous employment of artificial means, where natural means suffice. The attraction of pleasure; the succession of wants; the active desire of increasing happiness, will procure unceasingly, under the reign of security, new efforts towards new acquisitions. Wants, enjoyments, those universal agents of society, having begun with gathering the first sheaf of corn, proceed little by little, to build magazines of abundance, always increasing but never filled. Desires extend with means. The horizon elevates itself as we advance; and each new want, attended on the one hand by pain, on the other by pleasure, becomes a new principle of action. Opulence, which is only a comparative term, does not arrest this movement once begun. On the contrary, the greater our means, the greater the scale on which we labour; the greater is the recompense, and, consequently, the greater also the force of motive which animates to labour. Now what is the wealth of society, if not the sum of all individual wealth? And what more is necessary than the force of these natural motives, to carry wealth, by successive movements, to the highest possible point?

It appears that abundance is formed little by little, by the continued operation of the same causes which produce subsistence. Those who blame abundance under the name of luxury, have never looked at it from this point of view.

Bad seasons, wars, accidents of all kinds, attack so often the fund of subsistence, that a society which had nothing superfluous, and even if it had a good deal that was superfluous, would often be exposed to want what is necessary. We see this among savage tribes; it was often seen among all nations, during the times of ancient poverty. It is what happens even now, in countries little favoured by nature, such as Sweden; and in those where government restrains the operations of commerce, instead of confining itself to protection. But countries in which luxury abounds, and where governments are enlightened, are above the risk of famine. Such is the happy situation of England. With a free commerce, toys useless in themselves have their utility, as the means of obtaining bread. Manufactures of luxury furnish an assurance against famine. A brewery or a starch-factory might be changed into a means of subsistence.

How often have we heard declamations against dogs and horses, as devouring the food of men! Such declaimers rise but one degree above those apostles of disinterestedness, who set fire to the magazines in order to cause an abundance of corn.

CHAPTER VI

Pathological Propositions upon which the good of Equality is founded

Pathology is a term used in medicine. It has not been introduced into morals, where it is equally needed, though in a somewhat different sense. By *pathology*, I mean the study and the knowledge of the sensations, affections, passions, and of their effects upon happiness. Legislation, which hitherto has been founded in a great measure only upon the quicksands of prejudice and instinct, ought at last to be built upon the immoveable basis of sensations and experience. It is necessary to have a moral thermometer to make perceptible all the degrees of happiness and misery. This is a term of perfection which it is not possible to reach; but it is well to have it before our eyes. I know that a scrupulous examination of more or less, in the matter of pain or pleasure, will at first appear a minute undertaking. It will be said that in human affairs it is necessary to act in gross; to be contented with a vague approximation. This is the language of indifference or of incapacity. The sensations of men are sufficiently regular to become the objects of a science and an art. Yet hitherto we have seen but essays, blind attempts, and irregular efforts not well followed up. Medicine has for its foundation the axioms of physical pathology. Morality is the medicine of the soul; and legislation, which is the practical part of it, ought to have for its foundation the axioms of mental pathology.

To judge of the effect of a portion of wealth upon happiness, it is necessary to consider it in three different states: –

1st. When it has always been in the hands of the holder.

2nd. When it is leaving his hands.

3rd. When it is coming into them.

It is to be observed in general, that in speaking of the effect of a portion of wealth upon happiness, abstraction is always to be made of the particular sensibility of individuals, and of the exterior circumstances in which they may be placed. Differences of character are inscrutable; and such is the diversity of circumstances, that they are never the same for two individuals. Unless we begin by dropping these two considerations, it will be impossible to announce any general proposition. But though each of these propositions may prove false or inexact in a given individual case, that will furnish no argument against their speculative truth and practical utility. It is enough for the justification of these propositions – 1st, If they approach nearer the truth than any others which can be substituted for them; 2nd, If with less inconvenience than any others they can be made the basis of legislation.

I. Let us pass to the first case. The object being to examine the effect of a portion of wealth, when it has always been in the hands of the holder, we may lay down the following propositions: –

1st. *Each portion of wealth has a corresponding portion of happiness.*

2nd. *Of two individuals with unequal fortunes, he who has the most wealth has the most happiness.*

3rd. *The excess in happiness of the richer will not be so great as the excess of his wealth.*

4th. For the same reasons, *the greater the disproportion is between the two masses of wealth, the less is it probable that there exists a disproportion equally great between the corresponding masses of happiness.*

5th. *The nearer the actual proportion approaches to equality, the greater will be the total mass of happiness.*

It is not necessary to limit what is here said of wealth to the condition of those who are called wealthy. This word has a more extensive signification. It embraces everything which serves either for subsistence or abundance. It is for the sake of brevity that the phrase *portion of wealth* is used instead of *portion of the matter of wealth.*

I have said that for *each portion of wealth there is a corresponding portion of happiness.* To speak more exactly, it ought rather to be said, *a certain chance of happiness.* For the efficacy of a cause of happiness is always precarious; or, in other words, a cause of happiness has not its ordinary effect, nor the same effect, upon all persons. Here is the place for making an application of what has been said concerning the sensibility and the character of individuals, and the variety of circumstances in which they are found.

The second proposition is a direct consequence of the first. *Of two individuals, he who is the richer is the happier or has the greater chance of being so.* This is a fact proved by the experience of all the world. The first who doubts it shall be the very witness I will call to prove it. Let him give all his superfluous wealth to the first comer who asks him for it; for this superfluity, according to his system, is but dust in his hands; it is a burden and nothing more. The manna of the desert putrefied, if any one collected a greater quantity than he could eat. If wealth resembled that manna, and after passing a certain point was no longer productive in happiness, no one would wish for it; and the desire of accumulation would be a thing unknown.

The third proposition is less likely to be disputed. Put on one side a thousand farmers, having enough to live upon, and a little more. Put on the other side a king, or, not to be encumbered with the cares of government, a prince, well portioned, himself as rich as all the farmers taken together. It is probable, I say, that his happiness is greater than the average happiness of the thousand farmers; but it is by no means probable that it is equal to the sum total of their happiness, or, what amounts to the same thing, a thousand times greater than the average happiness of one of them. It would be remarkable if his happiness were ten times, or even five times greater. The man who is born in the bosom of opulence, is not so sensible of its pleasures as he who is the artisan of his own fortune. It is the pleasure of acquisition, not the satisfaction of possessing, which gives the greatest delights. The one is a lively sentiment, pricked on by the desires, and by anterior privations, which rushes toward an unknown good; the other is a feeble sentiment, weakened by use, which is not animated by contrasts, and which borrows nothing from the imagination. ...

Governments, profiting by the progress of knowledge, have favoured, in many respects, the principle of equality in the distribution of losses. It is thus that they have taken under the protection of the laws *policies of insurance*, those useful contracts by which individuals assess themselves beforehand to provide against possible losses. The principle of insurance, founded upon a calculation of probabilities, is but the art of distributing losses among so great a number of associates as to make them very light, and almost nothing.

The same spirit has influenced sovereigns when they have indemnified, at the expense of the state, those of their subjects who have suffered either by public calamities or by the devastations of war. We have seen nothing of this kind wiser or better managed than the administration of the great Frederic. It is one of the finest points of view under which the social art can be considered.

Some attempts have been made to indemnify individuals for losses caused by the offences of malefactors. But examples of this kind are yet very rare. It is an object which merits the attention of legislators; for it is the means of reducing almost to nothing the evil of offences which attack property. To prevent it from becoming injurious, such a system must be arranged with care. It will not do to encourage indolence and imprudence in the neglect of precautions against offences, by making them sure of an indemnification; and it is necessary to guard even more cautiously against fraud and secret connivances which might counterfeit offences, and even produce them, for the sake of the indemnity. The utility of this remedial process would depend entirely on the way in which it was administered; yet the rejection of a means so salutary can only originate in a culpable indifference, anxious to save itself the trouble of discovering expedients.

The principles we have laid down may equally serve to regulate the distribution of a loss among many persons charged with a common responsibility. If their respective contributions correspond to the respective quantity of their fortunes, their relative state will be the same as before; but if it is desired to improve this occasion for the purposes of an approach towards equality, it is necessary to adopt a different proportion. To levy an equal impost, without regard to differences of fortune, would be a third plan, which would be agreeable neither to equality nor security.

To place this subject in a clearer light, I shall present a mixed case, in which it is necessary to decide between two individuals, of whom one demands a profit at the expense of the other. The question is to determine the effect of a portion of wealth which, passing into the hands of one individual under the form of gain, must come out of the hands of another in the form of loss.

1st. *Among competitors of equal fortunes, when that which is gained by one must be lost by another, the arrangement productive of the greatest sum of good will be that which favours the old possessor to the exclusion of the new demandant.*

For, in the first place, the sum to be lost, bearing a greater proportion to the reduced fortune than the same sum to the augmented fortune, the diminution of happiness for the one will be greater than the augmentation of happiness for the other; in one word, equality will be violated by the contrary arrangement.

In the second place, the loser will experience a pain of disappointment; the other merely does not gain. Now the negative evil of not acquiring is not equal to the positive evil of losing. If it were, as every man would experience this evil for all that he does not acquire, the causes of suffering would be infinite, and men would be infinitely miserable.

In the third place, men in general appear to be more sensitive to pain than to pleasure, even when the cause is equal. To such a degree, indeed, does this extend, that a loss which diminishes a man's fortune by one-fourth, will take away more happiness than he could gain by doubling his property.

2nd. *Fortunes being unequal, if the loser is the poorer, the evil of the loss will be aggravated by that inequality.*

3rd. *If the loser is the richer, the evil done by an attack upon security will be compensated in part by a good which will be great in proportion to the progress towards equality.*

By the aid of these maxims, which, to a certain point, have the character and the certainty of mathematical propositions, there might be at last produced a regular and constant art of indemnities and satisfactions. Legislators have frequently shown a disposition to promote equality under the name of *equity*, a word to which a greater latitude has been given than to *justice.* But this idea of equity, vague and half developed, has rather appeared an affair of instinct than of calculation. It was only by much patience and method that it was found possible to reduce to rigorous propositions an incoherent multitude of confused sentiments.

CHAPTER VII
Of Security

We come now to the principal object of law, – the care of security. That inestimable good, the distinctive index of civilization, is entirely the work of law. Without law there is no security; and, consequently, no abundance, and not even a certainty of subsistence; and the only equality which can exist in such a state of things is an equality of misery.

To form a just idea of the benefits of law, it is only necessary to consider the condition of savages. They strive incessantly against famine; which sometimes cuts off entire tribes. Rivalry for subsistence produces among them the most cruel wars; and, like beasts of prey, men pursue men, as a means of sustenance. The fear of this terrible calamity silences the softer sentiments of nature; pity unites with insensibility in putting to death the old men who can hunt no longer.

Let us now examine what passes at those terrible epochs when civilized society returns almost to the savage state; that is, during war, when the laws on which security depends are in part suspended. Every instant of its duration is fertile in calamities; at every step which it prints upon the earth, at every movement which it makes, the existing mass of riches, the fund of abundance and of subsistence, decreases and disappears. The cottage is ravaged as well as the palace; and how often the rage, the caprice even of a moment, delivers up to destruction the slow produce of the labours of an age!

Law alone has done that which all the natural sentiments united have not the power to do. Law alone is able to create a fixed and durable possession which merits the name of property. Law alone can accustom men to bow their heads under the yoke of foresight, hard at first to bear, but afterwards light and agreeable. Nothing but law can encourage men to labours superfluous for the present, and which can be enjoyed only in the future. Economy has as many enemies as there are dissipators - men who wish to enjoy without giving themselves the trouble of producing. Labour is too painful for idleness; it is too slow for impatience. Fraud and injustice secretly conspire to appropriate its fruits. Insolence and audacity think to ravish them by open force. Thus security is assailed on every side - ever threatened, never tranquil, it exists in the midst of alarms. The legislator needs a vigilance always sustained, a power always in action, to defend it against this crowd of indefatigable enemies.

Law does not say to man, *Labour, and I will reward you;* but it says: *Labour, and I will assure to you the enjoyment of the fruits of your labour - that natural and sufficient recompense which without me you cannot preserve; I will insure it by arresting the hand which may seek to ravish it from you.* If industry creates, it is law which preserves; if at the first moment we owe all to labour, at the second moment, and at every other, we are indebted for everything to law.

To form a precise idea of the extent which ought to be given to the principle of security, we must consider that man is not like the animals, limited to the present, whether as respects suffering or enjoyment; but that he is susceptible of pains and pleasures by anticipation; and that it is not enough to secure him from actual loss, but it is necessary also to guarantee him, as far as possible, against future loss. It is necessary to prolong the idea of his security through all the perspective which his imagination is capable of measuring.

This presentiment, which has so marked an influence upon the fate of man, is called *expectation.* It is hence that we have the power of forming a general plan of conduct; it is hence that the successive instants which compose the duration of life are not like isolated and independent points, but become continuous parts of a whole. *Expectation* is a chain which unites our present existence to our future existence, and which passes beyond us to the generation which is to follow. The sensibility of man extends through all the links of this chain.

The principle of security extends to the maintenance of all these expectations; it requires that events, so far as they depend upon laws, should conform to the expectations which law itself has created.

Every attack upon this sentiment produces a distinct and special evil, which may be called a *pain of disappointment.*

It is a proof of great confusion in the ideas of lawyers, that they have never given any particular attention to a sentiment which exercises so powerful an influence upon human life. The word *expectation* is scarcely found in their vocabulary. Scarce a single argument founded upon that principle appears in their writings. They have followed it, without doubt, in many respects; but they have followed it by instinct rather than by reason. If they had known its extreme importance they would not have failed to *name* it and to mark it, instead of leaving it unnoticed in the crowd.

CHAPTER VIII
Of Property

The better to understand the advantages of law, let us endeavour to form a clear idea of *property*. We shall see that there is no such thing as natural property, and that it is entirely the work of law.

Property is nothing but a basis of expectation; the expectation of deriving certain advantages from a thing which we are said to possess, in consequence of the relation in which we stand towards it.

There is no image, no painting, no visible trait, which can express the relation that constitutes property. It is not material, it is metaphysical; it is a mere conception of the mind.

To have a thing in our hands, to keep it, to make it, to sell it, to work it up into something else; to use it – none of these physical circumstances, nor all united, convey the idea of property. A piece of stuff which is actually in the Indies may belong to me, while the dress I wear may not. The aliment which is incorporated into my very body may belong to another, to whom I am bound to account for it.

The idea of property consists in an established expectation; in the persuasion of being able to draw such or such an advantage from the thing possessed, according to the nature of the case. Now this expectation, this persuasion, can only be the work of law. I cannot count upon the enjoyment of that which I regard as mine, except through the promise of the law which guarantees it to me. It is law alone which permits me to forget my natural weakness. It is only through the protection of law that I am able to inclose a field, and to give myself up to its cultivation with the sure though distant hope of harvest.

But it may be asked, What is it that serves as a basis to law, upon which to begin operations, when it adopts objects which, under the name of property, it promises to protect? Have not men, in the primitive state, a *natural* expectation of enjoying certain things, - an expectation drawn from sources anterior to law?

Yes. There have been from the beginning, and there always will be, circumstances in which a man may secure himself, by his own means, in the enjoyment of certain things. But the catalogue of these cases is very limited. The savage who has killed a deer may hope to keep it for himself, so long as his cave is undiscovered; so long as he watches to defend it, and is stronger than his rivals; but that is all. How miserable and precarious is such a possession! If we suppose the least agreement among savages to respect the acquisitions of each other, we see the introduction of a principle to which no name can be given but that of law. A feeble and momentary expectation may result from time to time from circumstances purely physical; but a strong and permanent expectation can result only from law. That which, in the natural state, was an almost invisible thread, in the social state becomes a cable.

Property and law are born together, and die together. Before laws were made there was no property; take away laws, and property ceases.

As regards property, security consists in receiving no check, no shock, no derangement to the expectation founded on the laws, of enjoying such and such a portion of good. The legislator owes the greatest respect to this expectation which he has himself produced. When he does not contradict it, he does what is essential to the happiness of society; when he disturbs it, he always produces a proportionate sum of evil.

CHAPTER IX
Answer to an Objection

But perhaps the laws of property are good for those who have property, and oppressive to those who have none. The poor man, perhaps, is more miserable than he would be without laws.

The laws, in creating property, have created riches only in relation to poverty. Poverty is not the work of the laws; it is the primitive condition of the human race. The man who subsists only from day to day is precisely the man of nature – the savage. The poor man, in civilized society, obtains nothing, I admit, except by painful labour; but, in the natural state, can he obtain anything except by the sweat of his brow? Has not the chase its fatigues, fishing its dangers, and war its uncertainties? And if man seems to love this adventurous life; if he has an instinct warm for this kind of perils; if the savage enjoys with delight an idleness so dearly bought; – must we thence conclude that he is happier than our cultivators? No. Their labour is more uniform, but their reward is more sure; the woman's lot is far more agreeable; childhood and old age have more resources; the species multiplies in a proportion a thousand times greater, – and that alone suffices to show on which side is the superiority of happiness. Thus the laws, in creating riches, are the benefactors of those who remain in the poverty of nature. All participate more or less in the pleasures, the advantages, and the resources of civilized society. The industry and the labour of the poor place them among the candidates of fortune. And have they not the pleasures of acquisition? Does not hope mix with their labours? Is the security which the law gives of no importance to them? Those who look down from above upon the inferior ranks see all objects smaller; but towards the base of the pyramid it is the summit which in turn is lost. Comparisons are never dreamed of; the wish of what seems impossible does not torment. So that, in fact, all things considered, the protection of the laws may contribute as much to the happiness of the cottage as to the security of the palace.

It is astonishing that a writer so judicious as Beccaria has interposed, in a work dictated by the soundest philosophy, a doubt subversive of social order. *The right of property*, he says, *is a terrible right, which perhaps is not necessary.* Tyrannical and sanguinary laws have been founded upon that right; it has been frightfully abused; but the right itself presents only ideas of pleasure, abundance, and security. It is that right which has vanquished the natural aversion to labour; which has given to man the empire of the earth; which has brought to an end the migratory life of nations; which has produced the love of country and a regard for posterity. Men universally desire to enjoy speedily – to enjoy without labour. It is that desire which is terrible; since it arms all who have not against all who have. The law which restrains that desire is the noblest triumph of humanity over itself.

CHAPTER X
Analysis of the Evils which result from Attacks upon Property

We have already seen that subsistence depends upon the laws which assure to the labourer the produce of his labour. But it is desirable more exactly to analyze the evils which result from violations of property. They may be reduced to four heads.

1st. *Evil of Non-Possession.* - If the acquisition of a portion of wealth is a good, it follows that the non-possession of it is an evil, though only a negative evil. Thus, although men in the condition of primitive poverty may not have specially felt the want of a good which they knew not, yet it is clear that they have lost all the happiness which might have resulted from its possession, and of which we have the enjoyment. The loss of a portion of good, though we knew nothing of it, is still a loss. Are you doing me no harm when, by false representations, you deter my friend from conferring upon me a favour which I did not expect? In what consists the harm? In the negative evil which results from not possessing that which, but for your falsehoods, I should have had.

2nd. *Pain of Losing.* - Everything which I possess, or to which I have a title, I consider in my own mind as destined always to belong to me. I make it the basis of my expectations, and of the hopes of those dependent upon me; and I form my plan of life accordingly. Every part of my property may have, in my estimation, besides its intrinsic value, a value of affection - as an inheritance from my ancestors, as the reward of my own labour, or as the future dependence of my children. Everything about it represents to my eye that part of myself which I have put into it - those cares, that industry, that economy which denied itself present pleasures to make provision for the future. Thus our property becomes a part of our being, and cannot be torn from us without rending us to the quick.

3rd. *Fear of Losing.* - To regret for what we have lost is joined inquietude as to what we possess, and even as to what we may acquire. For the greater part of the objects which compose subsistence and abundance being perishable matters, future acquisitions are a necessary supplement to present possessions. When insecurity reaches a certain point, the fear of losing prevents us from enjoying what we possess already. The care of preserving condemns us to a thousand sad and painful precautions, which yet are always liable to fail of their end. Treasures are hidden or conveyed away. Enjoyment becomes sombre, furtive, and solitary. It fears to show itself, lest cupidity should be informed of a chance to plunder.

4th. *Deadening of Industry.* - When I despair of making myself sure of the produce of my labour, I only seek to exist from day to day. I am unwilling to give myself cares which will only be profitable to my enemies. Besides, the will to labour is not enough; means are wanting. While waiting to reap, in the meantime I must live. A single loss may deprive me of the capacity of action, without having quenched the spirit of industry, or without having paralyzed my will. Thus the three first evils affect the passive faculties of the individual, while the fourth extends to his active faculties, and more or less benumbs them.

It appears from this analysis that the two first evils do not go beyond the individual injured; while the two latter spread through society, and occupy an indefinite space. An attack upon the property of an individual excites alarm among other proprietors. This sentiment spreads from neighbour to neighbour, till at last the contagion possesses the entire body of the state.

Power and *will* must unite for the development of industry. Will depends upon encouragement; *power* upon means. These means are what is called, in the language of political economy, *productive capital*. When the question relates only to an individual, his productive capital may be annihilated by a single loss, while his spirit of industry is not extinguished, nor even weakened. When the question is of a nation, the annihilation of its productive capital is impossible; but a long time before that fatal term is approached, the evil may infect the will; and the spirit of industry may fall into a fatal lethargy, in the midst of natural resources offered by a rich and fertile soil. The will, however, is excited by so many stimulants, that it resists an abundance of discouragements and losses. A transitory calamity, though great, never destroys the spirit of industry. It is seen to spring up, after devouring wars which have impoverished nations, as a robust oak, mutilated by tempests, repairs its losses in a few years and covers itself with new branches. Nothing is sufficient to deaden industry, except the operation of a domestic and permanent cause, such as a tyrannical government, bad legislation, an intolerant religion which drives men from the country, or a minute superstition which stupifies them.

A first act of violence produces immediately a certain degree of apprehension; some timid spirits are already discouraged. A second violence, which soon succeeds, spreads a more considerable alarm. The more prudent begin to retrench their enterprises, and little by little to abandon an uncertain career. In proportion as these attacks are repeated, and the system of oppression takes a more habitual character, the dispersion increases. Those who fly are not replaced; those who remain fall into a state of languor. Thus the field of industry, beaten by perpetual storms, at last becomes a desert.

Asia Minor, Greece, Egypt, the coasts of Africa, so rich in agriculture, in commerce, and in population, at the flourishing epoch of the Roman empire, what have they become under the absurd despotism of the Turkish government? Palaces have been changed into cabins, and cities into hamlets. That government, odious to every thinking man, has never known that a state cannot grow rich except by an inviolable respect for property. It has never had but two secrets of statesmanship, - to sponge the people, and to stupify them. Thus the finest countries of the earth, wasted, barren, and almost abandoned, can hardly be recognized under the hands of barbarous conquerors.

These evils ought not to be attributed to foreign causes. Civil wars, invasions, natural scourges, may dissipate wealth, put the arts to flight, and swallow up cities. But choked harbours are opened again; communications are re-established; manufactures revive; cities rise from their ruins. All ravages are repaired by time, while men continue to be men; but there are no men to be found in those unhappy countries, where the slow but fatal despair of long insecurity has destroyed all the active faculties of the soul.

If we trace the history of this contagion, we shall see its first attacks directed against that part of society which is easy and well off. Opulence is the object of the first depredations. Apparent superfluity vanishes little by little. Absolute need makes itself be obeyed in spite of obstacles. We must live; but when man limits himself to living, the state languishes, and the lamp of industry throws out only a dying flame. Besides, abundance is never so distinct from subsistence, that one can be destroyed without a dangerous blow at the other. While some lose only what is superfluous, others lose a part of what is necessary; for by the infinitely complicated system of economical connections, the opulence of a part of the citizens is the only fund upon which a part more numerous depends for subsistence.

But another picture may be traced, more smiling and not less instructive. It is the picture of the progress of *security*, and of prosperity, its inseparable companion. North America presents to us a most striking contrast. Savage nature may be seen there, side by side with civilized nature. The interior of that immense region offers only a frightful solitude, impenetrable forests or sterile plains, stagnant waters and impure vapours; such is the earth when left to itself. The fierce tribes which rove through those deserts without fixed habitations, always occupied with the pursuit of game, and animated against each other by implacable rivalries, meet only for combat, and often succeed in destroying each other. The beasts of the forest are not so dangerous to man as he is to himself. But on the borders of these frightful solitudes, what different sights are seen! We appear to comprehend in the same view the two empires of good and evil. Forests give place to cultivated fields; morasses are dried up, and the surface, grown firm, is covered with meadows, pastures, domestic animals, habitations healthy and smiling. Rising cities are built upon regular plans; roads are constructed to communicate between them; everything announces that men, seeking the means of intercourse, have ceased to fear and to murder each other. Harbours filled with vessels receive all the productions of the earth, and assist in the exchange of all kinds of riches. A numerous people, living upon their labour in peace and abundance, has succeeded to a few tribes of hunters, always placed between war and famine. What has wrought these prodigies? Who has renewed the surface of the earth? Who has given to man this domain over nature – over nature embellished, fertilized, and perfected? That beneficent genius is *Security*. It is security which has wrought this great metamorphosis. And how rapid are its operations? It is not yet two centuries since William Penn landed upon those savage coasts, with a colony of true conquerors, men of peace, who did not soil their establishments with blood, and who made themselves respected by acts of beneficence and justice.

CHAPTER XI
Opposition between Security and Equality

In consulting the grand principle of security, what ought the legislator to decree respecting the mass of property already existing?

He ought to maintain the distribution as it is actually established. It is this which, under the name of *justice*, is regarded as his first duty. This is a general and simple rule, which applies itself to all states; and which adapts itself to all places, even those of the most opposite character. There is nothing more different than the state of property in America, in England, in Hungary, and in Russia. Generally, in the first of these countries, the cultivator is a proprietor; in the second, a tenant; in the third, attached to the glebe; in the fourth, a slave. However, the supreme principle of security commands the preservation of all these distributions, though their nature is so different, and though they do not produce the same sum of happiness. How make another distribution without taking away from each that which he has? And how despoil any without attacking the security of all? When your new repartition is disarranged – that is to say, the day after its establishment – how avoid making a second? Why not correct it in the same way? And in the meantime, what becomes of security? Where is happiness? Where is industry?

When security and equality are in conflict, it will not do to hesitate a moment. Equality must yield. The first is the foundation of life; subsistence, abundance, happiness, everything depends upon it. Equality produces only a certain portion of good. Besides, whatever we may do, it will never be perfect; it may exist a day; but the revolutions of the morrow will overturn it. The establishment of perfect equality is a chimera; all we can do is to diminish inequality.

If violent causes, such as a revolution of government, a division, or a conquest, should bring about an overturn of property, it would be a great calamity; but it would be transitory; it would diminish; it would repair itself in time. Industry is a vigorous plant which resists many amputations, and through which a nutritious sap begins to circulate with the first rays of returning summer. But if property should be overturned with the direct intention of establishing an equality of possessions, the evil would be irreparable. No more security, no more industry, no more abundance! Society would return to the savage state whence it emerged. ...

CHAPTER XII
Means of uniting Security and Equality

Is it necessary that between these two rivals, *Security* and *Equality*, there should be an opposition, an eternal war? To a certain point they are incompatible; but with a little patience and address they may, in a great measure, be reconciled.

The only mediator between these contrary interests is time. Do you wish to follow the counsels of equality without contravening those of security? – await the natural epoch which puts an end to hopes and fears, the epoch of death.

When property by the death of the proprietor ceases to have an owner, the law can interfere in its distribution, either by limiting in certain respects the testamentary power, in order to prevent too great an accumulation of wealth in the hands of an individual; or by regulating the succession in favour of equality in cases where the deceased has left no consort, nor relation in the direct line, and has made no will. The question then relates to new acquirers who have formed no expectations; and equality may do what is best for all without disappointing any. At present I only indicate the principle: the development of it may be seen in the second book.

When the question is to correct a kind of civil inequality, such as slavery, it is necessary to pay the same attention to the right of property; to submit it to a slow operation, and to advance towards the subordinate object without sacrificing the principal object. Men who are rendered free by these gradations, will be much more capable of being so than if you had taught them to tread justice under foot, for the sake of introducing a new social order.

It is worthy of remark that, in a nation prosperous in its agriculture, its manufactures, and its commerce, there is a continual progress towards equality. If the laws do nothing to combat it, if they do not maintain certain monopolies, if they put no shackles upon industry and trade, if they do not permit entails, we see great properties divided little by little, without effort, without revolution, without shock, and a much greater number of men coming to participate in the moderate favours of fortune. This is the natural result of the opposite habits which are formed in opulence and in poverty. The first, prodigal and vain, wishes only to enjoy without labour; the second, accustomed to obscurity and privations, finds pleasures even in labour and economy. Thence the change which has been made in Europe by the progress of arts and commerce, in spite of legal obstacles. We are at no great distance from those ages of feudality, when the world was divided into two classes: a few great proprietors, who were everything, and a multitude of serfs, who were nothing. These pyramidal heights have disappeared or have fallen; and from their ruins industrious men have formed those new establishments, the great number of which attests the comparative happiness of modern civilization. Thus we may conclude that *Security*, while preserving its place as the supreme principle, leads indirectly to *Equality*; while equality, if taken as the basis of the social arrangement, will destroy both itself and security at the same time.

5 / KARL MARX

From the early nineteenth century on, as the dehumanizing effects of industrial capitalism became increasingly evident, opposition to the received justification of property came from many quarters – utopian socialists (St Simon, Fourier, Owen), young Hegelians (Feuerbach, Hess), philosophic anarchists (Proudhon), Christian socialists (F.D. Maurice, Charles Kingsley), romantic celebrators of pre-industrial society (Carlyle), and closer analysts of the society and economy of their time (Marx and Engels). By far the most influential of these was Marx. His incisive analysis of the political economy of capitalism, his outraged ethical rejection of its reduction of human beings to commodities, and his argument that that reduction was required by the property relations of capitalism, gave his work a strength which is more formidable in the twentieth century than it was when he wrote. He followed Rousseau, and many of the early nineteenth century socialists, in giving a historical dimension to the institution of property and to human nature, but his analysis of that history was better informed and more solidly based than theirs.

Marx wrote so much that it is difficult to choose a few extracts which could convey the richness of his thinking. To appreciate it at all fully one would need to consult, in addition to the extracts presented here, the *Economic-Philosophic Manuscripts* (1844), and the *Critique of the Gotha Programme* (1875). Here there is only room to present his popular analysis in the famous *Communist Manifesto* (1848), and a brief but striking part of the fuller analysis, in part VIII of volume I of *Capital* (1867), which gives much more historical depth.

Bourgeois Property and Capitalist Accumulation

1 / From the *Communist Manifesto*

The abolition of existing property relations is not at all a distinctive feature of Communism.

All property relations in the past have continually been subject to historical change consequent upon the change in historical conditions.

The French Revolution, for example, abolished feudal property in favor of bourgeois property.

The distinguishing feature of Communism is not the abolition of property generally, but the abolition of bourgeois property. But modern bourgeois private property is the final and most complete expression of the system of producing and appropriating products, that is based on class antagonism, on the exploitation of the many by the few.

In this sense, the theory of the Communists may be summed up in the single sentence: Abolition of private property.

We Communists have been reproached with the desire of abolishing the right of personally acquiring property as the fruit of a man's own labor, which property is alleged to be the ground work of all personal freedom, activity and independence.

Hard-won, self-acquired, self-earned property! Do you mean the property of the petty artisan and of the small peasant, a form of property that preceded the bourgeois form? There is no need to abolish that; the development of industry has to a great extent already destroyed it, and is still destroying it daily.

Or do you mean modern bourgeois private property?

But does wage-labor create any property for the laborer? Not a bit. It creates capital, i.e., that kind of property which exploits wage-labor, and which cannot increase except upon condition of getting a new supply of wage-labor for fresh exploitation. Property, in its present form, is based on the antagonism of capital and wage-labor. Let us examine both sides of this antagonism.

To be a capitalist, is to have not only a purely personal, but a social status in production. Capital is a collective product, and only by the united action of many members, nay, in the last resort, only by the united action of all members of society, can it be set in motion.

Capital is therefore not a personal, it is a social power.

When, therefore, capital is converted into common property, into the property of all members of society, personal property is not thereby transformed into social property. It is only the social character of the property that is changed. It loses its class-character.

Let us now take wage-labor.

The average price of wage-labor is the minimum wage, i.e., that quantum of the means of subsistence, which is absolutely requisite to keep the laborer in bare existence as a laborer. What, therefore, the wage-laborer appropriates by means of his labor, merely suffices to prolong and reproduce a bare existence. We by no means intend to abolish this personal appropriation of the products of labor, an appropriation that is made for the maintenance and reproduction of human life, and that leaves no surplus wherewith to command the labor of others. All that we want to do away with is the miserable character of this appropriation, under which the laborer lives merely to increase capital, and is allowed to live only in so far as the interest of the ruling class requires it.

In bourgeois society, living labor is but a means to increase accumulated labor. In Communist society, accumulated labor is but a means to widen, to enrich, to promote the existence of the laborer.

In bourgeois society, therefore, the past dominates the present; in communist society, the present dominates the past. In bourgeois society capital is independent and has individuality, while the living person is dependent and has no individuality.

And the abolition of this state of things is called by the bourgeois, abolition of individuality and freedom! And rightly so. The abolition of bourgeois individuality, bourgeois independence, and bourgeois freedom is undoubtedly aimed at.

By freedom is meant, under the present bourgeois conditions of production, free trade, free selling and buying.

But if selling and buying disappears, free selling and buying disappears also. This talk about free selling and buying, and all the other 'brave words' of our bourgeoisie about freedom is general, have a meaning, if any, only in contrast with restricted selling and buying, with the fettered traders of the Middle Ages, but have no meaning when opposed to the Communistic abolition of buying and selling, of the bourgeois conditions of production, and of the bourgeoisie itself.

You are horrified at our intending to do away with private property. But in your existing society, private property is already done away with for nine-tenths of the population; its existence for the few is solely due to its non-existence in the hands of those nine-tenths. You reproach us, therefore, with intending to do away with a form of property, the necessary condition for whose existence is, the non-existence of any property for the immense majority of society.

In one word, you reproach us with intending to do away with your property. Precisely so; that is just what we intend.

From the moment when labor can no longer be converted into capital, money, or rent, into a social power capable of being monopolized, i.e., from the moment when individual property can no longer be transformed into bourgeois property, into capital, from that moment, you say, individuality vanishes.

You must, therefore, confess that by 'individual' you mean no other person than the bourgeois, than the middle-class owner of property. This person must, indeed, be swept out of the way, and made impossible.

Communism deprives no man of the power to appropriate the products of society: all that it does is to deprive him of the power to subjugate the labor of others by means of such appropriation.

It has been objected, that upon the abolition of private property all work will cease, and universal laziness will overtake us.

According to this, bourgeois society ought long ago to have gone to the dogs through sheer idleness; for those of its members who work, acquire nothing, and those who acquire anything, do not work. The whole of this objection is but another expression of the tautology: that there can no longer be any wage-labor when there is no longer any capital.

All objections urged against the Communistic mode of producing and appropriating material products, have, in the same way, been urged against the Communistic modes of producing and appropriating intellectual products. Just as, to the bourgeois, the disappearance of class property is the disappearance of production itself, so the disappearance of class culture is to him identical with the disappearance of all culture.

That culture, the loss of which he laments, is, for the enormous majority, a mere training to act as a machine.

But don't wrangle with us so long as you apply, to our intended abolition of bourgeois property, the standard of your bourgeois notions of freedom, culture, law, etc. Your very ideas are but the outgrowth of the conditions of your bourgeois production and bourgeois property, just as your jurisprudence is but the will of your class made into a law for all, a will, whose essential character and direction are determined by the economic conditions of existence of your class.

The selfish misconception that induces you to transform into eternal laws of nature and of reason, the social forms springing from your present mode of production and form of property – historical relations that rise and disappear in the progress of production – this misconception you share with every ruling class that has preceded you. What you see clearly in the case of ancient property, what you admit in the case of feudal property, you are of course forbidden to admit in the case of your own bourgeois form of property.

2 / From *Capital*, volume I

CHAPTER XXXII
Historical Tendency of Capitalist Accumulation

What does the primitive accumulation of capital, *i.e.*, its historical genesis, resolve itself into? In so far as it is not immediate transformation of slaves and serfs into wage-labourers, and therefore a mere change of form, it only means the expropriation of the immediate producers, *i.e.*, the dissolution of private property based on the labour of its owner. Private property, as the antithesis to social, collective property, exists only where the means of labour and the external conditions of labour belong to private individuals. But according as these private individuals are labourers or not labourers, private property has a different character. The numberless shades, that it at first sight presents, correspond to the intermediate stages lying between these two extremes. The private property of the labourer in his means of production is the foundation of petty industry, whether agricultural, manufacturing, or both; petty industry, again, is an essential condition for the development of social production and of the free individuality of the labourer himself. Of course, this petty mode of production exists also under slavery, serfdom, and other states of dependence. But it flourishes, it lets loose its whole energy, it attains its adequate classical form, only where the labourer is the private owner of his own means of labour set in action by himself: the peasant of the land which he cultivates, the artizan of the tool which he handles as a virtuoso. This mode of production presupposes parcelling of the soil, and scattering of the other means of production. As it excludes the concentration of these means of production, so also it excludes co-operation, division of labour within each separate process of production, the control over, and the productive application of the forces of Nature by society, and the free development of the social productive powers. It is compatible only with a system of production, and a society, moving within narrow and more or less primitive bounds. To perpetuate it would be, as Pecqueur rightly says, 'to decree universal mediocrity.' At a certain stage of development it brings forth the material agencies for its own dissolution. From that moment new forces and new passions spring up in the bosom of society; but the old social organisation fetters them and keeps them down. It must be annihilated; it is annihilated. Its annihilation, the transformation of the individualised and scattered means of production into socially concentrated ones, of the pigmy property of the many into the huge property of the few, the expropriation of the great mass of the people from the soil, from the means of subsistence, and from the means of labour, this fearful and painful expropriation of the mass of the people forms the prelude to the history of capital. It comprises a series of forcible methods, of which we have passed in review only those that have been epoch-making as methods of the primitive accumulation of capital. The expropriation of the immediate producers was accomplished with merciless Vandalism, and under the stimulus of passions the most infamous, the most sordid, the pettiest, the most meanly odious. Self-earned private property, that is based, so to say, on the fusing together of the isolated, independent labouring-individual with the conditions of his labour, is supplanted by capitalistic private property, which rests on exploitation of the nominally free labour of others, *i.e.*, on wages-labour.[1]

As soon as this process of transformation has sufficiently decomposed the old society from top to bottom, as soon as the labourers are turned into proletarians, their means of labour into capital, as soon as the capitalist mode of production stands on its own feet, then the further socialisation of labour and further transformation of the land and other means of production into socially exploited and, therefore, common means of production, as well as the further expropriation of private proprietors, takes a new form. That which is now to be expropriated is no longer the labourer working for himself, but the capitalist exploiting many labourers. This expropriation is accomplished by the action of the immanent laws of capitalistic production itself, by the centralisation of capital. One capitalist always kills many. Hand in hand with this centralisation, or this expropriation of many capitalists by few, develop, on an ever extending scale, the co-operative form of the labour-process, the conscious technical application of science, the methodical cultivation of the soil, the transformation of the instruments of labour into instruments of labour only usable in common, the economising of all means of production by their use as the means of production of combined, socialised labour, the entanglement of all peoples in

1 'Nous sommes dans une condition tout-à-fait nouvelle de la société ... nous tendons à séparer toute espèce de propriété d'avec toute espèce de travail.' (Sismondi: *Nouveaux Principes de l'Econ. Polit.* t. II., p. 434.)

the net of the world-market, and with this, the international character of the capitalistic régime. Along with the constantly diminishing number of the magnates of capital, who usurp and monopolise all advantages of this process of transformation, grows the mass of misery, oppression, slavery, degradation, exploitation; but with this too grows the revolt of the working-class, a class always increasing in numbers, and disciplined, united, organised by the very mechanism of the process of capitalist production itself. The monopoly of capital becomes a fetter upon the mode of production, which has sprung up and flourished along with, and under it. Centralisation of the means of production and socialisation of labour at last reach a point where they become incompatible with their capitalist integument. This integument is burst asunder. The knell of capitalist private property sounds. The expropriators are expropriated.

The capitalist mode of appropriation, the result of the capitalist mode of production, produces capitalist private property. This is the first negation of individual private property, as founded on the labour of the proprietor. But capitalist production begets, with the inexorability of a law of Nature, its own negation. It is the negation of negation. This does not re-establish private property for the producer, but gives him individual property based on the acquisitions of the capitalist era: *i.e.*, on co-operation and the possession in common of the land and of the means of production.

The transformation of scattered private property, arising from individual labour, into capitalist private property is, naturally, a process, incomparably more protracted, violent, and difficult, than the transformation of capitalistic private property, already practically resting on socialised production, into socialised property. In the former case, we had the expropriation of the mass of the people by a few usurpers; in the latter, we have the expropriation of a few usurpers by the mass of the people.[1]

1 The advance of industry, whose involuntary promoter is the bourgeoisie, replaces the isolation of the labourers, due to competition, by their revolutionary combination, due to association. The development of Modern Industry, therefore, cuts from under its feet, the very foundation on which the bourgeoisie produces and appropriates products. What the bourgeoisie therefore, produces, above all, are its own grave-diggers. Its fall and the victory of the proletariat are equally inevitable. ... Of all the classes, that stand face to face with the bourgeoisie to-day, the proletariat alone is a really revolutionary class. The other classes perish and disappear in the face of Modern Industry, the proletariat is its special and essential product. ... The lower middle-classes, the small manufacturers, the shopkeepers, the artisan, the peasant, all these fight against the bourgeoisie, to save from extinction their existence as fractions of the middle-class ... they are reactionary, for they try to roll back the wheel of history. 'Karl Marx and Frederick Engels, Manifest der Kommunistischen Partei,' London, 1848, pp. 9, 11.

CHAPTER XXXIII
The Modern Theory of Colonisation*

Political economy confuses on principle two very different kinds of private property, of which one rests on the producers' own labour, the other on the employment of the labour of others. It forgets that the latter not only is the direct antithesis of the former, but absolutely grows on its tomb only. In Western Europe, the home of political economy, the process of primitive accumulation is more or less accomplished. Here the capitalist régime has either directly conquered the whole domain of national production, or, where economic conditions are less developed, it, at least, indirectly controls those strata of society which, though belonging to the antiquated mode of production, continue to exist side by side with it in gradual decay. To this ready-made world of capital, the political economist applies the notions of law and of property inherited from a pre-capitalistic world with all the more anxious zeal and all the greater unction, the more loudly the facts cry out in the face of his ideology. It is otherwise in the colonies. There the capitalist régime everywhere comes into collision with the resistance of the producer, who, as owner of his own conditions of labour, employs that labour to enrich himself, instead of the capitalist. The contradiction of these two diametrically opposed economic systems, manifests itself here practically in a struggle between them. Where the capitalist has at his back the power of the mother-country, he tries to clear out of his way by force, the modes of production and appropriation, based on the independent labour of the producer. The same interest, which compels the sycophant of capital, the political economist, in the mother-country, to proclaim the theoretical identity of the capitalist mode of production with its contrary, that same interest compels him in the colonies to make a clean breast of it, and to proclaim aloud the antagonism of the two modes of production. To this end he proves how the development of the social productive power of labour, co-operation, division of labour, use of machinery on a large scale, & c., are impossible without the expropriation of the labourers, and the corresponding transformation of their means of production into capital. In the interest of the so-called national wealth, he seeks for artificial means to ensure the poverty of the people. Here his apologetic armour crumbles off, bit by bit, like rotten touchwood. It is the great merit of E.G. Wakefield to have discovered, not anything new about the Colonies,[1] but to have discovered in the Colonies the

* We treat here of real Colonies, virgin soils, colonised by free immigrants. The United States are, speaking economically, still only a Colony of Europe. Besides, to this category belong also such old plantations as those in which the abolition of slavery has completely altered the earlier conditions.

1 Wakefield's few glimpses on the subject of Modern Colonisation are fully anticipated by Mirabeau Père, the physiocrat, and even much earlier by English economists.

truth as to the conditions of capitalist production in the mother-country. As the system of protection at its origin[2] attempted to manufacture capitalists artificially in the mother-country, so Wakefield's colonisation theory, which England tried for a time to enforce by Acts of Parliament, attempted to effect the manufacture of wage-workers in the Colonies. This he calls 'systematic colonisation.'

First of all, Wakefield discovered that in the Colonies, property in money, means of subsistence, machines, and other means of production, does not as yet stamp a man as a capitalist if there be wanting the correlative – the wage-worker, the other man who is compelled to sell himself of his own free-will. He discovered that capital is not a thing, but a social relation between persons, established by the instrumentality of things.[3] Mr. Peel, he moans, took with him from England to Swan River, West Australia, means of subsistence and of production to the amount of £50,000. Mr. Peel had the foresight to bring with him, besides, 3000 persons of the working-class, men, women, and children. Once arrived at his destination, 'Mr. Peel was left without a servant to make his bed or fetch him water from the river.'[1] Unhappy Mr. Peel who provided for everything except the export of English modes of production to Swan River!

For the understanding of the following discoveries of Wakefield, two preliminary remarks: We know that the means of production and subsistence, while they remain the property of the immediate producer, are not capital. They become capital, only under circumstances in which they serve at the same time as means of exploitation and subjection of the labourer. But this capitalist soul of theirs is so intimately wedded, in the head of the political economist, to their material substance, that he christens them capital under all circumstances, even when they are its exact opposite. Thus is it with Wakefield. Further: the splitting up of the means of production into the individual property of many independent labourers, working on their own account, he calls equal division of capital. It is with the political economist as with the feudal jurist. The latter stuck on to pure monetary relations the labels supplied by feudal law.

'If,' says Wakefield, 'all the members of the society are supposed to possess

2 Later, it became a temporary necessity in the international competitive struggle. But, whatever its motive, the consequences remain the same.

3 A negro is a negro. In certain circumstances he becomes a slave. A mule is a machine for spinning cotton. Only under certain circumstances does it become capital. Outside these circumstances, it is no more capital than gold is intrinsically money, or sugar is the price of sugar. ... Capital is a social relation of production. It is a historical relation of production. (Karl Marx, 'Lohnarbeit und Kapital.' N. Rh. Z. No. 266, April 7, 1849.)

1 E.G. Wakefield: *England and America,* vol. ii., p. 33.

equal portions of capital ... no man would have a motive for accumulating more capital than he could use with his own hands. This is to some extent the case in new American settlements, where a passion for owning land prevents the existence of a class of labourers for hire.'[2] So long, therefore, as the labourer can accumulate for himself – and this he can do so long as he remains possessor of his means of production – capitalist accumulation and the capitalistic mode of production are impossible. The class of wage-labourers, essential to these, is wanting. How, then, in old Europe, was the expropriation of the labourer from his conditions of labour, *i.e.*, the co-existence of capital and wage-labour, brought about? By a social contract of a quite original kind. 'Mankind have adopted a ... simple contrivance for promoting the accumulation of capital,' which, of course, since the time of Adam, floated in their imagination as the sole and final end of their existence: 'they have divided themselves into owners of capital and owners of labour ... This division was the result of concert and combination.'[1] In one word: the mass of mankind expropriated itself in honour of the 'accumulation of capital.' Now, one would think, that this instinct of self-denying fanaticism would give itself full fling especially in the Colonies, where alone exist the men and conditions that could turn a social contract from a dream to a reality. But why, then, should 'systematic colonisation' be called in to replace its opposite, spontaneous, unregulated colonisation? But – but – 'In the Northern States of the American Union, it may be doubted whether so many as a tenth of the people would fall under the description of hired labourers ... In England ... the labouring class compose the bulk of the people.'[2] Nay, the impulse to self-expropriation, on the part of labouring humanity, for the glory of capital, exists so little, that slavery, according to Wakefield himself, is the sole natural basis of Colonial wealth. His systematic colonisation is a mere *pis aller*, since he unfortunately has to do with free men, not with slaves. 'The first Spanish settlers in Saint Domingo did not obtain labourers from Spain. But, without labourers, their capital must have perished, or, at least, must soon have been diminished to that small amount which each individual could employ with his own hands. This has actually occurred in the last Colony founded by Englishmen – the Swan River Settlement – where a great mass of capital, of seeds, implements, and cattle, has perished for want of labourers to use it, and where no settler has preserved much more capital than he can employ with his own hands.'[3]

We have seen that the expropriation of the mass of the people from the soil forms the basis of the capitalist mode of production. The essence of a free colony, on the contrary, consists in this – that the bulk of the soil is still public

2 l. c., p. 17.
1 l. c., vol. i., p. 18.
2 l. c., pp. 42, 43, 44.
3 l. c., vol. ii., p. 5.

property, and every settler on it therefore can turn part of it into his private property and individual means of production, without hindering the later settlers in the same operation.[1] This is the secret both of the prosperity of the colonies and of their inveterate vice – opposition to the establishment of capital. 'Where land is very cheap and all men are free, where every one who so pleases can easily obtain a piece of land for himself, not only is labour very dear, as respects the labourer's share of the produce, but the difficulty is to obtain combined labour at any price.'[2]

As in the colonies the separation of the labourer from the conditions of labour and their root, the soil, does not yet exist, or only sporadically, or on too limited a scale, so neither does the separation of agriculture from industry exist, nor the destruction of the household industry of the peasantry. Whence then is to come the internal market for capital? 'No part of the population of America is exclusively agricultural, excepting slaves and their employers who combine capital and labour in particular works. Free Americans, who cultivate the soil, follow many other occupations. Some portion of the furniture and tools which they use is commonly made by themselves. They frequently build their own houses, and carry to market, at whatever distance, the produce of their own industry. They are spinners and weavers; they make soap and candles, as well as, in many cases, shoes and clothes for their own use. In America the cultivation of land is often the secondary pursuit of a blacksmith, a miller or a shopkeeper.'[3] With such queer people as these, where is the 'field of abstinence' for the capitalists?

The great beauty of capitalist production consists in this – that it not only constantly reproduces the wage-worker as wage-worker, but produces always, in proportion to the accumulation of capital, a relative surplus population of wage-workers. Thus the law of supply and demand of labour is kept in the right rut, the oscillation of wages is penned within limits satisfactory to capitalist exploitation, and lastly, the social dependance of the labourer on the capitalist, that indispensable requisite, is secured; an unmistakable relation of dependence, which the smug political economist, at home, in the mother country, can transmogrify into one of free contract between buyer and seller, between equally independent owners of commodities, the owner of the commodity capital and the owner of the commodity labour. But in the colonies this pretty fancy is torn asunder. The absolute population here increases much more quickly than in the mother-country, because many labourers enter this world as ready-made adults, and yet the labour market is always understocked.

1 'Land, to be an element of colonization, must not only be waste, but it must be public property, liable to be converted into private property.' (l. c. Vol. II., p. 125.)
2 l. c. Vol. I. p. 247.
3 l. c. pp. 21, 22.

The law of the supply and demand of labour falls to pieces. On the one hand, the old world constantly throws in capital, thirsting after exploitation and 'abstinence;' on the other, the regular reproduction of the wage-labourer as wage-labourer comes into collision with impediments the most impertinent and in part invincible. What becomes of the production of wage-labourers, supernumerary in proportion to the accumulation of capital? The wage-worker of to-day is to-morrow an independent peasant, or artisan, working for himself. He vanishes from the labour-market, but not into the workhouse. This constant transformation of the wage-labourers into independent producers, who work for themselves instead of for capital, and enrich themselves instead of the capitalist gentry, reacts in its turn very perversely on the conditions of the labour-market. Not only does the degree of exploitation of the wage-labourer remain indecently low. The wage-labourer loses into the bargain, along with the relation of dependence, also the sentiment of dependence on the abstemious capitalist. Hence all the inconveniences that our E.G. Wakefield pictures so doughtily, so eloquently, so pathetically.

The supply of wage-labour, he complains, is neither constant, nor regular, nor sufficient. 'The supply of labour is always, not only small, but uncertain.'[1] 'Though the produce divided between the capitalist and the labourer be large, the labourer takes so great a share that he soon becomes a capitalist ... Few, even of those whose lives are unusually long, can accumulate great masses of wealth.'[1] The labourers most distinctly decline to allow the capitalist to abstain from the payment of the greater part of their labour. It avails him nothing, if he is so cunning as to import from Europe, with his own capital, his own wage-workers. They soon 'cease ... to be labourers for hire; they ... become independent landowners, if not competitors with their former masters in the labour market.'[2] Think of the horror! The excellent capitalist has imported bodily from Europe, with his own good money, his own competitors! The end of the world has come! No wonder Wakefield laments the absence of all dependence and of all sentiment of dependence on the part of the wage-workers in the colonies. On account of the high wages, says his disciple, Merivale, there is in the colonies 'the urgent desire for cheaper and more subservient labourers - for a class to whom the capitalist might dictate terms, instead of being dictated to by them. ... In ancient civilized countries the labourer, though free, is by a law of nature dependent on capitalists; in colonies this dependence must be created by artificial means.'[3]

1 l. c., Vol. II., p. 116.
1 l. c., Vol. I., p. 131.
2 l. c., Vol. II., p. 5.
3 Merivale, l. c., Vol. II., pp. 235-314 passim. Even the mild, free-trade, vulgar economist, Molinari, says: 'Dans les colonies où l'esclavage a été aboli sans que le travail forcé se trouvait remplacé par une quantité équivalente de travail libre, on a vu

What is now, according to Wakefield, the consequence of this unfortunate state of things in the colonies? A 'barbarising tendency of dispersion' of producers and national wealth.[1] The parcelling-out of the means of production among innumerable owners, working on their own account, annihilates, along with the centralisation of capital, all the foundations of combined labour. Every long-winded undertaking, extending over several years and demanding outlay of fixed capital, is prevented from being carried out. In Europe, capital invests without hesitating a moment, for the working-class constitutes its living appurtenance, always in excess, always at disposal. But in the colonies! Wakefield tells an extremely doleful anecdote. He was talking with some capitalists of Canada and the state of New York, where the immigrant wave often becomes stagnant and deposits a sediment of 'supernumerary' labourers. 'Our capital,' says one of the characters in the melodrama, 'was ready for many operations which require a considerable period of time for their completion; but we could not begin such operations with labour which, we knew, would soon leave us. If we had been sure of retaining the labour of such emigrants, we should have been glad to have engaged it at once, and for a high price: and we should have engaged it, even though we had been sure it would leave us, provided we had been sure of a fresh supply whenever we might need it.'[2]

After Wakefield has contrasted the English capitalist agriculture and its 'combined' labour with the scattered cultivation of American peasants, he unwittingly gives us a glimpse at the reverse of the medal. He depicts the mass of the American people as well-to-do, independent, enterprising and comparatively cultured, whilst 'the English agricultural labourer is a miserable wretch, a

s'opérer la contre-partie du fait qui se réalise tous les jours sous nos yeux. On a vu les simples travailleurs exploiter à leur tour les entrepreneurs d'industrie, exiger d'eux des salaires hors de toute proportion avec la part légitime qui leur revenait dans le produit. Les planteurs, ne pouvant obtenir de leurs sucres un prix suffisant pour couvrir la hausse de salaire, ont été obligés de fournir l'excédant, d'abord sur leurs profits, ensuite sur leurs capitaux mêmes. Une foule de planteurs ont été ruinés de la sorte, d'autres ont fermé leurs ateliers pour échapper à une ruine imminente ... Sans doute, il vaut mieux voir périr des accumulations de capitaux que des générations d'hommes [how generous of Mr. Molinari!] : mais ne vaudrait-il pas mieux que ni les uns ni les autres périssent?' (Molinari l. c. pp. 51, 52.) Mr. Molinari, Mr. Molinari! What then becomes of the ten commandments, of Moses and the prophets, of the law of supply and demand, if in Europe the 'entrepreneur' can cut down the labourer's legitimate part, and in the West Indies, the labourer can cut down the entrepreneur's? And what, if you please, is this 'legitimate part,' which on your own showing the capitalist in Europe daily neglects to pay? Over yonder, in the colonies where the labourers are so 'simple' as to 'exploit' the capitalist, Mr. Molinari feels a strong itching to set the law of supply and demand, that works elsewhere automatically, on the right road by means of the police.

1 Wakefield, l. c., Vol. II., p. 52.

2 l. c. pp. 191, 192.

pauper. ... In what country, except North America and some new colonies, do the wages of free labour employed in agriculture, much exceed a bare subsistence for the labourer? ... Undoubtedly, farm-horses in England, being a valuable property, are better fed than English peasant.'[3] But, never mind, national wealth is, once again, by its very nature, identical with misery of the people.

How, then, to heal the anti-capitalistic cancer of the colonies? If men were willing, at a blow, to turn all the soil from public into private property, they would destroy certainly the root of the evil, but also – the colonies. The trick is how to kill two birds with one stone. Let the Government put upon the virgin soil an artificial price, independent of the law of supply and demand, a price that compels the immigrant to work a long time for wages before he can earn enough money to buy land, and turn himself into an independent peasant.[1] The funds resulting from the sale of land at a price relatively prohibitory for the wage-workers, this fund of money extorted from the wages of labour by violation of the sacred law of supply and demand, the Government is to employ, on the other hand, in proportion as it grows, to import have-nothings from Europe into the colonies, and thus keep the wage-labour market full for the capitalists. Under these circumstances, tout sera pour le mieux dans le meilleur des mondes possibles. This is the great secret of 'systematic colonisation.' By this plan, Wakefield cries in triumph, 'the supply of labour *must* be constant and regular, because, first, as no labourer would be able to procure land until he had worked for money, all immigrant labourers, working for a time for wages and in combination, would produce capital for the employment of more labourers; secondly, because every labourer who left off working for wages and became a landowner would, by purchasing land, provide a fund for bringing fresh labour to the colony.'[2] The price of the soil imposed by the State must, of course, be a 'sufficient price' – *i.e.*, so high 'as to prevent the labourers from becoming independent land-owners until others had followed to take their place.'[1] This 'sufficient price for the land' is nothing but a euphemistic circumlocution for the ransom which the labourer pays to the capitalist for leave to retire from the wage-labour market to the land. First, he must create for the capitalist 'capital,' with which the latter may be able to ex-

3 l. c., Vol. I., pp. 47, 246.

1 'C'est, ajoutez-vous, grâce à l'appropriation du sol et des capitaux que l'homme, qui n'a que ses bras, trouve de l'occupation, et se fait un revenu ... c'est au contraire, grâce à l'appropriation individuelle du sol qu'il se trouve des hommes n'ayant que leurs bras. ... Quand vous mettez un homme dans le vide, vous vous emparez de l'atmosphère. Ainsi faites-vous, quand vous vous emparez du sol. ... C'est le mettre dans le vide de richesses, pour ne le laisser vivre qu'à votre volonté.' (Colins, l. c., t. III., pp. 268-271, passim.)

2 Wakefield, l. c., Vol. II., p. 192.

1 l. c., p. 45.

ploit more labourers; then he must place, at his own expense, a *locum tenens* on the labour market, whom the Government forwards across the sea for the benefit of his old master, the capitalist.

It is very characteristic that the English Government for years practised this method of 'primitive accumulation,' prescribed by Mr Wakefield expressly for the use of the colonies. The fiasco was, of course, as complete as that of Sir Robert Peel's Bank Act. The stream of emigration was only diverted from the English colonies to the United States. Meanwhile, the advance of capitalistic production in Europe, accompanied by increasing Government pressure, has rendered Wakefield's recipe superfluous. On the one hand, the enormous and ceaseless stream of men, year after year driven upon America, leaves behind a stationary sediment in the east of the United States, the wave of immigration from Europe throwing men on the labour market there more rapidly than the wave of emigration westwards can wash them away. On the other hand, the American Civil War brought in its train a colossal national debt, and, with it, pressure of taxes, the rise of the vilest financial aristocracy, the squandering of a huge part of the public land on speculative companies for the exploitation of railways, mines, & c., in brief, the most rapid centralisation of capital. The great republic has, therefore, ceased to be the promised land for emigrant labourers. Capitalistic production advances there with giant strides, even though the lowering of wages and the dependence of the wage-worker are yet far from being brought down to the normal European level. The shameless lavishing of uncultivated colonial land on aristocrats and capitalists by the Government, so loudly denounced even by Wakefield, has produced, especially in Australia,[2] in conjunction with the stream of men that the gold-diggings attract and with the competition that the importation of English commodities causes even to the smallest artisan, an ample 'relative surplus labouring population,' so that almost every mail brings the Job's news of a 'glut of the Australian labour-market,' and prostitution in some places there flourishes as wantonly as in the London Haymarket.

However, we are not concerned here with the condition of the colonies. The only thing that interests us is the secret discovered in the new world by the political economy of the old world, and proclaimed on the house-tops; that the capitalist mode of production and accumulation, and therefore capitalist private property, have for their fundamental condition the annihilation of self-earned private property; in other words, the expropriation of the labourer.

2 As soon as Australia became her own law-giver, she passed, of course laws favourable to the settlers, but the squandering of the land, already accomplished by the English Government, stands in the way. 'The first and main object at which the new Land Act of 1862 aims is to give increased facilities for the settlement of the people.' (The Land Law of Victoria, by the Hon. O.G. Duffy, Minister of Public Lands. Lond. 1862.)

6 / JOHN STUART MILL

In the same year as the *Communist Manifesto* (1848) Mill published his *Principles of Political Economy*, which set the limits of his subsequent books on political theory, notably his *Considerations on Representative Government* (1861) and his *On Liberty* (1859). Mill was apparently not aware, either in 1848 or in all his subsequent revisions of the *Political Economy*, of Marx's critique. But he was alert to the critiques of established property by other socialists – St Simon, Fourier, Louis Blanc, and Robert Owen – and did try to come to terms with them. He wavered between admitting their critiques and upholding the justice or necessity of the existing, or a slightly modified, institution of property. On the whole, he came down in favour of the latter. The gross inequity of the existing system was, he argued, due not to anything inherent in the principle of private property and market freedom of accumulation, but only to accidental historical features that had been built into the prevailing system and could be removed from it.

In making this argument, Mill was trying to extricate himself from the Benthamist position in which he had been educated from his early youth. He offered instead a revised and humanized utilitarianism which was more to the taste of late nineteenth and twentieth century liberals. In spite of his failure to resolve the contradiction in his principle of property (on which see my *Life and Times of Liberal Democracy*, chap. III) his position is still widely shared.

This extract is reprinted from his *Principles of Political Economy with Some of Their Applications to Social Philosophy*, in *Collected Works of John Stuart Mill*, Volume II, edited by John M. Robson (University of Toronto Press, and London: Routledge and Kegan Paul, 1965), with the permission of the editor and publisher. This is the text of the seventh edition, 1871, the last revised by

Mill. One footnote by Mill which merely reproduces a long passage from Sismondi is omitted, as are annotations on variants in the editions. The extract comprises the following sections of the *Principles*: book II, chapter I, sections 2 and 3; and book II, chapter II (complete).

Of Property

BOOK II, CHAPTER I

2. [*Statement of the question concerning Property*] Private property, as an institution, did not owe its origin to any of those considerations of utility, which plead for the maintenance of it when established. Enough is known of rude ages, both from history and from analogous states of society in our own time, to show, that tribunals (which always precede laws) were originally established, not to determine rights, but to repress violence and terminate quarrels. With this object chiefly in view, they naturally enough gave legal effect to first occupancy, by treating as the aggressor the person who first commenced violence, by turning, or attempting to turn, another out of possession. The preservation of the peace, which was the original object of civil government, was thus attained; while by confirming, to those who already possessed it, even what was not the fruit of personal exertion, a guarantee was incidentally given to them and others that they would be protected in what was so.

In considering the institution of property as a question in social philosophy, we must leave out of consideration its actual origin in any of the existing nations of Europe. We may suppose a community unhampered by any previous possession; a body of colonists, occupying for the first time an uninhabited country; bringing nothing with them but what belonged to them in common, and having a clear field for the adoption of the institutions and polity which they judged most expedient; required, therefore, to choose whether they would conduct the work of production on the principle of individual property, or on some system of common ownership and collective agency.

If private property were adopted, we must presume that it would be accompanied by none of the initial inequalities and injustices which obstruct the beneficial operation of the principle in old societies. Every full grown man or woman, we must suppose, would be secured in the unfettered use and disposal of his or her bodily and mental faculties; and the instruments of production, the land and tools, would be divided fairly among them, so that all might start, in respect to outward appliances, on equal terms. It is possible also to conceive that in this original apportionment, compensation might be made for the injuries of nature, and the balance redressed by assigning to the less robust members of the community advantages in the distribution, sufficient to put them on a par with the rest. But the division, once made, would not again be interfered with; individuals would be left to their own exertions and to the ordinary chances, for making an advantageous use of what was assigned to them. If individual property, on the contrary, were excluded, the plan which must be adopted would be to hold the land and all instruments of production as the joint property of the community, and to carry on the operations of industry on the common account. The direction of the labour of the community would devolve upon a magistrate or magistrates, whom we may suppose elected by the suffrages of the community, and whom we must assume to be voluntarily obeyed by them. The division of the produce would in like manner be a public act. The principle might either be that of complete equality, or of apportionment to the necessities or deserts of individuals, in whatever manner might be conformable to the ideas of justice or policy prevailing in the community.

Examples of such associations, on a small scale, are the monastic orders, the Moravians, the followers of Rapp, and others: and from the hopes which they hold out of relief from the miseries and iniquities of a state of much inequality of wealth, schemes for a larger application of the same idea have reappeared and become popular at all periods of active speculation on the first principles of society. In an age like the present, when a general reconsideration of all first principles is felt to be inevitable, and when more than at any former period of history the suffering portions of the community have a voice in the discussion, it was impossible but that ideas of this nature should spread far and wide. The late revolutions in Europe have thrown up a great amount of speculation of this character, and an unusual share of attention has consequently been drawn to the various forms which these ideas have assumed: nor is this attention likely to diminish, but on the contrary, to increase more and more.

The assailants of the principle of individual property may be divided into two classes: those whose scheme implies absolute equality in the distribution of the physical means of life and enjoyment, and those who admit inequality, but grounded on some principle, or supposed principle, of justice or general expediency, and not, like so many of the existing social inequalities, dependent on accident alone. At the head of the first class, as the earliest of those belonging to the present generation, must be placed Mr. Owen and his followers. M. Louis Blanc and M. Cabet have more recently become conspicuous as apostles of similar doctrines (though the former advocates equality of distribution only as a transition to a still higher standard of justice, that all should work according to their capacity, and receive according to their wants). The characteristic name for this economical system is Communism, a word of continental origin, only of late introduced into this country. The word Socialism, which originated among the English Communists, and was assumed by them as a name to designate their own doctrine, is now, on the Continent, employed in a larger sense; not necessarily implying Communism, or the entire abolition of private property, but applied to any system which requires that the land and the instruments of production should be the property, not of individuals, but of communities or associations, or of the government. Among such systems, the two of highest intellectual pretension are those which, from the names of their real or reputed authors, have been called St. Simonism and Fourierism; the former defunct as a system, but which during the few years of its public promulgation, sowed the seeds of nearly all the Socialist tendencies which have since spread so widely in France: the second, still flourishing in the number, talent, and zeal of its adherents.

3. [*Examination of Communism*] Whatever may be the merits or defects of these various schemes, they cannot be truly said to be impracticable. No reasonable person can doubt that a village community, composed of a few thousand inhabitants cultivating in joint ownership the same extent of land which at present feeds that number of people, and producing by combined labour and the most improved processes the manufactured articles which they required, could raise an amount of productions sufficient to maintain them in comfort; and would find the means of obtaining, and if need be, exacting, the quantity of labour necessary for this purpose, from every member of the association who was capable of work.

The objection ordinarily made to a system of community of property and equal distribution of the produce, that each person would be incessantly occupied in evading his fair share of the work, points, undoubtedly, to a real difficulty. But those who urge this objection, forget to how great an extent the same difficulty exists under the system on which nine-tenths of the business of society is now conducted. The objection supposes, that honest and efficient labour is only to be had from those who are themselves individually to reap the benefit of their own exertions. But how small a part of all the labour performed in England, from the lowest-paid to the highest, is done by persons working for their own benefit. From the Irish reaper or hodman to the chief justice or the minister of state, nearly all the work of society is remunerated by day wages or fixed salaries. A factory operative has less personal interest in his work than a member of a Communist association, since he is not, like him, working for a partnership of which he is himself a member. It will no doubt be said, that though the labourers themselves have not, in most cases, a personal interest in their work, they are watched and superintended, and their labour directed, and the mental part of the labour performed, by persons who have. Even this, however, is far from being universally the fact. In all public, and many of the largest and most successful private undertakings, not only the labours of detail but the control and superintendence are entrusted to salaried officers. And though the 'master's eye,' when the master is vigilant and intelligent, is of proverbial value, it must be remembered that in a Socialist farm or manufactory, each labourer would be under the eye not of one master, but of the whole community. In the extreme case of obstinate perseverance in not performing the due share of work, the community would have the same resources which society now has for compelling conformity to the necessary conditions of the association. Dismissal, the only remedy at present, is no remedy when any other labourer who may be engaged does no better than his predecessor: the power of dismissal only enables an employer to obtain from his workmen the customary amount of labour, but that customary labour may be of any degree of inefficiency. Even the labourer who loses his employment by idleness or negligence, has nothing worse to suffer, in the most unfavourable case, than the discipline of a workhouse, and if the desire to avoid this be a sufficient motive in the one system, it would be sufficient in the other. I am not undervaluing the strength of the incitement given to labour when the whole or a large share of the benefit of extra exertion belongs to the labourer. But under the present system of industry this incitement, in the great majority of cases, does not exist. If Communistic labour might be less vigorous than that of a peasant proprietor, or a workman labouring on his own account, it would probably be more energetic than that of a labourer for hire, who has no personal interest in the matter at all. The neglect by the uneducated classes of labourers for hire, of the duties which they engage to perform, is in the present state of society most flagrant. Now it is an admitted condition of the Communist scheme that all shall be educated: and this being supposed, the duties of the members of the association would doubtless be as diligently performed as those of the generality of salaried officers in the middle or higher classes; who are not supposed to be necessarily unfaithful to their trust, because so long as they are not dismissed, their pay is the same in however lax a manner their duty is fulfilled. Undoubtedly, as a general rule, remuneration by fixed salaries does not in any class of functionaries produce the maximum of zeal: and this is as much as can be reasonably alleged against Communistic labour.

That even this inferiority would necessarily exist, is by no means so certain as is assumed by those who are little used to carry their minds beyond the state of things with which they are familiar. Mankind are capable of a far greater amount of public spirit than the present age is accustomed to suppose possible. History bears witness to the success with which large bodies of human beings may be trained to feel the public interest their own. And no soil could be more favourable to the growth of such a feeling, than a Communist association, since all the ambition, and the bodily and mental activity, which are now exerted in the pursuit of separate and self-regarding interests, would require another sphere of employment, and would naturally find it in the pursuit of the general benefit of the community. The same cause, so often assigned in explanation of the devotion of the Catholic priest or monk to the interest of his order - that he has no interest apart from it - would, under Communism, attach the citizen to the community. And independently of the public motive, every member of the association would be amenable to the most universal, and one of the strongest, of personal motives, that of public opinion. The force of this motive in deterring from any act or omission positively reproved by the community, no one is likely to deny; but the power also of emulation, in exciting to the most strenuous exertions for the sake of the approbation and admiration of others, is borne witness to by experience in every situation in which human beings publicly compete with one another, even if it be in things frivolous, or from which the public derive no benefit. A contest, who can do most for the common good, is not the kind of competition which Socialists repudiate. To what extent, therefore, the energy of labour would be diminished by Communism, or whether in the long run it would be diminished at all, must be considered for the present an undecided question.

Another of the objections to Communism is similar to that, so often urged against poor-laws: that if every member of the community were assured of subsistence for himself and any number of children, on the sole condition of willingness to work, prudential restraint on the multiplication of mankind would be at an end, and population would start forward at a rate which would reduce the community, through successive stages of increasing discomfort, to actual starvation. There would certainly be much ground for this apprehension if Communism provided no motives to restraint, equivalent to those which it would take away. But Communism is precisely the state of things in which opinion might be expected to declare itself with greatest intensity against this kind of selfish intemperance. Any augmentation of numbers which diminished the comfort or increased the toil of the mass, would then cause (which now it does not) immediate and unmistakeable inconvenience to every individual in the association; inconvenience which could not then be imputed to the avarice of employers, or the unjust privileges of the rich. In such altered circumstances opinion could not fail to reprobate, and if reprobation did not suffice, to repress by penalties of some description, this or any other culpable self-indulgence at the expense of the community. The Communistic scheme, instead of being peculiarly open to the objection drawn from danger of over-population, has the recommendation of tending in an especial degree to the prevention of that evil.

A more real difficulty is that of fairly apportioning the labour of the community among its members. There are many kinds of work, and by what standard are they to be measured one against another? Who is to judge how much cotton spinning, or distributing goods from the stores, or brick-laying, or chimney sweeping, is equivalent to so much ploughing? The difficulty of making the adjustment between different qualities of labour is so strongly felt by Communist writers, that they have usually thought it necessary to provide that all should work by turns at every description of useful labour: an arrangement which, by putting an end to the division of employments, would sacrifice so much of the advantage of co-operative production as greatly to diminish the productiveness of labour. Besides, even in the same kind of work, nominal equality of labour would be so great a real inequality, that the feeling of justice would revolt against its being enforced. All persons are not equally fit for all labour; and the same quantity of labour is an unequal burthen on the weak and the strong, the hardy and the delicate, the quick and the slow, the dull and the intelligent.

But these difficulties, though real, are not necessarily insuperable. The apportionment of work to the strength and capacities of individuals, the mitigation of a general rule to provide for cases in which it would operate harshly, are not problems to which human intelligence, guided by a sense of justice, would be inadequate. And the worst and most unjust arrangement which could be made of these points, under a system aiming at equality, would be so far short of the inequality and injustice with which labour (not to speak of remuneration) is now apportioned, as to be scarcely worth counting in the comparison. We must remember too, that Communism, as a system of society, exists only in idea; that its difficulties, at present, are much better understood than its resources; and that the intellect of mankind is only beginning to contrive the means of organizing it in detail, so as to overcome the one and derive the greatest advantage from the other.

If, therefore, the choice were to be made between Communism with all its chances, and the present state of society with all its sufferings and injustices; if the institution of private property necessarily carried with it as a consequence, that the produce of labour should be apportioned as we now see it, almost in an inverse ratio to the labour – the largest portions to those who have never worked at all, the next largest to those whose work is almost nominal, and so in a descending scale, the remuneration dwindling as the work grows harder and more disagreeable, until the most fatiguing and exhausting bodily labour cannot count with certainty on being able to earn even the necessaries of life; if this or Communism were the alternative, all the difficulties, great or small, of Communism would be but as dust in the balance. But to make the comparison applicable, we must compare Communism at its best, with the régime of individual property, not as it is, but as it might be made. The principle of private property has never yet had a fair trial in any country; and less so, perhaps, in this country than in some others. The social arrangements of modern Europe commenced from a distribution of property which was the result, not of just partition, or acquisition by industry, but of conquest and violence: and notwithstanding what industry has been doing for many centuries to modify the work of force, the system still retains many and large traces of its origin. The laws of property have never yet conformed to the principles on which the justification of private property rests. They have made property of things which never ought to be property, and absolute property where only a qualified property ought to exist. They have not held the balance fairly between human beings, but have heaped impediments upon some, to give advantage to others; they have purposely fostered inequalities, and prevented all from starting fair in the race. That all should indeed start on perfectly equal terms, is inconsistent with any law of private property: but if as much pains as has been taken to aggravate the inequality of chances arising from the natural working of the principle, had been taken to temper that inequality by every means not subversive of the principle itself; if the tendency of legislation had been to favour the diffusion, instead of the concentration of wealth – to encourage the subdivision of the large masses, instead of striving to keep them together; the principle of individual property would have been found to have no necessary connexion with the physical and social evils which almost all Socialist writers assume to be inseparable from it.

Private property, in every defence made of it, is supposed to mean, the guarantee to individuals of the fruits of their own labour and abstinence. The guarantee to them of the fruits of the labour and abstinence of others, transmitted to them without any merit or exertion of their own, is not of the essence of the institution, but a mere incidental consequence, which, when it reaches a certain height, does not promote, but conflicts with, the ends which render private property legitimate. To judge of the final destination of the institution of property, we must suppose everything rectified, which causes the institution to work in a manner opposed to that equitable principle, of proportion between remuneration and exertion, on which in every vindication of it that will bear the light, it is assumed to be grounded. We must also suppose two conditions realized, without which neither Communism nor any other laws or institutions could make the condition of the mass of mankind other than degraded and miserable. One of these conditions is, universal education; the other, a due limitation of the numbers of the community. With these, there could be no poverty, even under the present social institutions: and these being supposed, the question of Socialism is not, as generally stated by Socialists, a question of flying to the sole refuge against the evils which now bear down humanity; but a mere question of comparative advantages, which futurity must determine. We are too ignorant either of what individual agency in its best form, or Socialism in its best form, can accomplish, to be qualified to decide which of the two will be the ultimate form of human society.

If a conjecture may be hazarded, the decision will probably depend mainly on one consideration, viz. which of the two systems is consistent with the greatest amount of human liberty and spontaneity. After the means of subsistence are assured, the next in strength of the personal wants of human beings is liberty; and (unlike the physical wants, which as civilization advances become more moderate and more amenable to control) it increases instead of diminishing in intensity, as the intelligence and the moral faculties are more developed. The perfection both of social arrangements and of practical morality would be, to secure to all persons complete independence and freedom of action, subject to no restriction but that of not doing injury to others: and the education which taught or the social institutions which required them to exchange the control of their own actions for any amount of comfort or affluence, or to renounce liberty for the sake of equality, would deprive them of one of the most elevated characteristics of human nature. It remains to be discovered how far the preservation of this characteristic would be found compatible with the Communistic organization of society. No doubt, this, like all the other objections to the Socialist schemes, is vastly exaggerated. The members of the association need not be required to live together more than they do now, nor need they be controlled in the disposal of their individual share of the produce, and of the probably large amount of leisure which, if they limited their production to things really worth producing, they would possess. Individuals need not be chained to an occupation, or to a particular locality. The restraints of Communism would be freedom in comparison with the present condition of the majority of the human race. The generality of labourers in this and most other countries, have as little choice of occupation or freedom of locomotion, are practically as dependent on fixed rules and on the will of others, as they could be on any system short of actual slavery; to say nothing of the entire domestic subjection of one half the species, to which it is the signal honour of Owenism and most other forms of Socialism that they assign equal rights, in all respects, with those of the hitherto dominant sex. But it is not by comparison with the present bad state of society that the claims of Communism can be estimated; nor is it sufficient that it should promise greater personal and mental freedom than is now enjoyed by those who have not enough of either to deserve the name. The question is, whether there would be any asylum left for individuality of character; whether public opinion would not be a tyrannical yoke; whether the absolute dependence of each on all, and surveillance of each by all, would not grind all down into a tame uniformity of thoughts, feelings, and actions. This is already one of the glaring evils of the existing state of society, notwithstanding a much greater diversity of education and pursuits, and a much less absolute dependence of the individual on the mass, than would exist in the Communistic régime. No society in which eccentricity is a matter of reproach, can be in a wholesome state. It is yet to be ascertained whether the Communistic scheme would be consistent with that multiform development of human nature, those manifold unlikenesses, that diversity of tastes and talents, and variety of intellectual points of view, which not only form a great part of the interest of human life, but by bringing intellects into stimulating collision, and by presenting to each innumerable notions that he would not have conceived of himself, are the mainspring of mental and moral progression.

BOOK II, CHAPTER II

1. [*The institution of property implies freedom of acquisition by contract*] It is next to be considered, what is included in the idea of private property, and by what considerations the application of the principle should be bounded.

The institution of property, when limited to its essential elements, consists in the recognition, in each person, of a right to the exclusive disposal of what he or she have produced by their own exertions, or received either by gift or by fair agreement, without force or fraud, from those who produced it. The foundation of the whole is, the right of producers to what they themselves have produced. It may be objected, therefore, to the institution as it now exists, that it recognises rights of property in individuals over things which they have not produced. For example (it may be said) the operatives in a manufactory create, by their labour and skill, the whole produce; yet, instead of its belonging to them, the law gives them only their stipulated hire, and transfers the produce to some one who has merely supplied the funds, without perhaps contributing anything to the work itself, even in the form of superintendence. The answer to this is, that the labour of manufacture is only one of the conditions which must combine for the production of the commodity. The labour cannot be carried on without materials and machinery, nor without a stock of necessaries provided in advance, to maintain the labourers during the production. All these things are the fruits of previous labour. If the labourers were possessed of them, they would not need to divide the produce with any one; but while they have them not, an equivalent must be given to those who have, both for the antecedent labour, and for the abstinence by which the produce of that labour, instead of being expended on indulgences, has been reserved for this use. The capital may not have been, and in most cases was not, created by the labour and abstinence of the present possessor; but it was created by the labour and abstinence of some former person, who may indeed have been wrongfully dispossessed of it, but who, in the present age of the world, much more probably transferred his claims to the present capitalist by gift or voluntary contract: and the abstinence at least must have been continued by each successive owner, down to the present. If it be said, as it may with truth, that those who have inherited the savings of others have an advantage which they may have in no way deserved, over the industrious whose predecessors have not left them anything; I not only admit, but strenuously contend, that this unearned advantage should be curtailed, as much as is consistent with justice to those who thought fit to dispose of their savings by giving them to their descendants. But while it is true that the labourers are at a disadvantage compared with those whose predecessors have saved, it is also true that the labourers are far better off than if those predecessors had not saved. They share in the advantage, though not to an equal extent with the inheritors. The terms of co-operation between present labour and the fruits of past labour and saving, are a subject for adjustment between the two parties. Each is necessary to the other. The capitalists can do nothing without labourers, nor the labourers without capital. If the labourers compete for employment, the capitalists on their part compete for labour, to the full extent of the circulating capital of the country. Competition is often spoken of as if it were necessarily a cause of misery and degradation to the labouring class; as if high wages were not precisely as much a product of competition as low wages. The remuneration of labour is as much the result of the law of competition in the United States, as it is in Ireland, and much more completely so than in England.

The right of property includes then, the freedom of acquiring by contract. The right of each to what he has produced, implies a right to what has been produced by others, if obtained by their free consent; since the producers must either have given it from good will, or exchanged it for what they esteemed an equivalent, and to prevent them from doing so would be to infringe their right of property in the product of their own industry.

2. [*The institution of property implies the validity of prescription*] Before proceeding to consider the things which the principle of individual property does not include, we must specify one more thing which it does include: and this is that a title, after a certain period, should be given by prescription. According to the fundamental idea of property, indeed, nothing ought to be treated as such, which has been acquired by force or fraud, or appropriated in ignorance of a prior title vested in some other person; but it is necessary to the security of rightful possessors, that they should not be molested by charges of wrongful acquisition, when by the lapse of time witnesses must have per-

ished or been lost sight of, and the real character of the transaction can no longer be cleared up. Possession which has not been legally questioned within a moderate number of years, ought to be, as by the laws of all nations it is, a complete title. Even when the acquisition was wrongful, the dispossession, after a generation has elapsed, of the probably *bonâ fide* possessors, by the revival of a claim which had been long dormant, would generally be a greater injustice, and almost always a greater private and public mischief, than leaving the original wrong without atonement. It may seem hard that a claim, originally just, should be defeated by mere lapse of time; but there is a time after which (even looking at the individual case, and without regard to the general effect on the security of possessors), the balance of hardship turns the other way. With the injustices of men, as with the convulsions and disasters of nature, the longer they remain unrepaired, the greater become the obstacles to repairing them, arising from the aftergrowths which would have to be torn up or broken through. In no human transactions, not even in the simplest and clearest, does it follow that a thing is fit to be done now, because it was fit to be done sixty years ago. It is scarcely needful to remark, that these reasons for not disturbing acts of injustice of old date, cannot apply to unjust systems or institutions; since a bad law or usage is not one bad act, in the remote past, but a perpetual repetition of bad acts, as long as the law or usage lasts.

Such, then, being the essentials of private property, it is now to be considered, to what extent the forms in which the institution has existed in different states of society, or still exists, are necessary consequences of its principle, or are recommended by the reasons on which it is grounded.

3. [*The institution of property implies the power of bequest, but not the right of inheritance. Question of inheritance examined*] Nothing is implied in property but the right of each to his (or her) own faculties, to what he can produce by them, and to whatever he can get for them in a fair market; together with his right to give this to any other person if he chooses, and the right of that other to receive and enjoy it.

It follows, therefore, that although the right of bequest, or gift after death, forms part of the idea of private property, the right of inheritance, as distinguished from bequest, does not. That the property of persons who have made no disposition of it during their lifetime, should pass first to their children, and failing them, to the nearest relations, may be a proper arrangement or not, but is no consequence of the principle of private property. Although there belong to the decision of such questions many considerations besides those of political economy, it is not foreign to the plan of this work to suggest, for the judgment of thinkers, the view of them which most recommends itself to the writer's mind.

No presumption in favour of existing ideas on this subject is to be derived from their antiquity. In early ages, the property of a deceased person passed to his children and nearest relatives by so natural and obvious an arrangement, that no other was likely to be even thought of in competition with it. In the first place, they were usually present on the spot: they were in possession, and if they had no other title, had that, so important in an early state of society, of first occupancy. Secondly, they were already, in a manner, joint owners of his property during his life. If the property was in land, it had generally been conferred by the State on a family rather than on an individual: if it consisted of cattle or moveable goods, it had probably been acquired, and was certainly protected and defended, by the united efforts of all members of the family who were of an age to work or fight. Exclusive individual property in the modern sense, scarcely entered into the ideas of the time; and when the first magistrate of the association died, he really left nothing vacant but his own share in the division, which devolved on the member of the family who succeeded to his authority. To have disposed of the property otherwise, would have been to break up a little commonwealth, united by ideas, interest, and habits, and to cast them adrift on the world. These considerations, though rather felt than reasoned about, had so great an influence on the minds of mankind, as to create the idea of an inherent right in the children to the possessions of their ancestor; a right which it was not competent to himself to defeat. Bequest, in a primitive state of society, was seldom recognised; a clear proof, were there no other, that property was conceived in a manner totally different from the conception of it in the present time.

But the feudal family, the last historical form of patriarchal life, has long perished, and the unit of society is not now the family or clan, composed of all the reputed descendants of a common ancestor, but the individual; or at most a pair of individuals, with their unemancipated children. Property is now inherent in individuals, not in families: the children when grown up do not follow the occupations or fortunes of the parent: if they participate in the parent's pecuniary means it is at his or her pleasure, and not by a voice in the ownership and government of the whole, but generally by the exclusive enjoyment of a part; and in this country at least (except as far as entails or settlements are an obstacle) it is in the power of parents to disinherit even their children, and leave their fortune to strangers. More distant relatives are in general almost as completely detached from the family and its interests as if they were in no way connected with it. The only claim they are supposed to have on their richer relations, is to a preference, *caeteris paribus,* in good offices, and some aid in case of actual necessity.

So great a change in the constitution of society must make a considerable difference in the grounds on which the disposal of property by inheritance should rest. The reasons usually assigned by modern writers for giving the property of a person who dies intestate, to the children, or nearest relatives, are, first, the supposition that in so disposing of it, the law is more likely than in any other mode to do what the proprietor would have done, if he had done anything; and secondly, the hardship, to those who lived with their parents and partook in their opulence, of being cast down from the enjoyments of wealth into poverty and privation.

There is some force in both these arguments. The law ought, no doubt, to do for the children or dependents of an intestate, whatever it was the duty of the parent or protector to have done, so far as this can be known by any one besides himself. Since, however, the law cannot decide on individual claims, but must proceed by general rules, it is next to be considered what these rules should be.

We may first remark, that in regard to collateral relatives, it is not, unless on grounds personal to the particular individual, the duty of any one to make a pecuniary provision for them. No one now expects it, unless there happen to be no direct heirs; nor would it be expected even then, if the expectation were not created by the provisions of the law in case of intestacy. I see, therefore, no reason why collateral inheritance should exist at all. Mr. Bentham long ago proposed, and other high authorities have agreed in the opinion, that if there are no heirs either in the descending or in the ascending line, the property, in case of intestacy, should escheat to the State. With respect to the more remote degrees of collateral relationship, the point is not very likely to be disputed. Few will maintain that there is any good reason why the accumulations of some childless miser should on his death (as every now and then happens) go to enrich a distant relative who never saw him, who perhaps never knew himself to be related to him until there was something to be gained by it, and who had no moral claim upon him of any kind, more than the most entire stranger. But the reason of the case applies alike to all collaterals, even in the nearest degree. Collaterals have no real claims, but such as may be equally strong in the case of non-relatives; and in the one case as in the other, where valid claims exist, the proper mode of paying regard to them is by bequest.

The claims of children are of a different nature: they are real, and indefeasible. But even of these, I venture to think that the measure usually taken is an erroneous one: what is due to children is in some respects underrated, in others, as it appears to me, exaggerated. One of the most binding of all obligations, that of not bringing children into the world unless they can be maintained in comfort during childhood, and brought up with a likelihood of supporting themselves when of full age, is both disregarded in practice and made light of in theory in a manner disgraceful to human intelligence. On the other hand, when the parent possesses property, the claims of the children upon it seem to me to be the subject of an opposite error. Whatever fortune a parent may have inherited, or still more, may have acquired, I cannot admit that he owes to his children, merely because they are his children, to leave them rich, without the necessity of any exertion. I could not admit it, even if to be so left were always, and certainly, for the good of the children themselves. But this is in the highest degree uncertain. It depends on individual character. Without supposing extreme cases, it may be affirmed that in a majority of instances the good not only of society but of the individuals would be better consulted by bequeathing to them a moderate, than a large provision. This, which is a commonplace of moralists ancient and modern, is felt to be true by many intelligent parents, and would be acted upon much more frequently, if they did not allow themselves to consider less what really is, than what will be thought by others to be, advantageous to the children.

The duties of parents to their children are those which are indissolubly attached to the fact of causing the existence of a human being. The parent owes to society to endeavour to make the child a good and valuable member of it, and owes to the children to provide, so far as depends on him, such education, and such appliances and means, as will enable them to start with a fair chance of achieving by their own exertions a successful life. To this every child has a claim; and I cannot admit, that as a child he has a claim to more. There is a case in which these obligations present themselves in their true light, without any extrinsic circumstances to disguise or confuse them: it is that of an illegitimate child. To such a child it is generally felt that there is due from the parent, the amount of provision for his welfare which will enable him to make his life on the whole a desirable one. I hold that to no child, merely as such, anything more is due, than what is admitted to be due to an illegitimate child: and that no child for whom thus much has been done, has, unless on the score of previously raised expectations, any grievance, if the remainder of the parent's fortune is devoted to public uses, or to the benefit of individuals on whom in the parent's opinion it is better bestowed.

In order to give the children that fair chance of a desirable existence, to which they are entitled, it is generally necessary that they should not be brought up from childhood in habits of luxury which they will not have the means of indulging in after-life. This, again, is a duty often flagrantly violated by possessors of terminable incomes, who have little property to leave. When the children of rich parents have lived, as it is natural they should do, in habits corresponding to the scale of expenditure in which the parents indulge, it is generally the duty of the parents to make a greater provision for them, than would suffice for children otherwise brought up. I say generally, because even here there is another side to the question. It is a proposition quite capable of being maintained, that to a strong nature which has to make its way against narrow circumstances, to have known early some of the feelings and experiences of wealth, is an advantage both in the formation of character and in the happiness of life. But allowing that children have a just ground of complaint, who have been brought up to require luxuries which they are not afterwards likely to obtain, and that their claim, therefore, is good to a provision bearing some relation to the mode of their bringing up; this, too, is a claim which is particularly liable to be stretched further than its reasons warrant. The case is exactly that of the younger children of the nobility and landed gentry, the bulk of whose fortune passes to the eldest son. The other sons, who are usually numerous, are brought up in the same habits of luxury as the future heir, and they receive as a younger brother's portion, generally what the reason of the case dictates, namely, enough to support, in the habits of life to which they are accustomed, themselves, but not a wife or children. It really is no grievance to any man, that for the means of marrying and of supporting a family, he has to depend on his own exertions.

A provision, then, such as is admitted to be reasonable in the case of illegitimate children, for younger children, wherever in short the justice of the case, and the real interests of the individuals and of society, are the only things considered, is, I conceive, all that parents owe to their children, and all, therefore, which the State owes to the children of those who die intestate. The surplus, if any, I hold that it may rightfully appropriate to the general purposes of the community. I would not, however, be supposed to recommend that parents should never do more for their children than what, merely as children, they have a moral right to. In some cases it is imperative, in many laudable, and in all allowable, to do much more. For this, however, the means are afforded by the liberty of bequest. It is due, not to the children but to the parents, that they should have the power of showing marks of affection, of requiting services and sacrifices, and of bestowing their wealth according to their own preferences, or their own judgment of fitness.

4. [*Should the right of bequest be limited, and how?*] Whether the power of bequest should itself be subject to limitation, is an ulterior question of great importance. Unlike inheritance *ab intestato*, bequest is one of the attributes of property: the ownership of a thing cannot be looked upon as complete without the power of bestowing it, at death or during life, at the owner's pleasure: and all the reasons, which recommend that private property should exist, recommend *pro tanto* this extension of it. But property is only a means to an end, not itself the end. Like all other proprietary rights, and even in a greater degree than most, the power of bequest may be so exercised as to conflict with the permanent interests of the human race. It does so, when, not content with bequeathing an estate to A, the testator prescribes that on A's death it shall pass to his eldest son, and to that son's son, and so on for ever. No doubt, persons have occasionally exerted themselves more strenuously to acquire a fortune from the hope of founding a family in perpetuity; but the mischiefs to society of such perpetuities outweigh the value of this incentive to exertion, and the incentives in the case of those who have the opportunity

of making large fortunes are strong enough without it. A similar abuse of the power of bequest is committed when a person who does the meritorious act of leaving property for public uses, attempts to prescribe the details of its application in perpetuity; when in founding a place of education (for instance) he dictates, for ever, what doctrines shall be taught. It being impossible that any one should know what doctrines will be fit to be taught after he has been dead for centuries, the law ought not to give effect to such dispositions of property, unless subject to the perpetual revision (after a certain interval has elapsed) of a fitting authority.

These are obvious limitations. But even the simplest exercise of the right of bequest, that of determining the person to whom property shall pass immediately on the death of the testator, has always been reckoned among the privileges which might be limited or varied, according to views of expediency. The limitations, hitherto, have been almost solely in favour of children. In England the right is in principle unlimited, almost the only impediment being that arising from a settlement by a former proprietor, in which case the holder for the time being cannot indeed bequeath his possessions, but only because there is nothing to bequeath, he having merely a life interest. By the Roman law, on which the civil legislation of the Continent of Europe is principally founded, bequest originally was not permitted at all, and even after it was introduced, a *legitima portio* was compulsorily reserved for each child; and such is still the law in some of the Continental nations. By the French law since the Revolution, the parent can only dispose by will, of a portion equal to the share of one child, each of the children taking an equal portion. This entail, as it may be called, of the bulk of every one's property upon the children collectively, seems to me as little defensible in principle as an entail in favour of one child, though it does not shock so directly the idea of justice. I cannot admit that parents should be compelled to leave to their children even that provision which, as children, I have contended that they have a moral claim to. Children may forfeit that claim by general unworthiness, or particular ill-conduct to the parents: they may have other resources or prospects: what has been previously done for them, in the way of education and advancement in life, may fully satisfy their moral claim; or others may have claims superior to theirs.

The extreme restriction of the power of bequest in French law, was adopted as a democratic expedient, to break down the custom of primogeniture, and counteract the tendency of inherited property to collect in large masses. I agree in thinking these objects eminently desirable; but the means used are not, I think, the most judicious. Were I framing a code of laws according to what seems to me best in itself, without regard to existing opinions and sentiments, I should prefer to restrict, not what any one might bequeath, but what any one should be permitted to acquire, by bequest or inheritance. Each person should have power to dispose by will of his or her whole property; but not to lavish it in enriching some one individual, beyond a certain maximum, which should be fixed sufficiently high to afford the means of comfortable independence. The inequalities of property which arise from unequal industry, frugality, perseverance, talents, and to a certain extent even opportunities, are inseparable from the principle of private property, and if we accept the principle, we must bear with these consequences of it: but I see nothing objectionable in fixing a limit to what any one may acquire by the mere favour of others, without any exercise of his faculties, and in requiring that if he desires any further accession of fortune, he shall work for it. I do not conceive that the degree of limitation which this would impose on the right of bequest, would be felt as a burthensome restraint by any testator who estimated a large fortune at its true value, that of the pleasures and advantages that can be purchased with it: on even the most extravagant estimate of which, it must be apparent to every one, that the difference to the happiness of the possessor between a moderate independence and five times as much, is insignificant when weighed against the enjoyment that might be given, and the permanent benefits diffused, by some other disposal of the four-fifths. So long indeed as the opinion practically prevails, that the best thing which can be done for objects of affection is to heap on them to satiety those intrinsically worthless things on which large fortunes are mostly expended, there might be little use in enacting such a law, even if it were possible to get it passed, since if there were the inclination, there would generally be the power of evading it. The law would be unavailing unless the popular sentiment went energetically along with it; which (judging from the tenacious adherence of public opinion in France to the law of compulsory division) it would in some states of society and government be very likely to do, however much the contrary may be the fact in England and at the present time. If the restriction could be made practically effectual, the benefit would be great. Wealth which could no longer be employed in over-enriching a few, would either be devoted to objects of public usefulness, or if bestowed on individuals, would be distributed among a larger number. While those enormous fortunes which no one needs for any personal purpose but ostentation or improper power, would become much less numerous, there would be a great multiplication of persons in easy circumstances, with the advantages of leisure, and all the real enjoyments which wealth can give, except those of vanity; a class by whom the services which a nation having leisured classes is entitled to expect from them, either by their direct exertions or by the tone they give to the feelings and tastes of the public, would be rendered in a much more beneficial manner than at present. A large portion also of the accumulations of successful industry would probably be devoted to public uses, either by direct bequests to the State, or by the endowment of institutions; as is already done very largely in the United States, where the ideas and practice in the matter of inheritance seem to be unusually rational and beneficial.*

5. [*Grounds of property in land are different from those of property in moveables*] The next point to be considered is, whether the reasons on which the institution of property rests, are applicable to all things in which a right of exclusive ownership is at present recognised; and if not, on what other grounds the recognition is defensible.

The essential principle of property being to assure to all persons what they have produced by their labour and accumulated by their abstinence, this principle cannot apply to what is not the produce of labour, the raw material of the earth. If the land derived its productive power wholly from nature, and not at all from industry, or if there were any means of discriminating what is derived from each source, it not only would not be necessary, but it would be the height of injustice, to let the gift of nature be engrossed by individuals. The use of the land in agriculture must indeed, for the time being, be of necessity exclusive; the same person who has ploughed and sown must be permitted to reap: but the land might be occupied for one season only, as among the ancient Germans; or might be periodically redivided as population increased: or the State might be the universal landlord, and the cultivators tenants under it, either on lease or at will.

But though land is not the produce of industry, most of its valuable qualities are so. Labour is not only requisite for using, but almost equally so for fashioning, the instrument. Considerable labour is often required at the commencement, to clear the land for cultivation. In many cases, even when cleared, its productiveness is wholly the effect of labour and art. The Bedford Level produced little or nothing until artificially drained. The bogs of Ireland, until the same thing is done to them, can produce little besides fuel. One of the barrenest soils in the world, composed of the material of the Goodwin Sands, the

* 'Munificent bequests and donations for public purposes, whether charitable or educational, form a striking feature in the modern history of the United States, and especially of New England. Not only is it common for rich capitalists to leave by will a portion of their fortune towards the endowment of national institutions, but individuals during their lifetime make magnificent grants of money for the same objects. There is here no compulsory law for the equal partition of property among children, as in France, and on the other hand, no custom of entail or primogeniture, as in England, so that the affluent feel themselves at liberty to share their wealth between their kindred and the public; it being impossible to found a family, and parents having frequently the happiness of seeing all their children well provided for and independent long before their death. I have seen a list of bequests and donations made during the last thirty years for the benefit of religious, charitable, and literary institutions in the state of Massachusetts alone, and they amounted to no less a sum than six millions of dollars, or more than a million sterling.' – Lyell's *Travels in America*, vol. i. p. 263.

Pays de Waes in Flanders, has been so fertilized by industry, as to have become one of the most productive in Europe. Cultivation also requires buildings and fences, which are wholly the produce of labour. The fruits of this industry cannot be reaped in a short period. The labour and outlay are immediate, the benefit is spread over many years, perhaps over all future time. A holder will not incur this labour and outlay when strangers and not himself will be benefited by it. If he undertakes such improvements, he must have a sufficient period before him in which to profit by them: and he is in no way so sure of having always a sufficient period as when his tenure is perpetual.

6. [*Grounds of property in land are only valid on certain conditions, which are not always realized. The limitations considered*] These are the reasons which form the justification in an economical point of view, of property in land. It is seen, that they are only valid, in so far as the proprietor of land is its improver. Whenever, in any country, the proprietor, generally speaking, ceases to be the improver, political economy has nothing to say in defence of landed property, as there established. In no sound theory of private property was it ever contemplated that the proprietor of land should be merely a sinecurist quartered on it.

In Great Britain, the landed proprietor is not unfrequently an improver. But it cannot be said that he is generally so. And in the majority of cases he grants the liberty of cultivation on such terms, as to prevent improvements from being made by any one else. In the southern parts of the island, as there are usually no leases, permanent improvements can scarcely be made except by the landlord's capital; accordingly the South, compared with the North of England, and with the Lowlands of Scotland, is still extremely backward in agricultural improvement. The truth is, that any very general improvement of land by the landlords, is hardly compatible with a law or custom of primogeniture. When the land goes wholly to the heir, it generally goes to him severed from the pecuniary resources which would enable him to improve it, the personal property being absorbed by the provision for younger children, and the land itself often heavily burthened for the same purpose. There is therefore but a small proportion of landlords who have the means of making expensive improvements, unless they do it with borrowed money, and by adding to the mortgages with which in most cases the land was already burthened when they received it. But the position of the owner of a deeply mortgaged estate is so precarious; economy is so unwelcome to one whose apparent fortune greatly exceeds his real means, and the vicissitudes of rent and price which only trench upon the margin of his income, are so formidable to one who can call little more than the margin his own, that it is no wonder if few landlords find themselves in a condition to make immediate sacrifices for the sake of future profit. Were they ever so much inclined, those alone can prudently do it, who have seriously studied the principles of scientific agriculture: and great landlords have seldom seriously studied anything. They might at least hold out inducements to the farmers to do what they will not or cannot do themselves; but even in granting leases, it is in England a general complaint that they tie up their tenants by covenants grounded on the practices of an obsolete and exploded agriculture; while most of them, by withholding leases altogether, and giving the farmer no guarantee of possession beyond a single harvest, keep the land on a footing little more favourable to improvement than in the time of our barbarous ancestors,

> ——— immetata quibus jugera liberas
> Fruges et Cererem ferunt,
> Nec cultura placet longior annuâ.*

Landed property in England is thus very far from completely fulfilling the conditions which render its existence economically justifiable. But if insufficiently realized even in England, in Ireland those conditions are not complied with at all. With individual exceptions (some of them very honourable ones), the owners of Irish estates do nothing for the land but drain it of its produce. What has been epigrammatically said in the discussions on 'peculiar burthens' is literally true when applied to them; that the greatest 'burthen on land' is the landlords. Returning nothing to the soil, they consume its whole produce, minus the potatoes strictly necessary to keep the inhabitants from dying of famine; and when they have any purpose of improvement, the preparatory step usually consists in not leaving even this pittance, but turning out the people to beggary if not to starvation. When landed property has placed itself upon this footing it ceases to be defensible, and the time has come for making some new arrangement of the matter.

When the 'sacredness of property' is talked of, it should always be remembered, that any such sacredness does not belong in the same degree to landed property. No man made the land. It is the original inheritance of the whole species. Its appropriation is wholly a question of general expediency. When private property in land is not expedient, it is unjust. It is no hardship to any one, to be excluded from what others have produced: they were not bound to produce it for his use, and he loses nothing by not sharing in what otherwise would not have existed at all. But it is some hardship to be born into the world and to find all nature's gifts previously engrossed, and no place left for the new-comer. To reconcile people to this, after they have once admitted into their minds the idea that any moral rights belong to them as human beings, it

* [Far better live the Getae stern] whose unallotted acres bring forth fruits and corn for all in common; nor with them in tillage binding longer than a year. Horace, *Odes* III, 24, ll. [11] 12-14.

will always be necessary to convince them that the exclusive appropriation is good for mankind on the whole, themselves included. But this is what no sane human being could be persuaded of, if the relation between the landowner and the cultivator were the same everywhere as it has been in Ireland.

Landed property is felt, even by those most tenacious of its rights, to be a different thing from other property; and where the bulk of the community have been disinherited of their share of it, and it has become the exclusive attribute of a small minority, men have generally tried to reconcile it, at least in theory, to their sense of justice, by endeavouring to attach duties to it, and erecting it into a sort of magistracy, either moral or legal. But if the state is at liberty to treat the possessors of land as public functionaries, it is only going one step further to say, that it is at liberty to discard them. The claim of the landowners to the land is altogether subordinate to the general policy of the state. The principle of property gives them no right to the land, but only a right to compensation for whatever portion of their interest in the land it may be the policy of the state to deprive them of. To that, their claim is indefeasible. It is due to landowners, and to owners of any property whatever, recognised as such by the state, that they should not be dispossessed of it without receiving its pecuniary value, or an annual income equal to what they derived from it. This is due on the general principles on which property rests. If the land was bought with the produce of the labour and abstinence of themselves or their ancestors, compensation is due to them on that ground; even if otherwise, it is still due on the ground of prescription. Nor can it ever be necessary for accomplishing an object by which the community altogether will gain, that a particular portion of the community should be immolated. When the property is of a kind to which peculiar affections attach themselves, the compensation ought to exceed a bare pecuniary equivalent. But, subject to this proviso, the state is at liberty to deal with landed property as the general interests of the community may require, even to the extent, if it so happen, of doing with the whole, what is done with a part whenever a bill is passed for a railroad or a new street. The community has too much at stake in the proper cultivation of the land, and in the conditions annexed to the occupancy of it, to leave these things to the discretion of a class of persons called landlords, when they have shown themselves unfit for the trust. The legislature, which if it pleased might convert the whole body of landlords into fundholders or pensioners, might, *à fortiori*, commute the average receipts of Irish landowners into a fixed rent charge, and raise the tenants into proprietors; supposing always that the full market value of the land was tendered to the landlords, in case they preferred that to accepting the conditions proposed.

There will be another place for discussing the various modes of landed property and tenure, and the advantages and inconveniences of each; in this chapter our concern is with the right itself, the grounds which justify it, and (as a corollary from these) the conditions by which it should be limited. To me it seems almost an axiom that property in land should be interpreted strictly, and that the balance in all cases of doubt should incline against the proprietor. The reverse is the case with property in moveables, and in all things the product of labour: over these, the owner's power both of use and of exclusion should be absolute, except where positive evil to others would result from it: but in the case of land, no exclusive right should be permitted in any individual, which cannot be shown to be productive of positive good. To be allowed any exclusive right at all, over a portion of the common inheritance, while there are others who have no portion, is already a privilege. No quantity of moveable goods which a person can acquire by his labour, prevents others from acquiring the like by the same means; but from the very nature of the case, whoever owns land, keeps others out of the enjoyment of it. The privilege, or monopoly, is only defensible as a necessary evil; it becomes an injustice when carried to any point to which the compensating good does not follow it.

For instance, the exclusive right to the land for purposes of cultivation does not imply an exclusive right to it for purposes of access; and no such right ought to be recognised, except to the extent necessary to protect the produce against damage, and the owner's privacy against invasion. The pretension of two Dukes to shut up a part of the Highlands, and exclude the rest of mankind from many square miles of mountain scenery to prevent disturbance to wild animals, is an abuse; it exceeds the legitimate bounds of the right of landed property. When land is not intended to be cultivated, no good reason can in general be given for its being private property at all; and if any one is permitted to call it his, he ought to know that he holds it by sufferance of the community, and on an implied condition that his ownership, since it cannot possibly do them any good, at least shall not deprive them of any, which could have derived from the land if it had been unappropriated. Even in the case of cultivated land, a man whom, though only one among millions, the law permits to hold thousands of acres as his single share, is not entitled to think that all this is given to him to use and abuse, and deal with as if it concerned nobody but himself. The rents or profits which he can obtain from it are at his sole disposal; but with regard to the land, in everything which he does with it, and in everything which he abstains from doing, he is morally bound, and should whenever the case admits be legally compelled, to make his interest and pleasure consistent with the public good. The species at large still retains, of its original claim to the soil of the planet which it inhabits, as much as is compatible with the purposes for which it has parted with the remainder.

7. [*Rights of property in abuses*] Besides property in the produce of labour, and property in land, there are other things which are or have been sub-

jects of property, in which no proprietary rights ought to exist at all. But as the civilized world has in general made up its mind on most of these, there is no necessity for dwelling on them in this place. At the head of them, is property in human beings. It is almost superfluous to observe, that this institution can have no place in any society even pretending to be founded on justice, or on fellowship between human creatures. But, iniquitous as it is, yet when the state has expressly legalized it, and human beings, for generations, have been bought, sold, and inherited under sanction of law, it is another wrong, in abolishing the property, not to make full compensation. This wrong was avoided by the great measure of justice in 1833, one of the most virtuous acts, as well as the most practically beneficent, ever done collectively by a nation. Other examples of property which ought not to have been created, are properties in public trusts; such as judicial offices under the old French régime, and the heritable jurisdictions which, in countries not wholly emerged from feudality, pass with the land. Our own country affords, as cases in point, that of a commission in the army, and of an advowson, or right of nomination to an ecclesiastical benefice. A property is also sometimes created in a right of taxing the public; in a monopoly, for instance, or other exclusive privilege. These abuses prevail most in semibarbarous countries but are not without example in the most civilized. In France there are several important trades and professions, including notaries, attorneys, brokers, appraisers, printers, and (until lately) bakers and butchers, of which the numbers are limited by law. The *brevet* or privilege of one of the permitted number consequently brings a high price in the market. When such is the case, compensation probably could not with justice be refused, on the abolition of the privilege. There are other cases in which this would be more doubtful. The question would turn upon what, in the peculiar circumstances, was sufficient to constitute prescription; and whether the legal recognition which the abuse had obtained, was sufficient to constitute it an institution, or amounted only to an occasional licence. It would be absurd to claim compensation for losses caused by changes in a tariff, a thing confessedly variable from year to year; or for monopolies like those granted to individuals by the Tudors, favours of a despotic authority, which the power that gave was competent at any time to recall.

So much on the institution of property, a subject of which, for the purposes of political economy, it was indispensable to treat, but on which we could not usefully confine ourselves to economical considerations. We have now to inquire on what principles and with what results the distribution of the produce of land and labour is effected, under the relations which this institution creates among the different members of the community.

7/THOMAS HILL GREEN

A generation after Mill, the Idealist philosopher T.H. Green made a new analysis of the right of property, starting from quite a different ethical principle. Rejecting Utilitarianism, Green started from a concept of essentially human capacities. The essentially human quality which distinguished man from animals was man's ability to form and act upon a moral will. Everyone had a right to what was necessary to realize such a will. Property, of an extent beyond that required for the satisfaction of immediate, passing wants, is necessary for that, and so is an essential individual right. Property is a necessary extension of human personality. And because no limit could rightfully be put on the development of anyone's moral personality, the right of the individual to accumulate property either through trade or inheritance should not be limited. Here Green ran into much the same difficulty as Mill had encountered: what if the unlimited right produced a class with no property? Green's answer was much the same as Mill's: it wasn't the unlimited right but some accidental historical circumstances that had produced that result. Green's new justification of property was thus just as unsatisfactory as Mill's. But offering as it did an alternative moral basis for property, it has become, along with Mill's, one of the two mainstays of the twentieth century liberal justifications of modern property.

The extract is section N of Green's *Lectures on the Principles of Political Obligation*, which were given in Oxford in 1879-80, and were first published in volume II of his (posthumous) *Works*, 1885-8, London: Longmans Green.

The Right of the State in Regard to Property

211. We have now considered the ground of the right to free life, and what is the justification, if any, for the apparent disregard of that right, (*a*) in war, (*b*) in the infliction of punishment. We have also dealt with the question of the general office of the state in regard to the development of that capacity in individuals which is the foundation of the right, pointing out on the one hand the necessary limitation of its office in this respect, on the other hand the directions in which it may remove obstacles to that development. We have next to consider the rationale of the rights of property.

In discussions on the 'origin of property' two questions are apt to be mixed up which, though connected, ought to be kept distinct. One is the question how men have come to appropriate; the other the question how the idea of right has come to be associated with their appropriations. As the term 'property' not only implies a permanent possession of something, or a possession which can only be given up with the good will of the possessor, but also a possession recognised as a right, an inquiry into the origin of property must involve both these questions, but it is not the less important that the distinction between them should be observed. Each of them again has both its analytical and its historical side. In regard to the first question it is important to learn all that can be learnt as to the kind of things that were first, and afterwards at successive periods, appropriated; as to the mode in which, and the sort of persons or societies by whom, they were appropriated. This is an historical inquiry. But it cannot take the place of a metaphysical or psychological analysis of the conditions on the part of the appropriating subject implied in the fact that he does such a thing as appropriate. So, too, in regard to the second question, it is important to investigate historically the forms in which the right of men in their appropriations has been recognised; the parties, whether individuals or societies, to whom the right has been allowed; and the sort of objects, capable of appropriation, to which it has been considered to extend. But neither can these inquiries help us to understand, in the absence of a metaphysical or moral analysis, either what is implied in the ascription of a right to certain appropriations, or why there should be a right to them.

212. We have then two questions, as above stated, each requiring two different methods of treatment. But neither have the questions themselves, nor the different methods of dealing with them, been duly distinguished.

It is owing to confusion between them that the right of property in things has been supposed to originate in the first occupancy of them. This supposition, in truth, merely disguises the identical proposition that in order to property there must to begin with have been some appropriation. The truism that there could be no property in anything which had not been at some time and in some manner appropriated, tells us nothing as to how or why the property in it, as a right, came to be recognised, or why that right should be recognised. But owing to the confusion between the origin of appropriation and the origin of property as a right, an identical proposition as to the beginning of appropriation seemed to be an instructive statement as to the basis of the rights of property. Of late, in a revulsion from theories founded on identical propositions, 'historical' inquiries into the 'origin of property' have come into vogue. The right method of dealing with the question has been taken to lie in an investigation of the earliest forms in which property has existed. But such investigation, however valuable in itself, leaves untouched the questions, (1) what it is in the nature of men that makes it possible for them, and moves them, to appropriate; (2) why it is that they conceive of themselves and each other as having a right in their appropriations; (3) on what ground this conception is treated as a moral authority, - as one that should be acted on.

213. (1) Appropriation is an expression of will; of the individual's effort to give reality to a conception of his own good; of his consciousness of a possible self-satisfaction as an object to be attained. It is different from mere provision to supply a future want. Such provision appears to be made by certain animals, e.g. ants. It can scarcely be made under the influence of the imagination of pain incidental to future want derived from previous experience, for the ant lays up for the winter though it has not previously lived through the winter. It may be suggested that it does so from inherited habit, but that this habit has originally arisen from an experience of pain on the part of ants in the past. Whether this is the true account of the matter we have not, I think, - perhaps from the nature of the case we cannot have - the means of deciding. We conceal our ignorance by saying that the ant acts instinctively, which is in effect a merely negative statement, that the ant is not moved to make provision for winter either by imagination of the pain which will be felt in winter if it does not, or by knowledge (conception of the fact) that such pain

will be felt. In fact, we know nothing of the action of the ant from the inside, or as an expression of consciousness. If we are not entitled to deny dogmatically that it expresses consciousness at all, neither are we entitled to say that it does express consciousness, still less what consciousness it expresses. On the other hand we are able to interpret the acts of ourselves, and of those with whom we can communicate by means of signs to which we and they attach the same meaning, as expressions of consciousness of a certain kind, and thus by reflective analysis to assure ourselves that acts of appropriation in particular express a will of the kind stated; that they are not merely a passing employment of such materials as can be laid hands on to satisfy this or that want, present or future, felt or imagined, but reflect the consciousness of a subject which distinguishes itself from its wants; which presents itself to itself as still there and demanding satisfaction when this or that want, or any number of wants, have been satisfied; which thus not merely uses a thing to fill a want, and in so doing at once destroys the thing and for the time removes the want, but says to itself, 'This shall be mine to do as I like with, to satisfy my wants and express my emotions as they arise.'

214. One condition of the existence of property, then, is appropriation, and that implies the conception of himself on the part of the appropriator as a permanent subject for whose use, as instruments of satisfaction and expression, he takes and fashions certain external things, certain things external to his bodily members. These things, so taken and fashioned, cease to be external as they were before. They become a sort of extension of the man's organs, the constant apparatus through which he gives reality to his ideas and wishes. But another condition must be fulfilled in order to constitute property, even of the most simple and primitive sort. This is the recognition by others of a man's appropriations as something which they will treat as his, not theirs, and the guarantee to him of his appropriations by means of that recognition. What then is the ground of the recognition? The writers of the seventeenth and eighteenth centuries, who discussed the basis of the rights of property, took it for granted, and in so doing begged the question. Grotius makes the right of property rest on contract, but clearly until there is a recognised 'meum' and 'tuum' there can be no contract. Contract presupposes property. The property in a particular thing may be derived from a contract through which it has been obtained in exchange for another thing or for some service rendered, but that implies that it was previously the property of another, and that the person obtaining it had a property in something else, if only in the labour of his hands, which he could exchange for it.[1] Hobbes is so far more logical that he

1 Grotius, *De Jure, etc.* [*The Law of War and Peace*], Book II, chap. II, section 2, 5. [Green's quotations from Grotius are here translated from the Latin.] 'So we learn what was the origin of property ... from a kind of agreement, either expressed, as by a

does not derive property from contract, but treats property and 'the validity of covenants' as co-ordinately dependent on the existence of a sovereign power of compulsion.[1] But his account of this, as of all other forms of right, is open to the objection (before dwelt on) that if the sovereign power is merely a strongest force it cannot be a source of rights; and that if it is other than this, if it is a representative and maintainer of rights, its existence presupposes rights, which remain to be accounted for. As previously shown, Hobbes, while professing to make all rights dependent on the sovereign power, presupposes rights in his account of the institution of this power. The validity of contracts

division, or tacit, as by occupation. For as soon as living in common was no longer approved of, and no division had been made, it is to be supposed that there was agreement among all that whatever each one occupied would become his property.' But he supposes a previous process by which things had been appropriated (4), owing to the necessity of spending labour on them in order to satisfy desire for a more refined kind of living than could be supplied by spontaneous products of the earth. 'Thus we learn why it was that the primitive common ownership, first of moveable then of immoveable things, was abandoned. The reason was that men were not content to live off the spontaneous produce of nature, to dwell in caves ... but chose a more excellent way of life: this led to industry, which some applied to one thing, others to another.' ... The 'common ownership of things' thus departed from when labour came to be expended on things, Grotius had previously described (1) as a state of things in which everyone had a right to whatever he could lay hands on. 'All things were the common and undivided possession of all men, as if the earth were all a common inheritance. So each man could take what he wished for his own use, and could consume whatever was consumable; and such a use of this universal right served in place of property. For whatever each had taken for himself, another could not take from him without injustice.' Here then a virtual right of property, though not so called, seems to be supposed in two forms previous to the establishment of what Grotius calls the right of property by contract. There is (1) a right of property in what each can 'take to his use and consume' out of the raw material supplied by nature; (2) a further right of each man in that on which he has expended labour. Grotius does not indeed expressly call this a right, but if there is a right, as he says there is, on the part of each man to that which he is able 'to take to his own use,' much more must there be a right to that which he has not only taken but fashioned by his labour. On the nature and rationale of this right Grotius throws no light, but it is clearly presupposed by that right of property which he supposes to be derived from contract, and must be recognised before any such contract could be possible.

1 'There is annexed to the sovereignty the whole power of prescribing the rules whereby every man may know what goods he may enjoy and what actions he may do without being molested by any of his fellow-subjects: and this is it men call propriety. For before constitution of sovereign power all men had right to all things, which necessarily causeth war; and therefore this propriety, being necessary to peace, and depending on sovereign power, is the act of that power in order to the public peace.' (*Leviathan*, pt. II, chap. xviii.) 'The nature of justice consisteth in keeping of valid covenants, but the validity of covenants begins not but with the constitution of a civil power, sufficient to compel men to keep them; and then it is also that propriety begins.' (*Ibid.* chap. xv.)

'begins not but with its institution,' yet its own right is derived from an irrevocable contract of all with all in which each devolves his 'persona,' the body of his rights, upon it. Without pressing his particular forms of expression unfairly against him, it is clear that he could not really succeed in thinking of rights as derived simply from supreme force; that he could not associate the idea of absolute right with the sovereign without supposing prior rights which it was made the business of the sovereign to enforce, and in particular such a recognised distinction between 'meum' and 'tuum' as is necessary to a covenant. Nor when we have dropped Hobbes' notion of government or law-making power, as having originated in a covenant of all with all, shall we succeed any better in deriving rights of property, any more than other rights, from law or a sovereign which makes law, unless we regard the law or sovereign as the organ or sustainer of a general social recognition of certain powers, as powers which should be exercised.

215. Locke[1] treats property - fairly enough so long as only its simplest forms are in question - as derived from labour. By the same law of nature and reason by which a man has 'a property in his own person,' 'the labour of his body and the work of his hand are properly his' too. Now that the right to free life, which we have already dwelt on, carries with it a certain right to property, to a certain permanent apparatus beyond the bodily organs, for the maintenance and expression of that life, is quite true. But apart from the difficulty of tracing some kinds of property, in which men are in fact held to have a right, to the labour of anyone, even of someone from whom it has been derived by inheritance or bequest (a difficulty to be considered presently), to say that it is a 'law of nature and reason' that a man should have a property in the work of his hands is no more than saying that that on which a man has impressed his labour is recognised by others as something which should be his, just as he himself is recognised by them as one that should be his own master. The ground of the recognition is the same in both cases, and it is Locke's merit to have pointed this out; but what the ground is he does not consider, shelving the question by appealing to a law of nature and reason.

216. The ground of the right to free life, the reason why a man is secured in the free exercise of his powers through recognition of that exercise by others as something that should be, lay, as we saw, in the conception on the part of everyone who concedes the right to others and to whom it is conceded, of an identity of good for himself and others. It is only as within a society, as a relation between its members, though the society be that of all men, that there can be such a thing as a right; and the right to free life rests on the common will of the society, in the sense that each member of the society within

1 *Civil Government*, chap. V. The most important passages are quoted in Fox Bourne's *Life of Locke*, vol. II, pp. 171 and 172.

which the right subsists contributes to satisfy the others in seeking to satisfy himself, and that each is aware that the other does so; whence there results a common interest in the free play of the powers of all. And just as the recognised interest of a society constitutes for each member of it the right to free life, just as it makes each conceive of such life on the part of himself and his neighbour as what should be, and thus forms the basis of a restraining custom which secures it for each, so it constitutes the right to the instruments of such life, making each regard the possession of them by the other as for the common good, and thus through the medium first of custom, then of law, securing them to each.

217. Thus the doctrine that the foundation of the right of property lies in the will, that property is 'realised will,' is true enough if we attach a certain meaning to 'will'; if we understand by it, not the momentary spring of any and every spontaneous action, but a constant principle, operative in all men qualified for any form of society, however frequently overborne by passing impulses, in virtue of which each seeks to give reality to the conception of a well-being which he necessarily regards as common to himself with others. A will of this kind explains at once the effort to appropriate, and the restraint placed on each in his appropriations by a customary recognition of the interest which each has in the success of the life effort on the part of the other members of a society with which he shares a common well-being. This customary recognition, founded on a moral or rational will, requires indeed to be represented by some adequate force before it can result in a real maintenance of the rights of property. The wild beast in man will not otherwise yield obedience to the rational will. And from the operation of this compulsive force, very imperfectly controlled by the moral tendencies which need its co-operation, - in other words from the historical incidents of conquest and government, - there result many characteristics of the institution of property, as it actually exists, which cannot be derived from the spiritual principle which we have assigned as its foundation. Still, without that principle it could not have come into existence, nor would it have any moral justification at all.

218. It accords with the account given of this principle that the right of property, like every other form of right, should first appear within societies founded on kinship, these being naturally the societies within which the restraining conception of a common well-being is first operative. We are apt indeed to think of the state of things in which the members of a family or clan hold land and stock in common, as the antithesis of one in which rights of property exist. In truth it is the earliest stage of their existence, because the most primitive form of society in which the fruit of his labour is secured to the individual by the society, under the influence of the conception of a common well-being. The characteristic of primitive communities is not the absence of distinction between 'meum' and 'tuum,' without which no society of intel-

ligent as opposed to instinctive agents would be possible at all, but the common possession of certain materials, in particular land, on which labour may be expended. It is the same common interest which prevents the separate appropriation of these materials, and which secures the individual in the enjoyment and use of that which his labour can extract from them.

219. From the moral point of view, however, the clan-system is defective, because under it the restraint imposed upon the individual by his membership of a society is not, and has not the opportunity of becoming, a self-imposed restraint, a free obedience, to which, though the alternative course is left open to him, the individual submits, because he conceives it as his true good. The area within which he can shape his own circumstances is not sufficient to allow of the opposite possibilities of right and wrong being presented to him, and thus of his learning to love right for its own sake. And the other side of this moral tutelage of the individual, this withholding from him of the opportunity of being freely determined by recognition of his moral relations, is the confinement of those relations themselves, which under the clan-system have no actual existence except as between members of the same clan. A necessary condition at once of the growth of a free morality, i.e. a certain behaviour of men determined by an understanding of moral relations and by the value which they set on them as understood, and of the conception of those relations as relations between all men, is that free play should be given to every man's powers of appropriation. Moral freedom is not the same thing as a control over the outward circumstances and appliances of life. It is the end to which such control is a generally necessary means, and which gives it its value. In order to obtain this control, men must cease to be limited in their activities by the customs of the clan. The range of their appropriations must be extended; they must include more of the permanent material on which labour may be expended, and not merely the passing products of labour spent on unappropriated material; and they must be at once secured and controlled in it by the good-will, by the sense of common interest, of a wider society, of a society to which any and every one may belong who will observe its conditions, and not merely those of a particular parentage; in other words by the law, written or unwritten, of a free state.

220. It is too long a business here to attempt an account of the process by which the organisation of rights in the state has superseded that of the clan, and at the same time the restriction of the powers of appropriation implied in the latter has been removed. It is important to observe, however, that this process has by no means contributed unmixedly to the end to which, from the moral point of view, it should have contributed. That end is at once the emancipation of the individual from all restrictions upon the free moral life, and his provision with means for it. But the actual result of the development of rights of property in Europe, as part of its general political development,

has so far been a state of things in which all indeed *may* have property, but great numbers in fact cannot have it in that sense in which alone it is of value, viz. as a permanent apparatus for carrying out a plan of life, for expressing ideas of what is beautiful, or giving effect to benevolent wishes. In the eye of the law they have rights of appropriation, but in fact they have not the chance of providing means for a free moral life, of developing and giving reality or expression to a good will, an interest in social well-being. A man who possesses nothing but his powers of labour and who has to sell these to a capitalist for bare daily maintenance, might as well, in respect of the ethical purposes which the possession of property should serve, be denied rights of property altogether. Is the existence of so many men in this position, and the apparent liability of many more to be brought to it by a general fall of wages, if increase of population goes along with decrease in the productiveness of the earth, a necessary result of the emancipation of the individual and the free play given to powers of appropriation? or is it an evil incident, which may yet be remedied, of that historical process by which the development of the rights of property has been brought about, but in which the agents have for the most part had no moral objects in view at all?

221. Let us first be clear about the points in which the conditions of property, as it actually exists, are at variance with property according to its idea or as it should be. The rationale of property, as we have seen, is that everyone should be secured by society in the power of getting and keeping the means of realising a will, which in possibility is a will directed to social good. Whether anyone's will is actually and positively so directed, does not affect his claim to the power. This power should be secured to the individual irrespectively of the use which he actually makes of it, so long as he does not use it in a way that interferes with the exercise of like power by another, on the ground that its uncontrolled exercise is the condition of attainment by man of that free morality which is his highest good. It is not then a valid objection to the manner in which property is possessed among us, that its holders constantly use it in a way demoralising to themselves and others, any more than such misuse of any other liberties is an objection to securing men in their possession. Only then is property held in a way inconsistent with its idea, and which should, if possible, be got rid of, when the possession of property by one man interferes with the possession of property by another; when one set of men are secured in the power of getting and keeping the means of realising their will, in such a way that others are practically denied the power. In that case it may truly be said that 'property is theft.' The rationale of property, in short, requires that everyone who will conform to the positive condition of possessing it, viz. labour, and the negative condition, viz. respect for it as possessed by others, should, so far as social arrangements can make him so, be a possessor of property himself, and

of such property as will at least enable him to develope a sense of responsibility, as distinct from mere property in the immediate necessaries of life.

222. But then the question arises, whether the rationale of property, as thus stated, is not inconsistent with the unchecked freedom of appropriation, or freedom of appropriation checked only by the requirement that the thing appropriated shall not have previously been appropriated by another. Is the requirement that every honest man should be a proprietor to the extent stated, compatible with any great inequalities of possession? In order to give effect to it, must we not remove those two great sources of the inequality of fortunes, (1) freedom of bequest, and the other arrangements by which the profits of the labour of several generations are accumulated on persons who do not labour at all; (2) freedom of trade, of buying in the cheapest market and selling in the dearest, by which accumulated profits of labour become suddenly multiplied in the hands of a particular proprietor? Now clearly, if an inequality of fortunes, of the kind which naturally arises from the admission of these two forms of freedom, necessarily results in the existence of a proletariate, practically excluded from such ownership as is needed to moralise a man, there would be a contradiction between our theory of the right of property and the actual consequence of admitting the right according to the theory; for the theory logically necessitates freedom both in trading and in the disposition of his property by the owner, so long as he does not interfere with the like freedom on the part of others; and in other ways as well its realisation implies inequality.

223. Once admit as the idea of property that nature should be progressively adapted to the service of man by a process in which each, while working freely or for himself, i.e. as determined by a conception of his own good, at the same time contributes to the social good, and it will follow that property must be unequal. If we leave a man free to realise the conception of a possible well-being, it is impossible to limit the effect upon him of his desire to provide for his future well-being, as including that of the persons in whom he is interested, or the success with which at the prompting of that desire he turns resources of nature to account. Considered as representing the conquest of nature by the effort of free and variously gifted individuals, property must be unequal; and no less must it be so if considered as a means by which individuals fulfil social functions. As we may learn from Aristotle, those functions are various and the means required for their fulfilment are various. The artist and man of letters require different equipment and apparatus from the tiller of land and the smith. Either then the various apparatus needed for various functions must be provided for individuals by society, which would imply a complete regulation of life incompatible with that highest object of human attainment, a free morality; or we must trust for its provision to individual effort, which will imply inequality between the property of different persons.

224. The admission of freedom of trade follows from the same principle. It is a condition of the more complete adaptation of nature to the service of man by the free effort of individuals. 'To buy in the cheapest and sell in the dearest market' is a phrase which may no doubt be used to cover objectionable transactions, in which advantage is taken of the position of sellers who from circumstances are not properly free to make a bargain. It is so employed when the cheapness of buying arises from the presence of labourers who have no alternative but to work for 'starvation wages.' But in itself it merely describes transactions in which commodities are bought where they are of least use and sold where they are of most use. The trader who profits by the transaction is profiting by what is at the same time a contribution to social well-being.

In regard to the freedom which a man should be allowed in disposing of his property by will or gift, the question is not so simple. The same principle which forbids us to limit the degree to which a man may provide for his future, forbids us to limit the degree to which he may provide for his children, these being included in his forecast of his future. It follows that the amount which children may inherit may not rightly be limited; and in this way inequalities of property, and accumulations of it to which possessors have contributed nothing by their own labour, must arise. Of course the possessor of an estate, who has contributed nothing by his own labour to its acquisition, may yet by his labour contribute largely to the social good, and a well-organised state will in various ways elicit such labour from possessors of inherited wealth. Nor will it trust merely to encouraging the voluntary fulfilment of social functions, but will by taxation make sure of some positive return for the security which it gives to inherited wealth. But while the mere permission of inheritance, which seems implied in the permission to a man to provide unlimitedly for his future, will lead to accumulations of wealth, on the other hand, if the inheritance is to be equal among all children, and, failing children, is to pass to the next of kin, the accumulation will be checked. It is not therefore the right of inheritance, but the right of bequest, that is most likely to lead to accumulation of wealth, and that has most seriously been questioned by those who hold that universal ownership is a condition of moral well-being. Is a proprietor to be allowed to dispose of his property as he likes among his children (or, if he has none, among others), making one very rich as compared with the others, or is he to be checked by a law requiring approximately equal inheritance?

225. As to this, consider that on the same principle on which we hold that a man should be allowed to accumulate as he best can for his children, he should have discretion in distributing among his children. He should be allowed to accumulate, because in so doing he at once expresses and develops the sense of family responsibility, which naturally breeds a recognition of duties in many other directions. But if the sense of family responsibility is to have free

play, the man must have due control over his family, and this he can scarcely have if all his children as a matter of necessity inherit equally, however undutiful or idle or extravagant they may be. For this reason the true theory of property would seem to favour freedom of bequest, at any rate in regard to wealth generally. There may be special reasons, to be considered presently, for limiting it in regard to land. But as a general rule, the father of a family, if left to himself and not biassed by any special institutions of his country, is most likely to make that distribution among his children which is most for the public good. If family pride moves him to endow one son more largely than the rest, in order to maintain the honour of his name, family affection will keep this tendency within limits in the interest of the other children, unless the institutions of his country favour the one tendency as against the other. And this they will do if they maintain great dignities, e.g. peerages, of which the possession of large hereditary wealth is virtually the condition, and if they make it easy, when the other sons have been impoverished for the sake of endowing the eldest, to maintain the former at the public expense by means of appointments in the church or state.

It must be borne in mind, further, that the freedom of bequest which is to be justified on the above principles must not be one which limits that freedom in a subsequent generation. It must therefore be distinguished from the power of settlement allowed by English law and constantly exercised in dealing with landed estate; for this power, as exercised by the landowning head of a family in one generation, prevents the succeeding head of the family from being free to make what disposition he thinks best among his children and ties up the succession to the estate to his eldest son. The practice of settlement in England, in short, as applied to landed estate, cancels the freedom of bequest in the case of most landowners and neutralises all the dispersive tendency of family affection, while it maintains in full force all the accumulative tendency of family pride. This, however, is no essential incident of a system in which the rights of individual ownership are fully developed, but just the contrary.

226. The question then remains, whether the full development of those rights, as including that of unlimited accumulation of wealth by the individual and of complete freedom of bequest on his part, necessarily carries with it the existence of a proletariate, nominal owners of their powers of labour, but in fact obliged to sell these on such terms that they are owners of nothing beyond what is necessary from day to day for the support of life, and may at any time lose even that, so that, as regards the moral functions of property, they may be held to be not proprietors at all; or whether the existence of such a class is due to causes only accidentally connected with the development of rights of individual property.

We must bear in mind (1) that the increased wealth of one man does not naturally mean the diminished wealth of another. We must not think of wealth as a given stock of commodities of which a larger share cannot fall to one without taking from the share that falls to another. The wealth of the world is constantly increasing in proportion as the constant production of new wealth by labour exceeds the constant consumption of what is already produced. There is no natural limit to its increase except such as arises from the fact that the supply of the food necessary to sustain labour becomes more difficult as more comes to be required owing to the increase in the number of labourers, and from the possible ultimate exhaustion of the raw materials of labour in the world. Therefore in the accumulation of wealth, so far as it arises from the saving by anyone of the products of his labour, from his bequest of this capital to another who farther adds to it by saving some of the profit which the capital yields, as employed in the payment for labour or in trade either by the capitalist himself or someone to whom he lends it, and from the continuation of this process through generations, there is nothing which tends to lessen for anyone else the possibilities of ownership. On the contrary, supposing trade and labour to be free, wealth must be constantly distributed throughout the process in the shape of wages to labourers and of profits to those who mediate in the business of exchange.

227. It is true that the accumulation of capital naturally leads to the employment of large masses of hired labourers. But there is nothing in the nature of the case to keep these labourers in the condition of living from hand to mouth, to exclude them from that education of the sense of responsibility which depends on the possibility of permanent ownership. There is nothing in the fact that their labour is hired in great masses by great capitalists to prevent them from being on a small scale capitalists themselves. In their position they have not indeed the same stimulus to saving, or the same constant opening for the investment of savings, as a man who is *αὐτουργός* [self-employed]; but their combination in work gives them every opportunity, if they have the needful education and self-discipline, for forming societies for the investment of savings. In fact, as we know, in the well-paid industries of England the better sort of labourers do become capitalists, to the extent often of owning their houses and a good deal of furniture, of having an interest in stores, and of belonging to benefit-societies through which they make provision for the future. It is not then to the accumulation of capital, but to the condition, due to antecedent circumstances unconnected with that accumulation, of the men with whom the capitalist deals and whose labour he buys on the cheapest terms, that we must ascribe the multiplication in recent times of an impoverished and reckless proletariate.

228. It is difficult to summarise the influences to which is due the fact that in all the chief seats of population in Europe the labour-market is constantly thronged with men who are too badly reared and fed to be efficient labourers; who for this reason, and from the competition for employment with each other, have to sell their labour very cheap; who have thus seldom the means

to save, and whose standard of living and social expectation is so low that, if they have the opportunity of saving, they do not use it, and keep bringing children into the world at a rate which perpetuates the evil. It is certain, however, that these influences have no necessary connection with the maintenance of the right of individual property and consequent unlimited accumulation of capital, though they no doubt are connected with that régime of force and conquest by which existing governments have been established, - governments which do not indeed create the rights of individual property, any more than other rights, but which serve to maintain them. It must always be borne in mind that the appropriation of land by individuals has in most countries - probably in all where it approaches completeness - been originally effected, not by the expenditure of labour or the results of labour on the land, but by force. The original landlords have been conquerors.

229. This has affected the condition of the industrial classes in at least two ways: (1) When the application of accumulated capital to any work in the way of mining or manufacture has created a demand for labour, the supply has been forthcoming from men whose ancestors, if not themselves, were trained in habits of serfdom; men whose life has been one of virtually forced labour, relieved by church-charities or the poor law (which in part took the place of these charities); who were thus in no condition to contract freely for the sale of their labour, and had nothing of that sense of family-responsibility which might have made them insist on having the chance of saving. Landless countrymen, whose ancestors were serfs, are the parents of the proletariate of great towns. (2) Rights have been allowed to landlords, incompatible with the true principle on which rights of property rest, and tending to interfere with the development of the proprietorial capacity in others. The right to freedom in unlimited acquisition of wealth, by means of labour and by means of the saving and successful application of the results of labour, does not imply the right of anyone to do as he likes with those gifts of nature, without which there would be nothing to spend labour upon. The earth is just as much an original natural material necessary to productive industry, as are air, light, and water, but while the latter from the nature of the case cannot be appropriated, the earth can be and has been. The only justification for this appropriation, as for any other, is that it contributes on the whole to social well-being; that the earth as appropriated by individuals under certain conditions becomes more serviceable to society as a whole, including those who are not proprietors of the soil, than if it were held in common. The justification disappears if these conditions are not observed; and from government having been chiefly in the hands of appropriators of the soil, they have not been duly observed. Landlords have been allowed to 'do what they would with their own,' as if land were merely like so much capital, admitting of indefinite extension. The capital gained by one is not taken from another, but one man cannot acquire more

land without others having less; and though a growing reduction in the number of landlords is not necessarily a social evil, if it is compensated by the acquisition of other wealth on the part of those extruded from the soil, it is only not an evil if the landlord is prevented from so using his land as to make it unserviceable to the wants of men (e.g. by turning fertile land into a forest), and from taking liberties with it incompatible with the conditions of general freedom and health; e.g. by clearing out a village and leaving the people to pick up houseroom as they can elsewhere (a practice common under the old poor-law, when the distinction between close and open villages grew up), or, on the other hand, by building houses in unhealthy places or of unhealthy structure, by stopping up means of communication, or forbidding the erection of dissenting chapels. In fact the restraints which the public interest requires to be placed on the use of land if individual property in it is to be allowed at all, have been pretty much ignored, while on the other hand, that full development of its resources, which individual ownership would naturally favour, has been interfered with by laws or customs which, in securing estates to certain families, have taken away the interest, and tied the hands, of the nominal owner - the tenant for life - in making the most of his property.

230. Thus the whole history of the ownership of land in Europe has been of a kind to lead to the agglomeration of a proletariate, neither holding nor seeking property wherever a sudden demand has arisen for labour in mines or manufactures. This at any rate was the case down to the epoch of the French Revolution; and this, which brought to other countries deliverance from feudalism, left England, where feudalism had previously passed into unrestrained landlordism, almost untouched. And while those influences of feudalism and landlordism which tend to throw a shiftless population upon the centres of industry have been left unchecked, nothing till quite lately was done to give such a population a chance of bettering itself, when it had been brought together. Their health, housing, and schooling were unprovided for. They were left to be freely victimised by deleterious employments, foul air, and consequent craving for deleterious drinks. When we consider all this, we shall see the unfairness of laying on capitalism or the free development of individual wealth the blame which is really due to the arbitrary and violent manner in which rights over land have been acquired and exercised, and to the failure of the state to fulfil those functions which under a system of unlimited private ownership are necessary to maintain the conditions of a free life.

231. Whether, when those functions have been more fully recognised and executed, and when the needful control has been established in the public interest over the liberties which landlords may take in the use of their land, it would still be advisable to limit the right of bequest in regard to land, and establish a system of something like equal inheritance, is a question which cannot be answered on any absolute principle. It depends on circumstances. Prob-

ably the question should be answered differently in a country like France or Ireland, where the most important industries are connected directly with the soil, and in one like England where they are not so. The reasons must be cogent which could justify that interference with the control of the parent over his family, which seems to be implied in the limitation of the power of bequeathing land when the parent's wealth lies solely in land, and which arises, be it remembered, in a still more mischievous way from the present English practice of settling estates. But it is important to bear in mind that the question in regard to land stands on a different footing from that in regard to wealth generally, owing to the fact that land is a particular commodity limited in extent, from which alone can be derived the materials necessary to any industry whatever, on which men must find house-room if they are to find it at all, and over which they must pass in communicating with each other, however much water or even air may be used for that purpose. These are indeed not reasons for preventing private property in land or even free bequest of land, but they necessitate a special control over the exercise of rights of property in land, and it remains to be seen whether that control can be sufficiently established in a country where the power of great estates has not first been broken, as in France, by a law of equal inheritance.

232. To the proposal that 'unearned increment' in the value of the soil, as distinct from value produced by expenditure of labour and capital, should be appropriated by the state, though fair enough in itself, the great objection is that the relation between earned and unearned increment is so complicated, that a system of appropriating the latter to the state could scarcely be established without lessening the stimulus to the individual to make the most of the land, and thus ultimately lessening its serviceableness to society.

8 / THORSTEIN VEBLEN

Veblen, the iconoclastic American economist whose penetrating analyses of modern society were largely ignored when he was alive but became widely influential soon after, was the first to draw attention to a significant change that had taken place in the nature of property by the early twentieth century, a change which required a new defence of property. In his characteristically sardonic way he offered a defence which was a thinly veiled attack. The change was that with the rise of the modern corporation and of financial as distinct from directly productive property, more and more of the property in economically advanced countries had become essentially a claim on a revenue, and in large part on the revenue produced by the labour and ingenuity of others and by the accumulated knowledge or technology which was properly a joint stock of the whole society. The corporate owners of current productive plant (in which the technology of the whole society was embodied) are able, by withholding the plant, to impose their own terms or to make 'the community's workmanship useless,' and by the normal practice of business enterprise they steadily do this to a considerable extent. This Veblen called 'the Natural Right of Investment' and 'the larger meaning of the Security of Property' – a nice comment on the new inadequacy both of the natural-right justification of property and of the utilitarian case for security of property as essential to maximum productivity.

The Natural Right of Investment

The 'natural' right of property is grounded in the workmanship of the man who 'hath mixed his labor with' the materials out of which a valuable article has been created. By this right of ownership the owner is vested with power to dispose of his property by bargain and sale. He may sell for cash or for deferred payment, and he may also lend. In so lending, the use of the valuable article passes to the borrower (debtor) while the usufruct remains with the owner (creditor) in the way of a stated or customary payment for the use of the property. This is the simplest form of absentee ownership that arises out of the 'natural' right of property under the principles of the handicraft system. But the masterless men of the crafts had also the natural right to turn their workmanship to account for a valuable consideration in working up materials owned by another, without becoming owners of the resulting product; which gives rise to the wage relation and so brings on a second variant of absentee ownership, still securely guaranteed by the handicraft principle which derives ownership from workmanship and free contract. It was along these two lines – credit and hired labor – that absentee ownership chiefly found its way into the industrial system of recent times, until by degrees it has come to dominate the organisation of industry and has taken over the usufruct of the community's workmanship.

But included in the scheme of ownership as it stands in recent times there is also an alien strain, not warranted by the principles of Natural Right and not traceable to workmanship. Ownership of natural resources – lands, forests, mineral deposits, water-power, harbor rights, franchises, etc. – rests not on a natural right of workmanship but on the ancient feudalistic ground of privilege and prescriptive tenure, vested interest, which runs back to the right of seizure by force and collusion. The owners of these natural resources own them not by virtue of their having produced or earned them, nor on the workmanlike ground that they are making use of these useful things in productive work. These owners own these things because they own them. That is to say, title of ownership in these natural resources is traceable to an act of seizure, legalised by statute or confirmed by long undisturbed possession. All this is wholly foreign to the system of Natural Rights, altogether at cross purposes with the handicraft principle of workmanship, but quite securely incorporated in the established order of law and custom. It is, in effect, a remnant of feudalism; that is to say, absentee ownership without apology or afterthought.

Not that all ownership of natural resources is absentee ownership. Nor is it to be said that such ownership may not be grounded in the owner's workmanship. The small farmer, e.g., is not usually an absentee owner. The land owned and worked by the small farmer without hired help is raw material with which he mixes his labor in the work of producing crops, and so is to be counted in as a typical case of ownership based on workmanship. The like is true for other natural resources that are made use of in a similar way in other productive work. These things are not to be classed under the head of absentee ownership so long as these useful things are fully employed as ways and means of work by their owners alone. It is only when and in so far as such useful things are worked by the help of others than their owners, or so far as they are held out of productive use by their owners, that they are rightly to be classed under absentee ownership; only in so far as their productive use is disjoined from their usufruct, so that workmanship and ownership part company.

It follows that the small farmer's land-holding falls into the scheme of Natural Rights on an equal footing with the craftsmen's right to work for a living and to dispose of their product or their labor under the rule of free contract. It is not unusual to defend private property in land and other natural resources on the plea that the cultivator must have unhampered use of the land which is the raw material of his work. In the main, as things have turned in recent times, this plea is pettifoggery and subterfuge. It is not the small farmer's holding that needs apology or defense; and in the main the small farmer and his husbandry by self-help are already out of date in those communities where the machine system of industry has thoroughly taken effect. It is also to be noted that in the practical working-out of law and custom in all the civilised countries, absenteeism throws no cloud on the title to lands or other material resources. In this connection workmanship and the needs of productive work give no title, not even title to 'improvements.' Except by way of sophistication and *obiter dictum*, the tenure of lands and similar resources is not brought in under the 'natural' principle of creative workmanship, but remains a tenure by prescription, – that is to say by legalized seizure. It might perhaps be argued that 'squatter's rights' are a case of tenure arising out of workmanship, but closer attention to the question will show that the squatter's right, whatever it may amount to, rests on priority of seizure and possession.

Indeed, in the practical working-out of law and custom during the era of Natural Rights, the cultivator's 'natural' claim to the soil on grounds of workmanship has gone by default, even where a claim might have been sustained on that ground; for the reason, apparently, that there has been no sufficiently massive body of masterless men engaged in husbandry, such as would bend custom to its own habitual way of thinking about these things. On the other hand, the Landed Interest was vested with title by prescription and was a formidable spokesman for absentee ownership, tenacious of its prescriptive rights and full of an habitual conviction of the justice of its cause. So the feudalistic principle of absentee ownership by prescriptive right of seizure and possession still stands over as the accepted rule covering land and other natural resources.

As is well known, from the outset the handicraft system of industry included the petty trade, as a necessary factor in the work to be done. Therefore, that workday routine out of which the principles of Natural Right arose included also daily contact with the market and familiarity with the conduct of trade; so that all those preconceptions and usages of free contract and of bargain and sale which were involved in the conduct of the petty trade came to be worked into the texture of Natural Rights, by unbroken habit, and became a constituent part of the system. In the balanced order of the handicraft system, the trader, too, was counted in as a workman engaged in serviceable work and therefore entitled to a livelihood on the ground of work done. At the outset the petty trade runs along with handicraft as a traffic of give and take, a method of keeping the balance of work among the specialised workmen and between the body of these workmen and the world outside. It was a traffic in the nature of marketing, huckstering, or peddling, and much of it was not far removed from barter.

But the traffic presently grew greater in range, scale, and volume, and took on more of the character of 'business,' in that the necessary management of contracts, bargaining, and accounts became an occupation distinct from the handling and care of the merchandise in transit and in the market-place. The exigencies of the larger volume of traffic over longer distances and larger intervals of time necessarily removed the responsible merchant from personal contact with his merchantable goods; so that ever more and more he shifted from the footing of an itinerant huckster who handled his own wares in transit and in the market-place to that of an enterprising absentee investor who took care of the business; while agents, super-cargoes, factors took over the handling, carriage, and even the buying and selling of the goods, which so passed under the merchant's ownership without passing under his hand. By degrees, instead of an itinerant merchant he grew to be a 'merchant prince,' and instead of being an industrial occupation the trade became a business enterprise.[6] But even the 'merchant adventurer' of that time continued in close touch with the merchandising traffic from which his profits were drawn, as well as with the productive industry which supplied the merchantable goods.[7]

The growth of absentee ownership out of the craftsman's natural right grounded in his workmanship comes on first and most visibly in the merchandising trade. Investment, that is to say absentee ownership in the way of business enterprise, was commercial investment. It was in the shape of commercial enterprise that the modern world got used to the practice of investment for a profit and so learned to appreciate business principles and to value the investor and his work. But investment presently made its appearance also in industry proper, in the shape of ownership of industrial equipment and materials and the employment of hired labor.

By the time when the era of handicraft was drawing to a close and the transition to the machine industry and the factory system had set in, investment in industry was already a customary fact, particularly in certain of the leading industries, as, e.g., in textiles. It was absentee ownership, and would be recognised as such by anyone looking back to the facts of that time from the standpoint of the present; but it does not appear to have seemed so, at least not obtrusively so, to the men of that time, who had to do with the industrial situation as it then lay before them. Absenteeism was not the main and obvious feature of the case. It was still the tradition, and in great part the practical rule, that the owner of the works was on the ground in person and acted as overseer and director of the work in hand; although the work done was not the work of his own hands.[8]

But with the transition to the machine industry and the factory system the business organisation of industry gradually underwent such a change as to bring investment and absenteeism very practically into the foreground; so that since then, during the period which can properly be called 'recent times' in the industrial respect, absentee ownership has been the rule in industry and investment has been the type-form of ownership and control. By a slight stretch

6 Cf. Ehrenberg, *Das Zeitalter der Fugger*, where this transition is shown in syncopated form in the history of the House of Fugger, from the time when Jakob Fugger I came into Augsburg with a peddler's pack, to the great days of the third generation. A recent parallel may be found in the fortunes of the House of Guggenheim, which also shows the larger dimensions and swifter pace of the current facts in a felicitous way.

7 Cf. Thomas Mun, *England's Treasure by Forraign Trade*, which shows the qualifications and daily occupation of a merchant of the larger sort at the middle of the sixteenth Century.

8 Cf. Bücher, *Entstehung der Volkswirtschaft*, No. V, 'Niedergang des Handwerks'; Ashley, *Economic History and Theory*, Part II.

it can be said that in the days of handicraft absentee ownership was an incidental or adventitious feature of the case, while since that time it will hold true that it is the ordinary and typical practice; it now is that which is expected, and anything else is regarded as exceptional and sporadic.

Very much as was the case in the petty trade of the Middle Ages, so also in the handicraft industry; by degrees but unavoidably, absentee ownership came in so soon and so far as the scale of operation advanced to such a point that trade or industry became a matter of teamwork. With the advance of specialisation and division of labor the equipment required for carrying on any given line of work presently became larger than what a workman could ordinarily provide out of his own work as he went along, at the same time that the equipment took on more and more of the character of a 'plant' designed for the joint use of a number of workmen. Such a plant would ordinarily be the property of a master workman or of a partnership of such masters, who thereby and in that degree became absentee owners of the plant. The like is true for the ownership of the materials employed and of the finished product.

Yet it was still the tradition in Adam Smith's time, at the close of the handicraft era in England, that the wealth so invested in trade and industry was, in the natural and normal run of things, an accumulation of useful goods saved out of the productive work of its owner, and it was likewise the tradition that the owner whose savings were so employed in production should 'naturally' direct and oversee the work in which his savings were employed. What was 'natural' in the Eighteenth Century was that which had the sanction of unbroken tradition; and so far as touches the economic life in that time, that was 'natural' which was attested by unbroken habituation under the régime of handicraft.

Adam Smith spoke the language of what was to him the historical present, that is to say the recent past of his time, and he has left a luminous record of the state of things economic in his time as formulated in terms of the habits of thought with which the recent past had invested that generation of men. But in the historical sequence of things he stood at the critical point of transition to a new order in industry and in ownership, and what was 'natural' in his view of things, therefore, ceased to be the common run of things from and after the date at which his luminous formulation of economic laws was drawn up. What had gone before was the era of handicraft and the petty trade, the habitual outlook of which had become (second) nature to the thoughtful men of that time; what has followed after is the era of the machine industry and business enterprise, in which the 'natural' laws and rights handed on from the era of handicraft are playing the rôle of a 'dead hand.'

From and after Adam Smith's date (last quarter of the eighteenth century) a new era sets in in industry and business. As an incident of the new era there sets in also a visible and widening division between industrial work and business enterprise. The era of the machine industry opens in England in that time, and it opens presently after for the other civilised peoples also; at the same time that the businesslike management of industrial concerns begins to shift from a footing of workday participation in the work done, to that of absentee ownership and control. Instead of continuing to act as foreman of the shop, according to the ancient tradition, the owner began to withdraw more and more from personal contact and direction of the work in hand and to give his attention to the financial end of the enterprise and to control the work by taking care of the running balance of bargains involved in procuring labor and materials and disposing of the product. Instead of a master workman, he became a business man engaged in a quest of profits, very much after the pattern of business men engaged in commercial enterprise. The result was that investment and absentee ownership presently became the rule in the mechanical industries, as it already was the rule in commerce and as it had long been the rule in husbandry.

This rearrangement of economic factors, and division of economic activities, was brought on by the increasing scale of the industrial plant and operations, wherever and so far as the new technology of the machine process took effect. And the characterisation just offered is intended to apply only so far and so fast as the new mechanistic technology gradually took over the industries of the country. There came on a progressive, but none the less revolutionary, change in the standard type of industrial business, as well as in the ways and means of industrial work; and the same line of change has gone forward unremittingly from that time to the present, as it is also visibly running on into the future.

If the word be defined to suit the case, 'capitalism' in industry may be said to have arisen in that time and out of the circumstances described. Until the machine process had made serious inroads in the standard industries, and until things had consequently begun to shift to the new scale, the business man in industry continued, in the typical case, to be personally concerned with the work in hand; and until this change took effect, therefore, the employer-owner answered quite reasonably to the character which Adam Smith assigned him, as a master workman who owned certain industrial appliances which he made use of with the help of hired workmen. But from this time on he became, in the typical case, an absentee manager with a funded interest in the works as a going business concern. The visible relation between the owner and the works shifted from a personal footing of workmanship to an impersonal footing of absentee ownership resting on an investment of funds. Under the new dispensation the owner's guiding interest centered on the earnings of the concern rather than on the workmen and their work. The works – mill, factory, or whatever word may be preferred – became a business concern, a 'going concern' which was valued and capitalised on its earning-capacity; and the businesslike management of industry, accordingly, centered upon the net earnings to be derived in a competitive market, - earnings derived from the margin of the sale price of the product over the purchase price of the labor, materials, and equipment employed in its production. Industrial business became a commercial enterprise, and the industrial plant became a going concern capitalised on its earning-capacity.[9]

It is not that nothing of the kind is to be found in the practice of earlier times. Indeed it is quite easy so to analyse the facts of property-holding in any age as to show that the value of absentee ownership always and everywhere is necessarily a matter of the capitalisation of the earning-capacity of the property so held. It is more difficult, perhaps it would prove impracticable, to apply the same line of reasoning to the same end in the case of other than absentee ownership. At any rate the matter is fairly obvious in the case of absentee ownership, early or late, to anyone who has occasion to see it from that point of view. But with the advance into the new era, into what is properly to be called recent times in business and industry, the capitalisation of earning-capacity comes to be the standard practice in the conduct of business finance, and calls attention to itself as a dominant fact in the situation that has arisen. The value of any investment is measured by its capitalised earning-capacity, and the endeavors of any businesslike management therefore unavoidably centre on net earnings.[10]

It should be worth while to take stock of this earning-capacity that underlies modern business enterprise, and see what it comes of and what it comes to. The earning-capacity of any given going concern is measured by the habitual excess of its income over its outlay. The net aggregate income, and therefore the net aggregate earnings, of the business community taken as a whole is derived from the margin of product by which the output of the industrial system exceeds its cost - counting cost and output in physical terms. This may

9 The economists and others who discuss business and industry as carried on in that time - late eighteenth and early nineteenth century - do not speak of 'capitalisation of earning-capacity"; but business practice at the time gives evidence of the fact. Then as always the theoretical discussions endeavored to formulate the new facts in terms derived from an earlier state of things. Indeed, it has taken something like a hundred years for the formulas of the economists to adapt themselves to the new run of facts in business and industry which set in in the days of Adam Smith. Right lately the economists have begun to recognise that 'capital' means 'capitalisation of earning-capacity'; but when seen in the long perspective of history it is evident that the business men who had to do with these things were learning to do business on that footing something over a hundred years ago.

10 Cf. *The Theory of Business Enterprise*, ch. vi; W.H. Lyon, *Capitalisation*, chs. ii and iii.

conveniently be called the net product of industry. So far as the country's industries have been placed on a business footing; that is to say, so far as the control of the industries has been taken over by business men on a basis of investment for a profit; so far the aggregate earnings of the business community will tend to coincide with the net product of the industrial system. This coincidence, or identity, between the net aggregate product of industry and the net aggregate earnings of business is by no means exact; but then, the whole system of absentee ownership and businesslike control is also not yet complete or altogether supreme, either in range or scope. Indeed, it is safe to affirm that the earnings of business come as near taking up the total net product of industry as one has a right to expect, regard being had to the present imperfect state of things.

It is this net product, counted in terms of its price, that makes up the earnings of business and so makes the basis of capitalisation; for earnings and capital, both, are counted in terms of price, and not otherwise. It is the ownership of materials and equipment that enables the capitalisation to be made; but ownership does not of itself create a net product, and so it does not give rise to earnings, but only to the legal claim by force of which the earnings go to the owners of the capitalised wealth. Production is a matter of workmanship, whereas earnings are a matter of business. And so the question returns: What are the circumstances by force of which industry yields a net product, which can be turned to account as earnings?

It will appear on analysis that there are two main circumstances which enable human industry to turn out a net product, and which govern its rate and volume: (*a*) the state of the industrial arts, and (*b*) the growth of population. Transiently, production will also be limited by the available stock of industrial appliances, materials, and means of subsistence; as well as by a variety of hindrances of a conventional or institutional nature, chief among them being a businesslike curtailment of production with a view to private gain. But always the state of the industrial arts and the state of man-power provided by the population will determine what will be the productive capacity of the industrial system; and in the absence of disturbing causes of an extraneous kind the effectual rate and volume of production will approach the limit so set by these two abiding factors of workmanship.

At the same time, by and large, the growth of population is governed by the state of the industrial arts, in such a way that the numbers of the population cannot exceed the carrying capacity of the industrial arts as known and practiced at the time, although the population may, and habitually does, fall somewhat short of that limit. It appears, therefore, that the prime creative factor in human industry is the state of the industrial arts; that is to say, the determining fact which enables human work to turn out a useful product is the accumulated knowledge, skill, and judgment that goes into the work, - also called technology or workmanship.

The dominant creative force of this accumulated industrial wisdom, within the sweep of which human workmanship lives and moves, has become evident more and more obtrusively since the era of the mechanical industry set in. The increasingly impersonal sweep of mechanical processes in industry during the past century has brought a realisation of the indispensably creative function of technology. But in the light of what the machine industry has made plain it is readily to be seen that the state of the industrial arts, the accumulated knowledge of ways and means, must in the nature of things always be the prime factor in human industry. So that in this respect the technology of this mechanistic era differs from what has gone before only in that the creative primacy of the state of the industrial arts is a more palpable fact today than ever before.

The state of the industrial arts determines what natural materials will be useful as well as how they will be made use of.[11] For the greater part the state of the industrial arts is a heritage out of the past, a knowledge of ways and means hit upon and tried out by past generations and from them handed on to their posterity; and for the greater part also any addition, extension, advance, or improvement in technology is a rearrangement of and a refinement upon the elements of such knowledge so handed down from the past. Industrial inventions and improvements invariably consist, in the main, of elements of knowledge drawn from common notoriety but turned to new and technologically unexpected uses. The novelties of today are a technologically later generation of the commonplaces of the day before yesterday.[12]

Evidently the state of the industrial arts is of the nature of a joint stock, worked out, held, carried forward, and made use of by those who live within the sweep of the industrial community. In this bearing the industrial community is a joint going-concern. And the 'industrial community' does not mean the Nation; since no nation is or can be self-sufficient in this matter of technology.

11 E.g., in prehistoric times men (or more probably women) invented the domestication of certain crop-plants, and presently also of certain animals. By virtue of these technological discoveries in ancient times these products of nature came to be ways and means of human industry. And they have continued to hold their place in the industrial system since then; so that the life of the civilised peoples still depends on the continued use of these industrial appliances, and those lands and soils which lend themselves to use in the resulting system of husbandry are valuable natural resources in the precise measure in which the domestication of plants and animals has made them so. So, again, in later times, within the era of the machine industry, petroleum and rubber, e.g., which were of no account a hundred years ago, have come to be indispensable factors in the industrial situation today, because technology has made them so. There is no end to the number of instances that might be adduced in illustration of this thesis, because the same proposition applies to all natural materials or processes that are or have been turned to human use. It holds true throughout that 'Invention is the mother of necessity' and that workmanship turns brute matter into natural resources, ways and means of productive industry.

12 Cf. *The Instinct of Workmanship*, chapter iii, especially pp. 103-112.

Of course, the patriotic spirit of nationalism drives men to imagine vain things of that kind; but all that is in the nature of a pathological make-believe, which has only a paranoiac relation to the facts of the case. And of course, the statesmen endeavor to hedge the nation about with restrictions designed to set up some sort of technological self-sufficiency and isolation; but all that is done in the service of technological sterilisation and decay, with a paranoiac view to the defeat of outsiders. It is only that the statesmen are running true to form. The industrial community as a technologically going concern is so much of mankind as is living in and by the industrial arts that go to make up the effectual system of technological knowledge and practice. And in this relation, as in most others, the national frontiers are the frontiers of the national futilities.

The state of the industrial arts is a joint stock of technological knowledge and practice worked out, accumulated, and carried forward by the industrial population which lives and moves within the sweep of this industrial system. As regards the modern mechanical industry this immaterial equipment of knowledge and training is held jointly by the peoples of Christendom. And the broad centre of its diffusion still is that community of peoples that cluster about the North Sea, together with their colonial extensions into newer lands. It is this joint stock of industrial knowledge and practice that makes the nations of Christendom formidable, and it is this same joint stock of technology that gives to the modern world's tangible assets whatever use and value they have. Tangible assets, considered simply as material objects, are inert, transient and trivial, compared with the abiding efficiency of that living structure of technology that has created them and continues to turn them to account.

But for the transient time being the material appliances of industry, the natural resources and the material equipment in hand, are indispensable to the conduct of industry; since the current state of the industrial arts does its creative work only by use of suitable mechanical apparatus. Modern industry is a system of mechanical processes devised and directed by expert knowledge and carried out by means of mechanical apparatus and raw materials. For the transient time being, therefore, any person who has a legal right to withhold any part of the necessary industrial apparatus or materials from current use will be in a position to impose terms and exact obedience, on pain of rendering the community's joint stock of technology inoperative to that extent. Ownership of industrial equipment and natural resources confers such a right legally to enforce unemployment, and so to make the community's workmanship useless to that extent. This is the Natural Right of Investment.

Ownership confers a legal right of sabotage, and absentee ownership vests the owner with the power of sabotage at a distance, by help of the constituted authorities whose duty it is to enforce the legal rights of citizens. This legal right of sabotage is commonly exercised only to the extent of a partial and fluctuating unemployment of the material equipment and therefore of the available workmanship; only to such an extent as seems wise for the enforcement of terms satisfactory to the owners, – only so far 'as the traffic will bear.' It is to the owner's interest to derive an income from these his legal rights; and in the long run there will be no income derivable from equipment or natural resources that are wholly unemployed,[13] or from man-power which is not allowed to work.

So the common practice has come to be partial employment of equipment and man-power on terms satisfactory to the owners; often rising to something near full employment for a limited time, but always with the reservation that the owner retains his legal right to withhold his property from productive use in whole or in part. Plainly, ownership would be nothing better than an idle gesture without this legal right of sabotage. Without the power of discretionary idleness, without the right to keep the work out of the hands of the workmen and the product out of the market, investment and business enterprise would cease. This is the larger meaning of the Security of Property.

By virtue of this legal right of sabotage which inheres as a natural right in the ownership of industrially useful things, the owners are able to dictate satisfactory terms; so that they come in for the usufruct of the community's industrial knowledge and practice, with such deductions as are necessary to enforce their terms and such concessions as will induce the underlying population to go on with the work. This making of terms is called 'Charging what the traffic will bear.' It consists, on the one hand, in stopping down production to such a volume as will bring the largest net returns in terms of price, and in allowing so much of a livelihood to the working force of technicians and workmen, on the other hand, as will induce them to turn out this limited output. It evidently calls for a shrewd balancing of production against price, such as is best served by a hard head and a cool heart. In the ideal case, in so far as the 'Law of Balanced Return' works out to a nicety, the output of production should be held to such a volume that the resulting price of the limited output will take up the entire purchasing power of the underlying population, at the same time that the livelihood which the owners allow their working force of technicians and workmen is held down to the 'subsistence minimum.' But such a precise balance is not commonly maintained in the practical management of affairs. The difficulties arising out of a very complex and fluctuating situation are very perplexing; so that in practice it is necessary to allow for a certain margin of error, which a businesslike (safe and sane) management will bring in on the conservative side, to the effect that the volume of production and the allowance of livelihood will commonly fall short of what the traffic would bear rather than exceed that amount.

13 This does not overlook the case of speculative real estate which is held quite idle for the time being with a view to a lump gain in the future, in which case sabotage is carried to perfection for the time being.

It appears, therefore (*a*) that industrial appliances and materials (tangible assets), as well as the industrial man-power, are productive agencies because and so far as the accumulated industrial knowledge and practice make them so; (*b*) that investment in industrial plant and natural resources is worth while to the investor because and so far as his ownership of these useful things enables him to control and limit the operation of the industrial arts which make these things useful, - that is to say, because and so far as his ownership of these things confers on him the usufruct of the community's workmanship; (*c*) the earning-capacity of these assets, which gives them their value as property, is measured by the net returns - in terms of price - which come to their owner as usufructuary or pensioner on the community's workmanship; (*d*) these valuable assets are assets to the amount of their capitalised value, that is to say to the amount of their funded earning-capacity; (*e*) their earning-capacity is determined by what the traffic will bear, that is to say by curtailing production to such an amount that the output multiplied by the price per unit will yield the largest net aggregate return; so that (*f*) the natural right of investment becomes, in effect, a vested right of use and abuse over the current industrial knowledge and practice.[14]

14 Cf. Two papers 'On the Nature of Capital,' in the *Quarterly Journal of Economics*, August and November, 1908; reprinted in *The Place of Science in Modern Civilisation and Other Essays*, pp. 324-386.

9 / R. H. TAWNEY

At about the same time as Veblen's critique, other criticisms of current theories justifying modern capitalist property were being developed by some moderate socialist theorists, notable among whom was the leading English economic historian, R.H. Tawney. Starting from a distinction that had often been made before, between the small property that one could work by oneself and modern property in capital as a right to an income regardless of services rendered by the owner, Tawney developed a general theory that private property is justified only in terms of function. Only those kinds of property which served functions judged by the whole society to be valuable were justified. One valuable function of individual property was that it enabled those who could save a little to provide some security against sickness, old age, etc., though that function could be better performed by the social security measures of a welfare state. In any case that was no justification of modern corporate property. Most property was now functionless property, which undermines the creative energy that originally produced property and which in earlier ages had been protected by the institution of property. Tawney's case, backed by his historical expertise and clearly related to Christian values, has had a considerable appeal ever since to those in the Christian humanist tradition.

Reprinted here is chapter V of Tawney's *The Sickness of An Acquisitive Society*, first published in 1920 by The Fabian Society and George Allen & Unwin. Reprinted by permission of the publishers.

Property and Creative Work

The application of the principle that society should be organised upon the basis of functions, is not recondite, but simple and direct. It offers in the first place, a standard for discriminating between those types of private property which are legitimate and those which are not. During the last century and a half, political thought has oscillated between two conceptions of property, both of which, in their different ways, are extravagant. On the one hand, the practical foundation of social organization has been the doctrine that the particular forms of private property which exist at any moment are a thing sacred and inviolable, that anything may properly become the object of property rights, and that, when it does, the title to it is absolute and unconditioned. The modern industrial system took shape in an age when this theory of property was triumphant. The American Constitution and the French Declaration of the Rights of Man both treated property as one of the fundamental rights which governments exist to protect. The English Revolution of 1688, undogmatic and reticent though it was, had in effect done the same. The great individualists from Locke to Turgot, Adam Smith and Bentham all repeated, in different language, a similar conception. Though what gave the Revolution its diabolical character in the eyes of the English upper classes was its treatment of property, the dogma of the sanctity of private property was maintained as tenaciously by French Jacobins as by English Tories; and the theory that property is an absolute, which is held by many modern Conservatives, is identical, if only they knew it, with that not only of the men of 1789, but of the Convention itself. On the other hand, the attack has been almost as undiscriminating as the defence. Private property has been the central position against which the social movement of the last hundred years has directed its forces. The criticism of it has ranged from an imaginative communism in the most elementary and personal of necessaries, to prosaic and partially realized proposals to transfer certain kinds of property from private to public ownership, or to limit their exploitation by restrictions imposed by the State. But, however varying in emphasis and in method, the general note of what may conveniently be called the Socialist criticism of property is what the word Socialism itself implies. Its essence is the statement that the economic evils of society are primarily due to the unregulated operation, under modern conditions of industrial organization, of the institution of private property.

The divergence of opinion is natural, since in most discussions of property the opposing theorists have usually been discussing different things. Property is the most ambiguous of categories. It covers a multitude of rights which have nothing in common except that they are exercised by persons and enforced by the State. Apart from these formal characteristics, they vary indefinitely in economic character, in social effect, and in moral justification. They may be conditional like the grant of patent rights, or absolute like the ownership of ground rents, terminable like copyright, or permanent like a freehold, as comprehensive as sovereignty or as restricted as an easement, as intimate and personal as the ownership of clothes and books, or as remote and intangible as shares in a goldmine or rubber plantation. It is idle, therefore, to present a case for or against private property without specifying the particular forms of property to which reference is made, and the journalist who says that 'private property is the foundation of civilization' agrees with Proudhon, who said it was theft, in this respect at least that, without further definition, the words of both are meaningless. Arguments which support or demolish certain kinds of property may have no application to others; considerations which are conclusive in one stage of economic organization may be almost irrelevant in the next. The course of wisdom is neither to attack private property in general nor to defend it in general; for things are not similar in quality, merely because they are identical in name. It is to discriminate between the various concrete embodiments of what, in itself, is, after all, little more than an abstraction.

The origin and development of different kinds of proprietary rights is not material to this discussion. Whatever may have been the historical process by which they have been established and recognized, the *rationale* of private property traditional in England is that which sees in it the security that each man will reap where he has sown. 'If I despair of enjoying the fruits of my labour,' said Bentham, 'I shall only live from day to day; I shall not undertake labours which will only benefit my enemies.' Property, it is argued, is a moral right, and not merely a legal right, because it ensures that the producer will not be deprived by violence of the result of his efforts. The period from which that doctrine was inherited differed from our own in three obvious, but significant, respects. Property in land and in the simple capital used in most industries was widely distributed. Before the rise of capitalist agriculture and capitalist industry, the ownership, or at any rate the secure and effective occupation, of land and tools by those who used them, was a condition precedent to effective work in the field or in the workshop. The forces which threatened property were the fiscal policy of governments and in some countries, for example France, the decaying relics of feudalism. The interference both of the one and of the other involved the sacrifice of those who carried on useful labour to those who did not. To resist them was to protect not only property but industry, which was indissolubly connected with it. Too often, indeed, resistance was ineffective. Accustomed to the misery of the rural proprietor in France, Voltaire remarked with astonishment that in England the peasant may be rich, and 'does not fear to increase the number of his beasts to or cover his roof with tiles.' And the English Parliamentarians and the French philosophers who made the inviolability of property rights the centre of their political theory, when they defended those who owned, were incidentally, if sometimes unintentionally, defending those who laboured. They were protecting the yeoman or the master craftsman or the merchant from seeing the fruits of his toil squandered by the hangers-on at St James or the courtly parasites of Versailles.

In such circumstances the doctrine which found the justification of private property in the fact that it enabled the industrious man to reap where he had sown, was not a paradox, but, as far as the mass of the population was concerned, almost a truism. Property was defended as the most sacred of rights. But it was defended as a right which was not only widely exercised, but which was indispensable to the performance of the active function of providing food and clothing. For it consisted predominantly of one of two types, land or tools which were used by the owner for the purpose of production, and personal possessions which were the necessities or amenities of civilized existence. The former had its *rationale* in the fact that the land of the peasant or the tools of the craftsman were the condition of his rendering the economic services which society required; the latter because furniture and clothes are indispensable to a life of decency and comfort. The proprietary rights – and, of course, they were numerous – which had their source, not in work, but in predatory force, were protected from criticism by the wide distribution of some kind of property among the mass of the population, and in England, at least, the cruder of them were gradually whittled down. When property in land and what simple capital existed were generally diffused among all classes of society, when, in most parts of England, the typical workman was not a labourer but a peasant farmer or small master, who could point to the strips which he had ploughed or the cloth which he had woven, when the greater part of the wealth passing at death consisted of land, household furniture and a stock in trade which was hardly distinguishable from it, the moral justification of the title to property was self-evident. It was obviously, what theorists said that it was, and plain men knew it to be, the labour spent in producing, acquiring and administering it.

Such property was not a burden upon society, but a condition of its health and efficiency, and indeed, of its continued existence. To protect it was to maintain the organization through which public necessities were supplied. If, as in Tudor England, the peasant was evicted from his holding to make room for sheep, or crushed, as in eighteenth century France, by arbitrary taxation and seigneurial dues, land went out of cultivation and the whole community was short of food. If the tools of the carpenter or smith were seized, ploughs were not repaired or horses shod. Hence, before the rise of a commercial civilization, it was the mark of statesmanship, alike in the England of the Tudors and in the France of Henry IV, to cherish the small property-owner even to the point of offending the great. Popular sentiment idealized the yeoman – 'the Joseph of the country who keeps the poor from starving' – not merely because he owned property, but because he worked on it, denounced that 'bringing of the livings of many into the hands of one' which capitalist societies regard with equanimity as an inevitable, and, apparently, a laudable result of economic development, cursed the usurer who took advantage of his neighbour's necessities to live without labour, was shocked by the callous indifference to public welfare shown by those who 'not having before their eyes either God or the profit and advantage of the realm, have enclosed with hedges and dykes towns and hamets,' and was sufficiently powerful to compel governments to intervene to prevent the laying of field to field, and the engrossing of looms – to set limits, in short, to the scale to which property might grow. When Bacon, who commended Henry VII. for protecting the tenant right of the small farmer, and pleaded in the House of Commons for more drastic land legislation, wrote 'Wealth is like muck. It is not good but if it be spread,' he was expressing in an epigram what was the commonplace of every writer on politics from Fortescue at the end of the fifteenth century to Harrington in the middle of the seventeenth. The modern conservative, who is inclined to take *au pied de la lettre* the vigorous argument in which Lord Hugh Cecil denounces the doctrine that the maintenance of proprietary rights ought to be contingent upon the use to which they are put, may be reminded that Lord Hugh's own theory is of a kind to make his ancestors turn in their graves. Of the two members of the family who achieved distinction before the nineteenth century, the elder advised the Crown to prevent landlords evicting tenants, and actually proposed to fix a pecuniary maximum to the property which different classes might possess, while the younger attacked enclosing in Parliament, and carried legislation compelling landlords to build cottages, to let them with small holdings, and to plough up pasture.

William and Robert Cecil were sagacious and responsible men, and their view that the protection of property should be accompanied by the enforcement of obligations upon its owners was shared by most of their contemporaries. The idea that the institution of private property involves the right of the owner to use it, or refrain from using it, in such a way as he may please, and that its principal significance is to supply him with an income, irrespective of any duties which he may discharge, would not have been understood by most public men of that age, and, if understood, would have been repudiated with indignation by the more reputable among them. They found the meaning of property in the public purposes to which it contributed, whether they were the production of food, as among the peasantry, or the management of public affairs, as among the gentry, and hesitated neither to maintain those kinds of property which met these obligations nor to repress those uses of it which appeared likely to conflict with them. Property was to be an aid to creative work, not an alternative to it. The patentee was secured protection for a new invention, in order to secure him the fruits of his own brain, but the monopolist who grew fat on the industry of others was to be put down. The law of the village bound the peasant to use his land, not as he himself might find most profitable, but to grow the corn the village needed. Long after political changes had made direct interference impracticable, even the higher ranks of English landowners continued to discharge, however capriciously and tyrannically, duties which were vaguely felt to be the contribution which they made to the public service in virtue of their estates. When as in France, the obligations of ownership were repudiated almost as completely as they have been by the owner of to-day, nemesis came in an onslaught upon the position of a *noblesse* which had retained its rights and abdicated its functions. Property reposed, in short, not merely upon convenience, or the appetite for gain, but on a moral principle. It was protected not only for the sake of those who owned, but for the sake of those who worked and of those for whom their work provided. It was protected, because, without security for property, wealth could not be produced or the business of society carried on.

Whatever the future may contain, the past has shown no more excellent social order than that in which the mass of the people were the masters of the holdings which they ploughed and of the tools with which they worked, and could boast, with the English freeholder, that 'it is a quietness to a man's mind to live upon his own and to know his heir certain.' With this conception of property and its practical expression in social institutions those who urge that society should be organized on the basis of function have no quarrel. It is in agreement with their own doctrine, since it justifies property by reference to the services which it enables its owner to perform. All that they need ask is that it should be carried to its logical conclusion.

The argument has evidently more than one edge. If it justifies certain types of property, it condemns others; and in the conditions of modern industrial civilization, what it justifies is less than what it condemns. For this theory of property and the institutions in which it is embodied have survived into an age in which the whole structure of society is radically different from that in which it was formulated, and which made it a valid argument, if not for all, at least for the most common and characteristic kinds of property. It is not merely that the ownership of any substantial share in the national wealth is concentrated to-day in the hands of a few hundred thousand families, and that at the end of an age which began with an affirmation of the rights of property, proprietary rights are, in fact, far from being widely distributed. Nor is it merely that what makes property insecure to-day is not the arbitrary taxation of unconstitutional monarchies or the privileges of an idle *noblesse*, but the insatiable expansion and aggregation of property itself, which menaces with absorption all property less than the greatest, the small master, the little shopkeeper, the country bank, and has turned the mass of mankind into a proletariat working under the agents and for the profit of those who own. The characteristic fact, which differentiates most modern property from that of the pre-industrial age, and which turns against it the very reasoning by which formerly it was supported, is that in modern economic conditions ownership is not active, but passive, that to most of those who own property to-day it is not a means of work but an instrument for the acquisition of gain or the exercise of power, and that there is no guarantee that gain bears any relation to service, or power to responsibility. For property which can be regarded as a condition of the performance of function, like the tools of the craftsman, or the holding of the peasant, or the personal possessions which contribute to a life of health and efficiency, forms an insignificant proportion, as far as its value is concerned, of the property rights existing at present. In modern industrial societies the great mass of property consists, as the annual review of wealth passing at death reveals, neither of personal acquisitions such as household furniture, nor of the owner's stock-in-trade, but of rights of various kinds, such as royalties, ground-rents, and, above all, of course, shares in industrial undertakings, which yield an income irrespective of any personal service rendered by their owners. Ownership and use are normally divorced. The greater part of modern property has been attenuated to a pecuniary lien or bond on the product of industry, which carries with it a right to payment, but which is normally valued precisely because it relieves the owner from any obligation to perform a positive or constructive function.

Such property may be called passive property, or property for acquisition, for exploitation, or for power, to distinguish it from the property which is actively used by its owner for the conduct of his profession or the upkeep of his household. To the lawyer the first is, of course, as fully property as the second. It is questionable, however, whether economists should call it 'Property' at all, and not rather, as Mr Hobson has suggested, 'Improperty,' since it is not identical with the rights which secure the owner the produce of his toil, but is the opposite of them. A classification of proprietary rights based upon this difference would be instructive. If they were arranged according to the closeness with which they approximate to one or other of these two extremes, it would be found that they were spread along a line stretching from property which is obviously the payment for, and condition of, personal services, to property which is merely a right to payment from the services rendered by others, in fact a private tax. The rough order which would emerge, if all details and qualification were omitted, might be something as follows: –

1. Property in payments made for personal services.
2. Property in personal possessions necessary to health and comfort.
3. Property in land and tools used by their owners.
4. Property in copyright and patent rights owned by authors and inventors.
5. Property in pure interest, including much agricultural rent.
6. Property in profits of luck and good fortune: 'quasi-rents.'
7. Property in monopoly profits.
8. Property in urban ground rents.
9. Property in royalties.

The first four kinds of property obviously accompany, and in some sense condition, the performance of work. The last four obviously do not. Pure interest has some affinities with both. It represents a necessary economic cost, the equivalent of which must be born, whatever the legal arrangements under which property is held, and is thus unlike the property represented by profits (other than the equivalent of salaries and payment for necessary risk), urban ground-rents and royalties. It relieves the recipient from personal services, and thus resembles them.

The crucial question for any society is, under which each of these two broad groups of categories the greater part (measured in value) of the proprietary rights which it maintains are at any given moment to be found. If they fall in the first group creative work will be encouraged and idleness will be depressed; if they fall in the second, the result will be the reverse. The facts vary widely from age to age and from country to country. Nor have they ever been fully revealed; for the lords of the jungle do not hunt by daylight. It is probable, at least, that in the England of 1550 to 1750, a larger proportion of the existing property consisted of land and tools used by their owners than either in contemporary France, where feudal dues absorbed a considerable proportion of the peasants' income, or than in the England of 1800 to 1850, where the new capitalist manufacturers made hundreds per cent while manual workers were goaded by starvation into ineffectual revolt. It is probable that in the nineteenth century, thanks to the Revolution, France and England changed places, and that in this respect not only Ireland but the British Dominions resemble the former rather than the latter. The transformation can be studied best of all in the United States, in parts of which the population of peasant proprietors and small masters of the early nineteenth century were converted in three generations into a capitalist plutocracy. The abolition of the economic privileges of agrarian feudalism, which, under the name of equality, was the driving force of the French Revolution, and which has taken place, in one form or another, in all countries touched by its influence, has been largely counterbalanced since 1800 by the growth of the inequalities springing from Industrialism.

In England the general effect of recent economic development has been to swell proprietary rights which entitle the owners to payment without work, and to diminish those which can properly be described as functional. The expansion of the former, and the process by which the simpler forms of property have been merged in them, are movements the significance of which it is hardly possible to over-estimate. There is, of course, a considerable body of property which is still of the older type. But though working landlords, and capitalists who manage their own businesses, are still in the aggregate a numerous body, the organization for which they stand is not that which is most representative of the modern economic world. The general tendency for the ownership and administration of property to be separated, the general refinement of property into a claim on goods produced by an unknown worker, is as unmistakeable as the growth of capitalist industry and urban civilization themselves. Villages are turned into towns and property in land changes from the holding worked by a farmer or the estate administered by a landlord into 'rents,' which are advertized and bought and sold like any other investment. Mines are opened and the rights of the land-owner are converted into a tribute for every ton of coal which is brought to the surface. As joint-Stock Companies take the place of the individual enterprise which was typical of the earlier years of the factory system, organization passes from the employer who both owns and manages his business, into the hands of salaried officials, and again the mass of property-owners is swollen by the multiplication of *rentiers* who put their wealth at the disposal of industry, but who have no other connection with it. The change is taking place in our day most conspicuously, perhaps, through the displacement in retail trade of the small shopkeeper by the multiple store, and the substitution in manufacturing industry of combines and amalgamations for separate businesses conducted by competing employers. And, of course, it is not only by economic development that such claims are created. 'Out of the eater came forth meat, and out of the strong came forth sweetness.' It is probable that war, which in barbarous ages used to be blamed as destructive of property, has recently created more titles to property than almost all other causes put together.

Infinitely diverse as are these proprietary rights, they have the common characteristic of being so entirely separated from the actual objects over which they are exercised, so rarified and generalized, as to be analogous almost to a form of currency rather than to the property which is so closely united to its owner as to seem a part of him. Their isolation from the rough environment of economic life, where the material objects of which they are the symbol are shaped and handled, is their charm. It is also their danger. The hold which a class has upon the future depends on the function which it performs. What nature demands is work: few working aristocracies, however tyrannical, have fallen; few functionless aristocracies have survived. In society, as in the world of organic life, atrophy is but one stage removed from death. In proportion as the landowner becomes a mere *rentier* and industry is conducted, not by the rude energy of the competing employers who dominated its infancy, but by the salaried servants of shareholders, the argument for private property which reposes on the impossibility of finding any organization to supersede them loses its application, for they are already superseded.

Whatever may be the justification of these types of property, it cannot be that which was given for the property of the peasant or the craftsman. It cannot be that they are necessary in order to secure to each man the fruits of his own labour. For if a legal right which gives £50,000 a year to a mineral owner in the North of England and to a ground landlord in London 'secures the fruits of labour' at all, the fruits are the proprietor's and the labour that of someone else. Property has no more insidious enemies than those well-meaning anarchists who, by defending all forms of it as equally valid, involve the institution in the discredit attaching to its extravagances. In reality, whatever conclusion may be drawn from the fact, the greater part of modern property, whether, like mineral rights and urban ground-rents, it is merely a form of private taxation which the law allows certain persons to levy on the industry of others, or whether, like property in capital, it consists of rights to payment for instruments which the capitalist cannot himself use but puts at the disposal of those who can, has as its essential feature that it confers upon its owners income unaccompanied by personal service. In this respect the ownership of land and the ownership of capital are normally similar, though from other points of view their differences are important. To the economist rent and interest are distinguished by the fact that the latter, though it is often accompanied by surplus elements which are merged with it in dividends, is the price of an instrument of production which would not be forthcoming for industry if the price were not paid, while the former is a differential surplus which does not affect the supply. To the business community and the solicitor land and capital are equally investments, between which, since they possess the common characteristic of yielding income without labour, it is inequitable to discriminate; and though their significance as economic categories may be different, their effect as social institutions is the same. It is to separate property from creative activity, and to divide society into two classes, of which one has its primary interest in passive ownership, while the other is mainly dependent upon active work.

Hence the real analogy to many kinds of modern property is not the simple property of the small landowner or the craftsman, still less the household gods and dear domestic amenities, which is what the word suggests to the guileless minds of clerks and shopkeepers, and which stampede them into displaying the ferocity of terrified sheep when the cry is raised that 'Property' is threatened. It is the feudal dues which robbed the French peasant of part of his produce till the Revolution abolished them. How do royalties differ from *quintaines* and *lods et ventes?* They are similar in their origin and similar in being a tax levied on each increment of wealth which labour produces. How do urban ground-rents differ from the payments which were made to English sinecurists before the Reform Bill of 1832? They are equally tribute paid by those who work to those who do not. If the monopoly profits of the owner of *banalités*, whose tenant must grind corn at his mill and make wine at his press, were an intolerable oppression, what is the sanctity attaching to the monopoly profits of the capitalists, who, as the Report of the Government Committee on trusts tells us, 'in soap, tobacco, wall-paper, salt, cement and in the textile trades ... are in a position to control output and prices,' or, in other words, can compel the consumer to buy from them, at the figure they fix, on pain of not buying at all?

All these rights - royalties, ground rents, monopoly profits - are 'Property.' The criticism most fatal to them is not that of Socialists. It is contained in the arguments by which property is usually defended. For if the meaning of the institution is to encourage industry by securing that the worker shall receive the produce of his toil, then precisely in proportion as it is important to preserve the property which a man has in the results of his own efforts, is it important to abolish that which he has in the results of the efforts of someone else. The considerations which justify ownership as a function are those which condemn it as a tax. Property is not theft, but a good deal of theft becomes property. The owner of royalties who, when asked why he should be paid £50,000 a year from minerals which he has neither discovered nor developed nor worked but only owned, replies 'But it's Property!' may feel all the awe which his language suggests. But in reality he is behaving like the snake which sinks into its background by pretending that it is the dead branch of a tree, or the lunatic who tried to catch rabbits by sitting behind a hedge and making a noise like a turnip. He is practising protective - and sometimes aggressive - mimicry. His sentiments about property are those of the simple toiler who fears that what he has sown another may reap. His claim is to be allowed to continue to reap what another has sown.

It is sometimes suggested that the less attractive characteristics of our industrial civilization, its combination of luxury and squalor, its class division and class warfare, are accidental maladjustments which are not rooted in the centre of its being, but are excrescences which economic progress itself may in time be expected to correct. That agreeable optimism will not survive an examination of the operation of the institution of private property in land and capital in industrialized communities. In countries where land is widely distributed, in France or in Ireland, its effect may be to produce a general diffusion of wealth among a rural middle class who at once work and own. In countries where the development of industrial organization has separated the ownership of property and the performance of work, the normal effect of private property is to transfer to functionless owners the surplus arising from the more fertile sites, the better machinery, the more elaborate organization. No clearer exemplifications of this 'law of rent' has been given than the figures supplied to the Coal Industry Commission by Sir Arthur Lowes Dickenson, which showed that in a given quarter the costs per ton of producing coal varied from 12/6 to 48/- per ton, and the profits from *nil* to 16/6. The distribution in dividends to shareholders of the surplus accruing from the working of richer and more accessible seams, from special opportunities and access to markets, from superior machinery, management and organization, involves the establishment of Privilege as a national institution, as much as the most arbitrary exactions of a feudal *seigneur.* It is the foundation of an inequality which is not accidental or temporary, but necessary and permanent. And on this inequality is erected the whole apparatus of class institutions, which make not only the income, but the housing, education, health and manners, indeed the very physical appearance of different classes of Englishmen almost as different from each other as though the minority were alien settlers established amid the rude civilization of a race of impoverished aborigines.

So the justification of private property traditional in England, which saw in it the security that each man would enjoy the fruits of his own labour, though largely applicable to the age in which it was formulated, has undergone the fate of most political theories. It has been refuted not by the doctrines of rival philosophers, but by the prosaic course of economic development. As far as the mass of mankind are concerned, the need which private property other than personal possessions does still often satisfy, though imperfectly and precariously, is the need for security. To the small investors, who are the majority of property-owners, though owning only an insignificant fraction of the property in existence, its meaning is simple. It is not wealth or power, or even leisure from work. It is safety. They work hard. They save a little money for old age, or sickness, or for their children. They invest it, and the interest stands between them and all that they dread most. Their savings are of convenience to industry, the income from them is convenient to themselves. 'Why' they ask, 'should we not reap in old age the advantage of energy and thrift in youth?' And this hunger for security is so imperious that those who suffer most from the abuses of property, as well as those who, if they could profit by them, would be least inclined to do so, will tolerate and even defend them, for fear lest the knife which trims dead matter should cut into the quick. They have seen too many men drown to be critical of dry land, though it be an inhospitable rock. They are haunted by the nightmare of the future, and, if a burglar broke it, would welcome a burglar.

This need for security is fundamental, and almost the gravest indictment of our civilization is that the mass of mankind are without it. Property is one way of securing it. It is quite comprehensible therefore, that the instrument should be confused with the end, and that any proposal to modify it should create dismay. In the past, human beings, roads, bridges and ferries, civil, judicial and clerical offices, and commissions in the army have all been private property. Whenever it was proposed to abolish the rights exercised over them, it was protested that their removal would involve the destruction of an institution in which thrifty men had invested their savings, and on which they depended for protection amid the chances of life and for comfort in old age. In fact, however, property is not the only method of assuring the future, nor, when it is the way selected, is security dependent upon the maintenance of all the rights which are at present normally involved in ownership. In so far as its psychological foundation is the necessity for securing an income which is stable and certain, which is forthcoming when its recipient cannot work, and which can be used to provide for those who cannot provide for themselves, what is really demanded is not the command over the fluctuating proceeds of some particular undertaking, which accompanies the ownership of capital, but the security which is offered by an annuity. Property is the instrument, security is the object, and when some alternative way is forthcoming of providing the latter, it does not appear in practice that any loss of confidence, or freedom or independence is caused by the absence of the former. Hence not only the manual workers, who since the rise of capitalism, have rarely in England been able to accumulate property sufficient to act as a guarantee of income when their period of active earning is past, but also the middle and professional classes, increasingly seek security to-day, not in investment, but in insurance against sickness and death, in the purchase of annuities, or in what is in effect the same thing, the accumulation of part of their salary towards a pension which is paid when their salary ceases. The professional man may buy shares in the hope of making a profit on the transaction. But when what he desires to buy is security, the form which his investment takes is usually one kind or another of insurance. The teacher, or nurse, or government servant looks forward to a pension. Women, who fifty years ago would have been regarded as dependent almost as completely as if femininity were an incurable disease with which they had been born, and whose fathers, unless rich men, would have been tormented with anxiety for fear lest they should not save sufficient to provide for them, now receive an education, support themselves in professions, and save in the same way. It is still only in comparatively few cases that this type of provision is made; almost all wage earners outside government employment, and many in it, as well as large numbers of professional men, have nothing to fall back upon in sickness or old age. But that does not alter the fact that, when it is made, it meets the need for security, which, apart, of course, from personal possessions and household furniture, is the principal meaning of property to by far the largest element in the population, and that it meets it more completely and certainly than property itself.

Nor, indeed, even when property is the instrument used to provide for the future, is such provision dependent upon the maintenance in its entirety of the whole body of rights which accompany ownership to-day. Property is not simple but complex. That of a man who has invested his savings as an ordinary shareholder comprises at least three rights, the right to interest, the right to profits, the right to control. In so far as what is desired is the guarantee for the maintenance of a stable income, not the acquisition of additional wealth without labour - in so far as his motive is not gain but security - the need is met by interest on capital. It has no necessary connection either with the right to residuary profits or the right to control the management of the undertaking from which the profits are derived, both of which are vested to-day in the shareholder. If all that were desired were to use property as an instrument for purchasing security, the obvious course - from the point of view of the investor desiring to insure his future the safest course - would be to assimilate his position as far as possible to that of a debenture holder or mortgagee, who obtains the stable income which is his motive for investment, but who neither incurs the risks nor receives the profits of the speculator. To insist that the elaborate apparatus of proprietary rights which distributes dividends of thirty per cent to the shareholders in Coats, and several thousands a year to the owner of mineral royalties and ground-rents, and then allows them to transmit the bulk of gains which they have not earned to descendants who in their turn will thus be relieved from the necessity of earning, must be maintained for the sake of the widow and the orphan, the vast majority of whom have neither and would gladly part with them all for a safe annuity if they had, is, to say the least of it, extravagantly *mal-à-propos*. It is like pitching a man into the water because he expresses a wish for a bath, or presenting a tiger cub to a householder who is plagued with mice, on the ground that tigers and cats both belong to the genus *felis*. The tiger hunts for itself not for its masters, and when game is scarce will hunt them. The classes who own little or no property may reverence it because it is security. But the classes who own much prize it for quite different reasons, and laugh in their sleeve at the innocence which supposes that anything as vulgar as the saving of the *petite bourgeosie* have, except at elections, any interest for them. They prize it because it is the order which quarters them on the community and which provides for the maintenance of a leisure class at the public expense.

'Possession,' said the Egoist, 'without obligation to the object possessed, approaches felicity.' Functionless property appears natural to those who believe that society should be organized for the acquisition of private wealth, and attacks upon it perverse or malicious, because the question which they ask of any institution is, 'What does it yield?' And such property yields much to those who own it. Those, however, who hold that social unity and effective work are possible only if society is organized and wealth distributed on the basis of function, will ask of an institution, not, 'What dividends does it pay?' but 'What service does it perform?' To them the fact that much property yields income irrespective of any service which is performed or obligation which is recognized by its owners will appear not a quality but a vice. They will see in the social confusion which it produces, payments disproportionate to service here, and payments without any service at all there, and dissatisfaction everywhere, a convincing confirmation of their argument that to build on a foundation of rights and of rights alone is to build on a quicksand. From the portentous exaggeration into an absolute of what once was, and still might be, a sane and social institution most other social evils follow, the power of those who do not work over those who do, the alternate subservience and rebelliousness of those who work towards those who do not, the starving of science and thought and creative effort for fear that expenditure upon them should impinge on the comfort of the sluggard and the *fainéant*, and the arrangement of society in most of its subsidiary activities to suit the convenience not of those who work usefully but of those who spend gaily, so that the most hideous, desolate and parsimonious places in the country are those in which the greatest wealth is produced, the Clyde valley, or the cotton towns of Lancashire, or the mining villages of Scotland and Wales, and the gayest and most luxurious those in which it is consumed. From the point of view of social health and economic efficiency, society should obtain its material equipment at the cheapest price possible, and after providing for depreciation and expansion should distribute the whole product to its working members and their dependents. What happens at present, however, is that its workers are hired at the cheapest price which the market (as modified by organization) allows, and that the surplus, somewhat diminished by taxation, is distributed to the owners of property. Profits may vary in a given year from a loss to 100 per cent. But wages are fixed at a level which will enable the marginal firm to continue producing one year with another; and the surplus, even when due partly to efficient management, goes neither to managers nor manual workers, but to shareholders. The meaning of the process becomes startlingly apparent when, as in Lancashire to-day, large blocks of capital change hands at a period of abnormal activity. The existing shareholders receive the equivalent of the capitalized expectation of future profits. The workers, as workers, do not participate in the immense increment in value; and when, in the future, they demand an advance in wages, they will be met by the answer that profits, which before the transaction would have been reckoned large, yield shareholders after it only a low rate of interest on their investment.

The truth is that whereas in earlier ages the protection of property was normally the protection of work, the relationship between them has come in the course of the economic development of the last two centuries to be very nearly reversed. The two elements which compose civilization are active effort and passive property, the labour of human things are the tools which human beings use. Of these two elements those who supply the first maintain and improve it, those who own the second normally dictate its character, its development and its administration. Hence, though politically free, the mass of mankind live in effect under rules imposed to protect the interests of the small section among them whose primary concern is ownership. From this subordination of creative activity to passive property, the worker who depends upon his brains, the organizer, inventor, teacher or doctor suffers almost as much embarrassment as the craftsman. The real economic cleavage is not, as is often said, between employers and employed, but between all who do constructive work, from scientist to labourer, on the one hand, and all whose main interest is the preservation of existing proprietary rights upon the other, irrespective of whether they contribute to constructive work or not. If the world is to be governed for the advantages of those who own, it is only incidentally and by accident that the results will be agreeable to those who work. In practice there is a constant collision between them. Turned into another channel, half the wealth distributed in dividends to functionless shareholders could secure every child a good education up to 18, could re-endow English Universities, and (since more efficient production is important) could equip English industries for more efficient production. Half the ingenuity now applied to the protection of property could have made most industrial diseases as rare as smallpox, and most English cities into places of health and even of beauty. What stands in the way is the doctrine that the rights of property are absolute, irrespective of any social function which its owners may perform. So the laws which are most stringently enforced are still the laws which protect property, though the protection of property is no longer likely to be equivalent to the protection of work, and the interests which govern industry and predominate in public affairs are proprietary interests. A mill-owner may poison or mangle a generation of operatives; but his brother magistrates will let him off with a caution or a nominal fine to poison and mangle the next. For he is an owner of property. A landowner may draw rents from slums in which young children die at the rate of 200 per 1000; but he will be none the less welcome in polite society. For property has no obligations and therefore can do no wrong. Urban land may be held from the market on the outskirts of cities in which human beings are living three to a room, and rural land may be used for sport when villagers are leaving it to overcrowd them still more. No public authority intervenes, for both are property. To those who believe that institutions which repudiate all moral significance must sooner or later collapse, a society which confuses the protection of property with the preservation of its functionless perversions will appear as precarious as that which has left the memorials of its tasteless frivolity and more tasteless ostentation in the gardens of Versailles.

Do men love peace? They will see the greatest enemy of social unity in rights which involve no obligation to co-operate for the service of society. Do they value equality? Property rights which dispense their owners from the common human necessity of labour make inequality an institution permeating every corner of society, from the distribution of material wealth to the training of intellect itself. Do they desire greater industrial efficiency? There is no more fatal obstacle to efficiency than the revelation that idleness has the same privileges as industry, and that for every additional blow with the pick or hammer an additional profit will be distributed among shareholders who wield neither. Indeed, functionless property is the greatest enemy of legitimate property itself. It is the parasite which kills the organism that produced it. Bad money drives out good, and, as the history of the last two hundred years shows, when property for acquisition or power and property for service or for use jostle each other freely in the market, without restrictions such as some legal systems have imposed on alienation and inheritance, the latter tends normally to be absorbed by the former, because it has less resisting power. Thus functionless property grows, and as it grows it undermines the creative energy which produced property and which in earlier ages it protected. It cannot unite men, for what unites them is the bond of service to a common purpose, and that bond it repudiates, since its very essence is the maintenance of rights irrespective of service. It cannot create; it can only spend, so that the number of scientists, inventors, artists or men of letters who have sprung in the course of the last century from hereditary riches can be numbered on one hand. It values neither culture nor beauty, but only the power which belongs to wealth and the ostentation which is the symbol of it.

So those who dread these qualities, energy and thought and the creative spirit - and they are many - will not discriminate, as we have tried to discriminate, between different types and kinds of property, in order that they may preserve those which are legitimate and abolish those which are not. They will endeavour to preserve all private property, even in its most degenerate forms. And those who value those things will try to promote them by relieving property of its perversions, and thus enabling it to return to its true nature. They will not desire to establish any visionary communism, for they will realize that the free disposal of a sufficiency of personal possessions is the condition of a healthy and self-respecting life, and will seek to distribute more widely the property rights which make them to-day the privilege of a minority. But they will refuse to submit to the naïve philosophy which would treat all proprietary rights as equal in sanctity merely because they are identical in name. They will distinguish sharply between property which is used by its owner for the conduct of his profession or the upkeep of his household, and property which is merely a claim on wealth produced by another's labour. They will insist that property is moral and healthy only when it is used as a condition not of idleness but of activity, and when it involves the discharge of definite personal obligations. They will endeavour, in short, to base it upon the principle of function.

10/MORRIS COHEN

Later in the 1920s an outstanding American jurist added a new dimension to the understanding of modern property. Less opposed to the contemporary institution of property than either Veblen or Tawney, Morris Cohen nevertheless made a re-assessment of it which added a forceful legal voice to their critical positions. Property, he argued, contrary to the then prevailing legal view, *is* sovereignty. He starts from the simplest proposition, that property is a right, not a thing. He then shows that while property is in the first instance a relation of rights between persons in reference to things it is also a relation of power between persons; and he shows that this is as true of property in a free-contract market society as in any previous society. Now, as earlier, property is a power to impose one's will on others. In this light he examines the various justifications of property and concludes that only a limited right is defensible. The actual limits he then proposed are not very confining, but the principles he established - that property is power over others, and that therefore the state is entitled to set such limits or impose such duties on it as may be deemed necessary by some test of the general welfare - could be taken to justify limits of almost any stringency. He may at least be said to have provided the theoretical basis to justify the measures enacted shortly afterwards by Roosevelt's New Deal.

This lecture was originally delivered at the Cornell Law School as the Irvine Lecture for 1927 and was reprinted, with slight changes, from the *Cornell Law Quarterly*, vol. XIII (1927) in *Law and the Social Order* by Morris Cohen (New York: Harcourt, Brace and Company, 1933). It is here reprinted by permission of the Estate of Morris R. Cohen.

Property and Sovereignty

Property and sovereignty, as every student knows, belong to entirely different branches of the law.[1] Sovereignty is a concept of political or public law and property belongs to civil or private law. This distinction between public and private law is a fixed feature of our law-school curriculum. It was expressed with characteristic eighteenth-century neatness and clarity by Montesquieu, when he said that by political laws we acquire liberty and by civil law property, and that we must not apply the principles of one of the other.[2] Montesquieu's view that political laws must in no way retrench on private property, because no public good is greater than the maintenance of private property, was echoed by Blackstone and became the basis of legal thought in America. Though Austin, with his usual prolix and near-sighted sincerity, managed to throw some serious doubts on this classical distinction,[3] it has continued to be regarded as one of the fixed divisions of the jural field. In the second volume of his *Genossenschaftsrecht* the learned Gierke treated us to some very interesting speculations as to how the Teutons became the founders of public law just as the Romans were the founders of private law. But in later years he somewhat softened this sharp distinction;[4] and common-law lawyers are inclined rather to regard the Roman system as giving more weight to public than to private law.

1 This lecture, originally delivered at the Cornell Law School as the Irvine Lecture for 1927, is reprinted, with slight changes, from *Cornell Law Quarterly*, Vol. XIII (1927), p. 8.

2 *L'Esprit des lois*, Book XXVI, Chap. 15, 1748.

3 Austin, *Lectures on Jurisprudence*, 5th ed., 1911, Vol. I, p. 457.

4 Holtzendorff-Kohler, *Enzyklopädie*, 1913-15, Vol. I, pp. 179-80. Continental jurists generally regard Roman law as more individualistic than Germanic law. Gierke, 'Der Entwurf eines bürgerlichen Gesetzbuches und das deutsche Recht,' *Schmollers*

The distinction between property and sovereignty is generally identified with the Roman discrimination between *dominium*, the rule over things by the individual, and *imperium*, the rule over all individuals by the prince. Like other Roman distinctions, this has been regarded as absolutely fixed in the nature of things. But early Teutonic law – the law of the Anglo-Saxons, Franks, Visigoths, Lombards, and other tribes – makes no such distinction; and the state long continued to be the prince's estate, so that even in the eighteenth century the Prince of Hesse could sell his subjects as soldiers to the King of England. The essence of feudal law – a system not confined to medieval Europe – is the inseparable connection between land tenure and personal homage involving often rather menial services on the part of the tenant and always genuine sovereignty over the tenant by the landlord.

The feudal baron had, for instance, the right to determine the marriage of the ward, as well as the right to nominate the priest; and the great importance of the former as a real property right is amply attested in Magna Carta and in the Statute Quia Emptores. Likewise was the administration of justice in the baron's court an incident of landownership; and if, unlike the French up to the Revolution, the English did not regard the office of judge as a revenue-producing incident of seigniorage to be sold in the open market (as army commissions were up to the time of Gladstone), the local squire did in fact continue to act as justice of the peace. Ownership of the land and local political sovereignty were inseparable.

Can we dismiss all this with the simple exclamation that all this is medieval and we have long outgrown it?

Well, right before our eyes the Law of Property Act of 1925 is sweeping away substantial remains of the complicated feudal land laws of England, by abolishing the difference between the descent of real and that of personal property, and by abolishing all legal (though not equitable) estates intermediate between leaseholds and fees simple absolute. These remains of feudalism have not been mere vestiges. They have played an important part in the national life of England. Their absurdities and indefensible abuses were pilloried with characteristic wit and learning by the peerless Maitland. The same thing had been done most judiciously by Joshua Williams, the teacher of several generations of English lawyers brought up on the seventeen editions of his great text-book on real property law. Yet these and similar efforts made no impres-

Jahrbuch für Gesetzgebung, Vol. XII (1888), pp. 843, 875; Menger, *Archiv für Soziale Gesetzgebung*, Vol. II (1889), p. 429; Rambaud, *Civilisation française*, Vol. I, p. 13; D'Arbois de Jubainville, *Académie d'Inscriptions*, February, 1887. This seems also the view of Maine, *Ancient Law*, p. 228. Maitland's remark that the whole constitutional history of England seems at times to be but an appendix to the laws of real property (*Constitutional History of England*, 1908, p. 538) only echoes the prevailing French attitude that their Civil Code is their real constitution.

sion on the actual law. What these great men did not see with sufficient clearness was that back of the complicated law of settlement, fee-tail, copyhold estates, of the heir-at-law, of the postponement of women, and other feudal incidents, there was a great and well-founded fear that by simplifying and modernizing the real property law of England the land might become more marketable. Once land becomes fully marketable it can no longer be counted on to remain in the hands of the landed aristocratic families; and this means the passing of their political power and the end of their control over the destinies of the British Empire. For if American experience has demonstrated anything, it is that the continued leadership by great families cannot be as well founded on a money as on a land economy. The same kind of talent that enables Jay Gould to acquire dominion over certain railroads enables Mr. Harriman to take it away from his sons. From the point of view of an established land economy, a money economy thus seems a state of perpetual war instead of a social order where son succeeds father. The motto that a career should be open to talent thus seems a justification of anarchy, just as the election of rulers (kings or priests) seems an anarchic procedure to those used to the regular succession of father by son.

That which was hidden from Maitland, Joshua Williams, and the other great ones, was revealed to a Welsh solicitor who in the budget of 1910 proposed to tax the land so as to force it on the market. The radically revolutionary character of this proposal was at once recognized in England. It was bitterly fought by all those who treasured what had remained of the old English aristocratic rule. When this budget finally passed, the basis of the old real property law and the effective power of the House of Lords was gone. The legislation of 1925–26 was thus a final completion in the realm of private law of the revolution that was fought in 1910 in the forum of public law, i.e., in the field of taxation and the power of the House of Lords.

As the terms 'medievalism' and 'feudalism' have become with us terms of opprobrium, we are apt to think that only unenlightened selfishness has until recently prevented English land law from cutting its medieval moorings and embarking on the sea of purely money or commercial economy. This light-hearted judgment, however, may be somewhat sobered by reflection on a second recent event – the Supreme Court decision on the Minimum Wage Law.[5] Without passing judgment at this point on the soundness of the reasoning whereby the majority reached its decision, the result may still fairly be characterized as a high-water mark of law in a purely money or commercial economy. For by that decision private monetary interests receive precedence over the sovereign duty of the state to maintain decent standards of living.

The state, which has an undisputed right to prohibit contracts against pub-

5 Adkins v. Children's Hospital, U.S. 261, 525; Supr. Ct. 43, 394 (1923).

lic morals or public policy, is here declared to have no right to prohibit contracts under which many receive wages less than the minimum of subsistence, so that if they are not the objects of humiliating public or private charity, they become centres of the physical and moral evils that result from systematic underfeeding and degraded standards of life. Now I do not wish here to argue the merits or demerits of the minimum wage decision. Much less am I concerned with any quixotic attempt to urge England to go back to medievalism. But the two events together show in strong relief how recent and in the main exceptional is the extreme position of the laissez faire doctrine, which, according to the insinuation of Justice Holmes, has led the Supreme Court to read Herbert Spencer's extreme individualism into the Fourteenth Amendment, and according to others, has enacted Cain's motto, 'Am I my brother's keeper?' as the supreme law of industry. Dean Pound has shown[6] that in making a property right out of the freedom to contract, the Supreme Court has stretched the meaning of the term 'property' to include what it has never before signified in the law or jurisprudence of any civilized country. But whether this extension is justified or not, it certainly means the passing of a certain domain of sovereignty from the state to the private employer of labour, who now has the absolute right to discharge and threaten to discharge any employee who wants to join a trade-union, and the absolute right to pay a wage that is injurious to a basic social interest.

It may be that economic forces will themselves correct the abuse which the Supreme Court does not allow the state to remove directly, that economic forces will eliminate parasitic industries which do not pay the minimum of subsistence, because such industries are not as economically efficient and profitable as those which pay higher wages. It was similarly argued that slavery was bound to disappear on account of its economic inefficiency. Meanwhile, however, the sovereignty of the state is limited by the manner in which the courts interpret the term 'property' in the Fifth and Fourteenth Amendments to the Federal Constitution and in the bills of rights in our state constitutions. This makes it imperative for us to consider the nature of private property with reference to the sovereign power of the state to look after the general welfare. A dispassionate scientific study of this requires an examination of the nature of property, its justification, and the ultimate meaning of the policies based on it.

I / PROPERTY AS POWER

Any one who frees himself from the crudest materialism readily recognizes that as a legal term 'property' denotes not material things but certain rights.

6 'Liberty of Contract,' *Yale Law Journal*, Vol. XVIII (1909), pp. 454, 482.

In the world of nature apart from more or less organized society, there are things but clearly no property rights.

Further reflection shows that a property right is not to be identified with the fact of physical possession. Whatever technical definition of property we may prefer, we must recognize that a property right is a relation not between an owner and a thing, but between the owner and other individuals in reference to things. A right is always against one or more individuals. This becomes unmistakably clear if we take specifically modern forms of property such as franchises, patents, goodwill, etc., which constitute such a large part of the capitalized assets of our industrial and commercial enterprises.

The classical view of property as a right over things resolves it into component rights such as the *jus utendi, jus disponendi*, etc. But the essence of private property is always the right to exclude others. The law does not guarantee me the physical or social ability of actually using what it calls mine. By public regulations it may indirectly aid me by removing certain general hindrances to the enjoyment of property. But the law of property helps me directly only to exclude others from using the things that it assigns to me. If, then, somebody else wants to use the food, the house, the land, or the plough that the law calls mine, he has to get my consent. To the extent that these things are necessary to the life of my neighbour, the law thus confers on me a power, limited but real, to make him do what I want. If Laban has the sole disposal of his daughters and his cattle, Jacob must serve him if he desires to possess them. In a régime where land is the principal source of obtaining a livelihood, he who has the legal right over the land receives homage and service from those who wish to live on it.

The character of property as sovereign power compelling service and obedience may be obscured for us in a commercial economy by the fiction of the so-called labour contract as a free bargain and by the frequency with which service is rendered indirectly through a money payment. But not only is there actually little freedom to bargain on the part of the steel-worker or miner who needs a job, but in some cases the medieval subject had as much power to bargain when he accepted the sovereignty of his lord. Today I do not directly serve my landlord if I wish to live in the city with a roof over my head, but I must work for others to pay him rent with which he obtains the personal services of others. The money needed for purchasing things must for the vast majority be acquired by hard labour and disagreeable service to those to whom the law has accorded dominion over the things necessary for subsistence.

To a philosopher this is of course not at all an argument against private property. It may well be that compulsion in the economic as well as the political realm is necessary for civilized life. But we must not overlook the actual fact that dominion over things is also *imperium* over our fellow human beings.

The extent of the power over the life of others which the legal order confers on those called owners is not fully appreciated by those who think of the law as merely protecting men in their possession. Property law does more. It determines what men shall acquire. Thus, protecting the property rights of a landlord means giving him the right to collect rent, protecting the property of a railroad or a public-service corporation means giving it the right to make certain charges. Hence the ownership of land and machinery, with the rights of drawing rent, interest, etc., determines the future distribution of the goods that will come into being - determines what share of such goods various individuals shall acquire. The average life of goods that are either consumable or used for production of other goods is very short. Hence a law that merely protected men in their possession and did not also regulate the acquisition of new goods would be of little use.

From this point of view it can readily be seen that when a court rules that a gas company is entitled to a return of 6 per cent on its investment, it is not merely protecting property already possessed, it is also determining that a portion of the future social produce shall under certain conditions go to that company. Thus not only medieval landlords but the owners of all revenue-producing property are in fact granted by the law certain powers to tax the future social product. When to this power of taxation there is added the power to command the services of large numbers who are not economically independent, we have the essence of what historically has constituted political sovereignty.

Though the sovereign power possessed by the modern large property owners assumes a somewhat different form from that formerly possessed by the lord of the land, they are not less real and no less extensive. Thus the ancient lord had a limited power to control the modes of expenditure of his subjects by direct sumptuary legislation. The modern captain of industry and of finance has no such direct power himself, though his direct or indirect influence with the legislature may in that respect be considerable. But those who have the power to standardize and advertise certain products do determine what we may buy and use. We cannot well wear clothes except within lines decreed by their manufacturers, and our food is becoming more and more restricted to the kinds that are branded and standardized.

This power of the modern owner of capital to make us feel the necessity of buying more and more of his material goods (that may be more profitable to produce than economical to use) is a phenomenon of the utmost significance to the moral philosopher. The moral philosopher must also note that the modern captain of industry or finance exercises great influence in setting the fashion of expenditure by his personal example. Between a landed aristocracy and the tenantry, the difference is sharp and fixed, so that imitation of the former's mode of life by the latter is regarded as absurd and even immoral. In a money or commercial economy differences of income and mode of life are more gradual and readily hidden, so that there is great pressure to engage in lavish expenditure in order to appear in a higher class than one's income really allows. Such expenditure may even advance one's business credit. This puts pressure not merely on ever greater expenditure but more specifically on expenditure for ostentation rather than for comfort. Though a landed aristocracy may be wasteful in keeping large tracts of land for hunting purposes, the need for discipline to keep in power compels the cultivation of a certain hardihood that the modern wealthy man can ignore. An aristocracy assured of its recognized superiority need not engage in the race of lavish expenditure regardless of enjoyment.

In addition to these indirect ways in which the wealthy few determine the mode of life of the many, there is the somewhat more direct mode that bankers and financiers exercise when they determine the flow of investment, e.g., when they influence building operations by the amount that they will lend on mortgages. This power becomes explicit and obvious when a needy country has to borrow foreign capital to develop its resources.

I have already mentioned that the recognition of private property as a form of sovereignty is not itself an argument against it. Some form of government we must always have. For the most part men prefer to obey and let others take the trouble to think out rules, regulations, and orders. That is why we are always setting up authorities; and when we cannot find any we write to the newspaper as the final arbiter. But although government is a necessity, not all forms of it are of equal value. At any rate it is necessary to apply to the law of property all those considerations of social ethics and enlightened public policy which ought to be brought to the discussion of any just form of government.

To do this, let us begin with a consideration of the usual justifications of private property.

II THE JUSTIFICATION OF PROPERTY

1 *The Occupation Theory*

The oldest and until recently the most influential defence of private property was based on the assumed right of the original discoverer and occupant to dispose of that which thus became his. This view dominated the thought of Roman jurists and of modern philosophers – from Grotius to Kant – so much so that the right of the labourer to the produce of his work was sometimes defended on the ground that the labourer 'occupied' the material that he fashioned into the finished product.

It is rather easy to find fatal flaws in this view. Few accumulations of great wealth were ever simply found. Rather were they acquired by the labour of many, by conquest, by business manipulation, and by other means. It is obvious that today at any rate few economic goods can be acquired by discovery and first occupancy.[7] Even in the few cases when they are, as in fishing and trapping, we are apt rather to think of the labour involved as the proper basis of the property acquired. Indeed, there seems nothing ethically self-evident in the motto 'Findings is keepings.' There seems nothing wrong in a law that a treasure trove shall belong to the king or the state rather than to the finder. Shall the finder of a river be entitled to all the water in it?

Moreover, even if we were to grant that the original finder or occupier should have possession as against any one else, it by no means follows that he may use it arbitrarily or that his rule shall prevail indefinitely after his death. The right of others to acquire the property from him, by bargain, by inheritance, or by testamentary disposition, is not determined by the principle of occupation.

Despite all these objections, however, there is a kernel of positive value in this principle. Protecting the discoverer or first occupant is really part of the more general principle that possession as such should be protected. There is real human economy in doing so until somebody shows a better claim than the possessor. It makes for certainty and security of transaction as well as for public peace – provided the law is ready to set aside possession acquired in ways that are inimical to public order. Various principles of justice may determine the distribution of goods and the retribution to be made for acts of injustice. But the law must not ignore the principle of inertia in human affairs. Continued possession creates expectations in the possessor and in others, and only a very poor morality would ignore the hardship of frustrating these expectations and rendering human relations insecure, even to correct some old flaws in the original acquisition. Suppose some remote ancestor of yours did acquire your property by fraud, robbery, or conquest, e.g., in the days of William of Normandy. Would it be just to take it away from you and your dependents who have held it in good faith? Reflection on the general insecurity that would result from such procedure leads us to see that as habit is the basis of individual life, continued practice must be the basis of social procedure. Any form of property that exists has therefore a claim to continue until it can be shown that the effort to change it is worth while. Continual changes in property laws would certainly discourage enterprise.

Nevertheless, it would be as absurd to argue that the distribution of property must never be modified by law as it would be to argue that the distribution of political power must never be changed. No less a philosopher than Aristotle argued against changing even bad laws, lest the habit of obedience be thereby impaired. There is something to be said for this, but only so long as we are in

7 In granting patents, copyrights, etc., the principle of reward for useful work or encouragement of productivity seems so much more relevant that the principle of discovery and first occupancy seems to have little force.

the realm of merely mechanical obedience. When we introduce the notion of free or rational obedience, Aristotle's argument loses its force in the political realm; and similar considerations apply to any property system that can claim the respect of rational beings.

2 *The Labour Theory*

That every one is entitled to the full produce of his labour is assumed as self-evident both by socialists and by conservatives who believe that capital is the result of the savings of labour. However, as economic goods are never the result of any one man's unaided labour, our maxim is altogether inapplicable. How shall we determine what part of the value of a table should belong to the carpenter, to the lumberman, to the transport worker, to the policeman who guarded the peace while the work was being done, and to the indefinitely large numbers of others whose coöperation was necessary? Moreover, even if we could tell what any one individual has produced - let us imagine a Robinson Crusoe growing up all alone on an island and in no way indebted to any community - it would still be highly questionable whether he has a right to keep the full produce of his labour when some shipwrecked mariner needs his surplus food to keep from starving.

In actual society no one ever thinks it unjust that a wealthy old bachelor should have part of his presumably just earnings taken away in the form of a tax for the benefit of other people's children, or that one immune to certain diseases should be taxed to support hospitals, etc. We do not think there is any injustice involved in such cases because social interdependence is so intimate that no man can justly say: 'This wealth is entirely and absolutely mine as the result of my own unaided effort.'

The degree of social solidarity varies, of course; and it is easy to conceive of a sparsely settled community, such as Missouri at the beginning of the nineteenth century, where a family of hunters or isolated cultivators of the soil might regard everything that it acquired as the product of its own labour. Generally, however, human beings start with a stock of tools or information acquired from others and they are more or less dependent upon some government for protection against foreign aggression, etc.

Yet despite these and other criticisms, the labour theory contains too much substantial truth to be brushed aside. The essential truth is that labour has to be encouraged and that property must be distributed in such a way as to encourage ever greater efforts at productivity.

As not all things produced are ultimately good, as even good things may be produced at an unjustified expense in human life and worth, it is obvious that other principles besides that of labour or productivity are needed for an adequate basis or justification of any system of property law. We can only say dialectically that all other things being equal, property should be distributed with due regard to the productive needs of the community. We must, however, recognize that a good deal of property accrues to those who are not productive,[8] and a good deal of productivity does not and perhaps should not receive its reward in property. Nor should we leave this theme without recalling the Hebrew-Christian view - and for that matter, the specifically religious view - that the first claim on property is by the man who needs it rather than the man who has created it. Indeed, the only way of justifying the principle of distribution of property according to labour is to show that it serves the larger social need.

The occupation theory has shown us the necessity for security of possession, and the labour theory the need for encouraging enterprise. These two needs are mutually dependent. Anything that discourages enterprise makes our possessions less valuable, and it is obvious that it is not worth while engaging in economic enterprise if there is no prospect of securely possessing the fruit of it. Yet there is also a conflict between these two needs. The owners of land, wishing to secure the continued possession by the family, oppose laws that make it subject to free financial transactions or make it possible that land should be taken away from one's heirs by a judgment creditor for personal debts. In an agricultural economy security of possession demands that the owner of a horse should be able to reclaim it no matter into whose hands it has fallen. But in order that markets should be possible, it becomes necessary that the innocent purchaser should have a good title. This conflict between static and dynamic security has been treated most suggestively by Demogue.[9]

3 *Property and Personality*

Hegel, Ahrens, Lorimer, and other idealists have tried to deduce the right of property from the individual's right to act as a free personality. To be free one must have a sphere of self-assertion in the external world. One's private property provides such an opportunity.

Waiving all traditional difficulties in applying the metaphysical idea of freedom to empirical legal acts, we may still object that the notion of personality is too vague to enable us to deduce definite legal consequences by means of it. How, for example, can the principle of personality help us to decide to what extent there shall be private rather than public property in railroads, mines, gas-works, and other public necessities?

Not the extremest communist would deny that in the interest of privacy certain personal belongings such as are typified by the toothbrush must be

8 Economists often claim that unearned increment is the greatest source of wealth. See H.J. Davenport, 'Extent and Significance of Unearned Increment,' *Bulletin of the American Economic Association*, Series 4, No. 2 (1911), pp. 322, 324-25.

9 Demogue, *Les notions fondamentales du droit privé*, 1911.

under the dominion of the individual owner, to the absolute exclusion of every one else. This, however, will not carry us far if we recall that the major effect of property in land, in the machinery of production, in capital goods, etc., is to enable the owner to exclude others from *their necessities*, and thus to compel them to serve him. Ahrens, one of the chief expounders of the personality theory, argues: 'It is undoubtedly contrary to the right of personality to have persons dependent on others on account of material goods.'[10] But if so, the primary effect of property on a large scale is to limit freedom, since the one thing that private property law does not do is to guarantee a minimum of subsistence or the necessary tools of freedom to every one. So far as a régime of private property fails to do the latter it rather compels people to part with their freedom.

It may well be argued in reply that just as restraining traffic rules in the end give us greater freedom of motion, so, by giving control over things to individual property owners, greater economic freedom is in the end assured to all. This is a strong argument, as can be seen by comparing the different degrees of economic freedom that prevail in lawless and in law-abiding communities. It is, however, an argument for legal order rather than for any particular form of government or private property. It argues for a régime where every one has a definite sphere of rights and duties, but it does not tell us where these lines should be drawn. The principle of freedom of personality certainly cannot justify a legal order wherein a few can, by virtue of their legal monopoly over necessities, compel others to work under degrading and brutalizing conditions. A government that limits the right of large landholders limits the rights of property, and yet may promote real freedom. Property owners, like other individuals, are members of a community and must subordinate their ambition to the larger whole of which they are a part. They may find their compensation in spiritually identifying their good with that of the larger life.

4 *The Economic Theory*

The economic justification of private property is that by means of it a maximum of productivity is promoted. The classical economic argument may be put thus: The successful business man, the one who makes the greatest profit, is the one who has the greatest power to foresee effective demand. If he has not that power his enterprise fails. He is therefore, in fact, the best director of economic activities.

There can be little doubt that if we take the whole history of agriculture and industry, or compare the economic output in Russia under the *mir* system with that in the United States, there is a strong *prima facie* case for the contention that more intensive cultivation of the soil and greater productiveness

10 *Cours de droit naturel*, 6th ed., 1868, p. 108.

of industry prevail under individual ownership. Many *a priori* psychologic and economic reasons can also be brought to explain why this must be so, why the individual cultivator will take greater care not to exhaust the soil, etc. All this, however, is so familiar that we may take it for granted and look at the other side of the case, at the considerations which show that there is a difference between socially desirable productivity and the desire for individual profits.

In the first place, let us note that of many things the supply is not increased by making them private property. This is obviously true of land in cities and of other monopoly or limited goods. Private ownership of land does not increase the amount of rainfall, and irrigation works to make the land more fruitful have been carried through by governments more than by private initiative. Nor was the productivity of French or Irish lands reduced when the property of their landlords in rent charges and other incidents of seigniorage was reduced or even abolished. In our own days, we frequently see tobacco, cotton, or wheat farmers in distress because they have succeeded in raising too plentiful crops; and manufacturers who are well informed know when greater profit is to be made by a decreased output. Patents for processes that would cheapen the product are often bought up by manufacturers and never used. Durable goods that are more economic to the consumer are very frequently crowded out of the market by shoddier goods which are more profitable to produce because of the larger turnover. Advertising campaigns often persuade people to buy the less economical goods and to pay the cost of the uneconomic advice.

In the second place, there are inherent sources of waste in a régime of private enterprise and free competition. If the biologic analogy of the struggle for existence were taken seriously, we should see that the natural survival of the economically fittest is attended, as in the biologic field, with frightful wastefulness. The elimination of the unsuccessful competitor may be a gain to the survivor, but all business failures are losses to the community.

Finally, a régime of private ownership in industry is too apt to sacrifice social interests to immediate monetary profits. This shows itself in speeding up industry to such a pitch that men are exhausted in a relatively few years, whereas a slower expenditure of their energy would prolong their useful years. It shows itself in the way in which private enterprise has wasted a good deal of the natural resources of the United States to obtain immediate profits. Even when the directors of a modern industrial enterprise see the uneconomic consequences of immediate profits, the demand of shareholders for immediate dividends,[11] and the ease with which men can desert a business and leave it to

11 Thus the leading brewers doubtless foresaw the coming of prohibition and could have saved millions in losses by separating their interests from that of the saloon. But the large temporary loss involved in such an operation was something to which stockholders could never have agreed.

others to stand the coming losses, tend to encourage ultimately wasteful and uneconomic activity. Possibly the best illustration of this is child labour, which by lowering wages increases immediate profits, but in the end is really wasteful of the most precious wealth of the country, its future manhood and womanhood.

Surveying our arguments thus far: We have seen the roots of property in custom, in the need for economic productivity, and in individual needs of privacy. But we have also noted that property, being only one among other human interests, cannot be pursued absolutely without detriment to human life. Hence we can no longer maintain Montesquieu's view that private property is sacrosanct and that the general government must in no way interfere with or retrench its domain. The issue before thoughtful people is therefore not the maintenance or abolition of private property, but the determination of the precise lines along which private enterprise must be given free scope and where it must be restricted in the interests of the common good.

III LIMITATIONS OF PROPERTY RIGHTS

The traditional theory of rights, and the one that still prevails in this country, was moulded by the struggle in the seventeenth and eighteenth centuries against restrictions on individual enterprise. These restrictions in the interest of special privilege were fortified by the divine (and therefore absolute) rights of kings. As is natural in all revolts, absolute claims on one side were met with absolute denials on the other. Hence the theory of the natural rights of the individual took not only an absolute but a negative form: men have *in*alienable rights, the state must never interfere with private property, etc. The state, however, must interfere in order that individual rights should become effective and not degenerate into public nuisances. To permit any one to do absolutely what he likes with his property in creating noise, smells, or danger of fire, would be to make property in general valueless. To be really effective, therefore, the right of property must be supported by restrictions or positive duties on the part of owners, enforced by the state, as much as by the right to exclude others that is the essence of property. Unfortunately, however, whether because of the general decline of juristic philosophy after Hegel or because law has become more interested in defending property against attacks by socialists, the doctrine of natural rights has remained in the negative state and has never developed into a doctrine of the positive contents of rights based upon an adequate notion of the function of these rights in society.[12]

12 Thus our courts are reluctant to admit that rules against unfair competition may be in the interest of the general public and not merely for those whose immediate prop-

Lawyers occupied with civil or private law have in any case continued the absolutistic conception of property; and in doing this, they are faithful to the language of the great eighteenth century codes, the French, Prussian, and Austrian, and even of nineteenth century codes like the Italian and German, which also begin with a definition of property as absolute or unlimited, though they subsequently introduce qualifying or limiting provisions.[13]

As, however, no individual rights can in fact be exercised in a community except under public regulation, it has been left mainly to publicists,[14] to writers on politics and constitutional and administrative law, to consider the limitations of private property necessary for public safety, peace, health, and morals, as well as for those enterprises like housing, education, the preservation of natural resources, etc., which the community finds it necessary to entrust to the state rather than to private hands. The fact, however, that in the United States the last word on law comes from judges, who, like other lawyers, are for the most part trained in private rather than in public law, is one of the reasons why with us traditional conceptions of property prevail over obvious national interests such as the freedom of labourers to organize, the necessity of preserving certain standards of living, of preventing the future manhood and womanhood of the country from being sacrificed to individual profits, and the like. Our students of property law need, therefore, to be reminded that not only has the whole law since the industrial revolution shown a steady growth in ever new restrictions upon the use of private property, but that the ideal of absolute laissez faire has never in fact been completely operative.

(1) Living in a free land economy we have lost the sense of how exceptional in the history of mankind is the absolutely free power of directing what shall be done with our property after our death. In the history of the common law, wills as to land begin only in the reign of Henry VIII. On the Continent it is still restrained by the system of the reserve. In England no formal restriction has been necessary because of the system of entails or strict settlement. Even in the United States we have kept such rules as that against perpetuities, which is certainly a restraint on absolute freedom of testamentary disposition.

Even as to the general power of alienating the land *inter vivos* history shows that some restrictions are always present. The persistence of dower rights in

erty interests are directly affected. Levy v. Walker, 10 Ch. D. 436 (1878); American Washboard Co. v. Saginaw Mfg. Co., 103 Fed. 281, 285 (C.C.A. 6th, 1900); Dickenson v. N.R. Co., 76 W. Va. 148, 151, 85 S.E. 71 (1915).

13 French Civil Code, 544; Prussian Landrecht I, 8, I; Austrian General Civil Code, 354; German Civil Code, 903; Italian Civil Code, 436. Cf. Markby, *Elements of Law*, 6th ed., 1905, 310; Aubry & Rau, *Cours de droit civil française*, 5th ed., 1897-1922, 190.

14 The great Jhering is an honorable exception. The distinction between property for use and property for power was developed by the Austrian jurist A. Menger, and made current by the German economist Adolf Wagner.

our own individualistic economy is a case in point. Land and family interest have been too closely connected to sacrifice the former completely to pure individualism. Though the interests of free exchange of goods and services have never been as powerful as in the last century, governments have not abandoned the right to regulate the rate of interest to be charged for the use of money, or to fix the price of certain other services of general public importance, e.g., railway rates, grain-elevator and warehouse charges, etc. The excuse that this applies only to business affected with a public interest, is a very thin one. What large business is there in which the public has not a real interest? Is coal less a public affair than gas, or electricity? Courts and conservative lawyers sometimes speak as if the regulation of wages by the state were a wild innovation that would upset all economic order as well as our legal tradition. Yet the direct regulation of wages has been a normal activity of English law; and we in fact regulate it indirectly by limiting hours of work, prohibiting payment in truck, enforcing certain periodic payments, etc.; and under the compensation acts the law compels an employer to pay his labourer when the latter cannot work at all on account of some accident.

(2) More important than the foregoing limitations upon the transfer of property are limitations on the use of property. Looking at the matter realistically, few will question the wisdom of Holdsworth's remarks, that 'at no time can the state be wholly indifferent to the use which the owners make of their property.'[15] There must be restrictions on the use of property not only in the interests of other property owners but also in the interests of the health, safety, religion, morals, and general welfare of the whole community. No community can view with indifference the exploitation of the needy by commercial greed. As under the conditions of crowded life the reckless or unconscionable use of one's property is becoming more and more dangerous, enlightened jurists find new doctrines to limit the abuse of ancient rights. The French doctrine of *abus de droit*, the prohibition of chicanery in the German Civil Code, and the rather vague use of 'malice' in the common law are all efforts in that direction.[16]

(3) Of greatest significance is the fact that in all civilized legal systems there is a great deal of just expropriation or confiscation without any direct compensation. This may sound shocking to those who think that for the state to take away the property of the citizen is not only theft or robbery but even worse, an act of treachery, since the state avowedly exists to protect people in those very rights.

As a believer in natural rights, I believe that the state can, and unfortunate-

15 Holdsworth, *History of English Law*, 1916, Vol. VIII, Chap. IV, p. 100.
16 Roussel, *L'Abus du droit*, 1913; German Civil Code, 226; Walton, 'Motive as an Element in Torts,' *Harvard Law Review*, Vol. XXII (1909), p. 501.

ly often does, enact unjust laws. But I think it is a sheer fallacy based on verbal illusion to think that the rights of the community against an individual owner are no better than the rights of a neighbour. Indeed, no one has in fact had the courage of this confusion to argue that the state has no right to deprive an individual of property to which he is so attached that he refuses any money for it. Though no neighbour has such a right, the public interest often justly demands that a proprietor shall part with his ancestral home, to which he may be attached by all the roots of his being.

When taking away a man's property, is the state always bound to pay a direct compensation? I submit that while this is generally advisable in order not to disturb the general feeling of security, no absolute principle of justice requires it. I have already suggested that there is no injustice in taxing an old bachelor to educate the children of others, or taxing one immune to typhoid for the construction of sewers or other sanitary measures. We may go further and say that the whole business of the state depends upon its rightful power to take away the property of some (in the form of taxation) and use it to support others, such as the needy, those invalided in the service of the state in war or peace, and those who are not yet able to produce but in whom the hope of humanity is embodied. Doubtless, taxation and confiscation may be actuated by malice and may impose needless and cruel hardship on some individuals or classes. But this is not to deny that taxation and confiscation are within the just powers of the state. A number of examples may make this clearer.

(a) Slavery. When slavery is abolished by law, the owners have their property taken away. Is the state ethically bound to pay them the full market value of their slaves? It is doubtless a grievous shock to a community to have a large number of slave-owners, whose wealth often makes them leaders of culture, suddenly deprived of their income. It may also be conceded that it is not always desirable for the slave himself to be suddenly taken away from his master and cut adrift on the sea of freedom. But when one reads of the horrible ways in which some of those slaves were violently torn from their homes in Africa and shamelessly deprived of their human rights, one is inclined to agree with Emerson that compensation should first be paid to the slaves. This compensation need not be in the form of a direct bounty to them. It may be more effectively paid in the form of rehabilitation and education for freedom; and such a charge may take precedence over the claims of the former owners. After all, the latter claims are no greater than those of a protected industry when the tariff is removed. If the state should decide that certain import duties, e.g., those on scientific instruments or hospital supplies, are unjustified and proceed to abolish them, many manufacturers may suffer. Are they entitled to compensation by the state?

It is undoubtedly for the general good to obviate as much as possible the effect of economic shock to a large number of people. The routine of life prospers on security. But when that security contains a large element of injustice the shock of an economic operation by law may be necessary and ethically justified.

This will enable us to deal with other types of confiscation:

(b) Financial loss through the abolition of public office. It is only in very recent times that we have come to forget that public office is and always has been regarded as a source of revenue like any other occupation. When, therefore, certain public offices are abolished for the sake of good government, a number of people are deprived of their expected income. In the older law and often in popular judgment today this does not seem fair. But reflection shows that the state is not obligated to pay any one when it finds that particular services of his are unnecessary. At best, it should help him to find a new occupation.

Part of the prerogative of the English or Scotch landlord was the right to nominate the priest for the parish on his land. To abolish this right of advowson is undoubtedly a confiscation of a definite property right. But while I cannot agree with my friend Mr. Laski[17] that the courts were wrong to refuse to disobey the law that subordinated the religious scruples of a church to the property rights of an individual, I do not see that there could have been any sound ethical objection to the legislature's changing the law without compensating the landlord.

(c) In our own day, we have seen the confiscation of many millions of dollars' worth of property through prohibition. Were the distillers and brewers entitled to compensation for their losses? We have seen that property on a large scale is power, and the loss of it, while evil to those who are accustomed to exercise it, may not be an evil to the community. In point of fact, the shock to the distillers and brewers was not as serious as to others, e.g., saloon-keepers and bartenders, who did not lose any legal property since they were only employees, but who found it difficult late in life to enter new employments.

History is full of examples of valuable property privileges abolished without any compensation, e.g., the immunity of nobles from taxation, their rights to hunt over other persons' lands, etc. It would be absurd to claim that all such legislation was unjust.

These and other examples of justifiable confiscation without compensation are inconsistent with the absolute theory of private property. An adequate theory of private property, however, should enable us to draw the line between justifiable and unjustifiable cases of confiscation. Such a theory I cannot here undertake to elaborate, though the doctrine of security of possession and avoidance of unnecessary shock seem to me suggestive. I wish, however,

17 Laski, *Studies in the Problem of Sovereignty*, 1917, Chap. II.

to urge that if the large property owner is viewed, as he ought to be, as a wielder of power over the lives of his fellow citizens, the law should not hesitate to develop a doctrine as to his positive duties in the public interest. The owner of a tenement house in a modern city is in fact a public official and has all sorts of positive duties. He must keep the halls lighted, he must see that the roof does not leak, that there are fire-escape facilities; he must remove tenants guilty of certain public immoralities, etc.; and he is compensated by the fees of his tenants, which the law is beginning to regulate. Similar is the case of a factory owner. He must install all sorts of safety appliances, hygienic conveniences; see that the workmen are provided with a certain amount of light, air, etc.

In general, there is no reason for the law's insisting that people should make the most economic use of their property. They have a motive in doing so themselves and the cost of the enforcing machinery may be a mischievous waste. Yet there may be times, such as occurred during the late war, when the state may insist that man shall cultivate the soil intensively and be otherwise engaged in socially productive work.

With considerations such as these in mind, it becomes clear that there is no unjustifiable taking away of property when railroads are prohibited from posting notices that they will discharge their employees if the latter join trade unions, and that there is no property taken away without due or just process of law when an industry is compelled to pay its labourers a minimum of subsistence instead of having subsistence provided for them by private or public charity or else systematically starving its workers.

IV POLITICAL VS. ECONOMIC SOVEREIGNTY

If the discussion of property by those interested in private law has suffered from a lack of realism and from too great a reliance on vague *a priori* plausibilities, much the same can be said about political discussion as to the proper limits of state action in regard to property and economic enterprise. Utterly unreal is all talk of men's being robbed of their power of initiative because the state undertakes some service, e.g., the building of a bridge across a river. Men are not deprived of opportunities for real self-reliance if the state lights their streets at night, fills up holes in the pavements, and removes other dangers to life and limb, or provides opportunities for education to all. The conditions of modern life are complex and distracting enough so that if we can ease the strain by simplifying some things through state action we are all the gainers by it. Certain things have to be done in a community and the question whether they should be left to private enterprise dominated by the profit motive, or to the government dominated by political considerations, is not a question of man versus the state, but simply a question of which organization and motive can best do the work. Both private and government enterprise are initiated and carried through by individual human beings. A realistic attitude would not begin with the assumption that all men in the government service are less or more intelligent or efficient than all those in private business. It would rather inquire what sort of people are drawn into government service and what attitudes their organization develops in contrast with that of private business. This is a matter for specific factual inquiry, unfortunately most sadly neglected. In the absence of such definite knowledge I can only venture a few guesses.

Government officials seem likely to be chosen more for their oratorical ability, popularly likable manners, and political availability, and less for their competence and knowledge of the problems with which they have to deal. The inheritance of wealth, however, may bring incompetent people for a while into control of private business. More serious is the fact that political officials have less incentive to initiate new ventures. Political leaders in touch with public sentiment are apt to be too conservative and prefer to avoid trouble by letting things alone. Their bureaucratic underlings, on whom they are more dependent than business executives are on theirs, are apt to overemphasize the value of red tape, i.e., to care more for uniformity of governmental procedure than for the diverse special needs to which they ought to minister. All business administration, however, also loses in efficiency as its volume increases. On the other hand, experience has shown all civilized peoples the indispensable need for communal control to prevent the abuse of private enterprise. Only a political or general government is competent to deal with a problem like city congestion, because only the general government can coördinate a number of activities some of which have no financial motive. Private business may be more efficient in saving money. It does so largely by paying smaller wages to the many and higher remuneration to those on top. From a social point of view this is not necessarily a good in itself. It is well to note that men of great ability and devotion frequently prefer to work for the government at a lower pay than they can obtain in private employment. There is something more than money in daily employment. Humanity prefers - not altogether unwisely - to follow the lead of those who are sensitive rather than those who are efficient. Business efficiency mars the beauty of our country-side with hideous advertising signs and would, if allowed, ruin the scenic grandeur of Niagara.

The subordination of everything to the single aim of monetary profit leads industrial government to take the form of absolute monarchy. Monarchy has a certain simplicity and convenience; but in the long run it is seldom the best for all concerned. Sooner or later it leads to insurrections. It is short-sighted to assume that an employer cannot possibly run his business without the absolute right to hire and fire his employees whenever he feels like doing so. It is interesting to note that even a modern army is run without giving the general the absolute right to hire and fire. The Shah of Persia was shocked when a British ambassador, Sir John Malcolm, informed him that the King of England could not at his pleasure behead any of his courtiers. But Sir John Malcolm was equally shocked to observe the elaborate precautions that the Shah had to take against assassination.[18] May not democratic or limited constitutional government in industry have some human advantages over unlimited monarchy?[19]

The main difficulty, however, with industrial and financial government is that the governors are released from all responsibility for the actual human effects of their policies. Formerly, the employer could observe and had an interest in the health and morals of his apprentice. Now, the owners or stockholders have lost all personal touch with all but few of those who work for them. The human element is thus completely subordinated to the profit motive. In some cases this even makes for industrial inefficiency, as when railroads or other businesses are run by financiers in the interest of stock manipulation. Very often our captains of finance exercise power by controlling other people's funds. This was strikingly shown when several millions of dollars were paid for some shares that promised little or no direct return but which enabled the purchaser to control the assets of a great life insurance company. Professor Ripley has recently thrown Wall Street into a turmoil by pointing out the extent to which promoters and financiers can with little investment of their own control great industrial undertakings.

There can be no doubt that our property laws do confer sovereign power on our captains of industry and even more so on our captains of finance.

Now it would be unworthy of a philosopher to shy at government by captains of industry and finance. Humanity has been ruled by priests, soldiers, hereditary landlords, and even antiquarian scholars. The results are not such as to make us view with alarm a new type of ruler. But if we are entering a new era involving a new set of rulers, it is well to recognize it and reflect on what is involved.

For the first time in the history of mankind the producer of things is in the saddle - not of course the actual physical producer, but the master mind that directs the currents of production. If this is contrary to the tradition of philosophy from Plato down, we may well be told that our philosophy needs revision. Great captains of industry and finance like the late James J. Hill deal with problems in many respects bigger than those which faced Caesar and Augustus in building the Roman Empire.

Still the fear may well be expressed that as modern life is becoming more

18 Malcolm, *Sketches of Persia*, 1861, pp. 215 *et seq.*

19 It used to be thought that there could be no credit transactions if the creditor could not acquire dominion over the body of the debtor in default. Yet credit transactions have not decreased with the development of homestead laws and the limitation of imprisonment for debt.

and more complex it is dangerous to give too much sovereignty to those who are after all dealing with the rather simpler aspects of life involved in economic relations.

It may, of course, rightly be contended that the modern captain of industry is not merely concerned with the creation of things, that his success is largely determined by his judgment and ability to manage the large numbers of human beings that form part of his organization. Against this, however, there is the obvious retort that the only ability taken account of in the industrial and financial world, the ability to make money, is a very specialized one; and when business men get into public office they are not notably successful. Too often they forget that while saving the money of the taxpayer may be an admirable incident, it is not the sole or even the principal end of communal life and government. The wise expenditure of money is a more complicated problem than the mere saving it, and a no less indispensable task to those who face the question of how to promote a better communal life. To do this effectively we need a certain liberal insight into the more intangible desires of the human heart. Preoccupation with the management of property has not in fact advanced this kind of insight.

Many things are produced to the great detriment of the health and morals of the consumers as well as the producers. This refers not only to things that are inherently deleterious or enervating to those who create them and those who use them. It includes also many of the things of which people buy more than they need and more than is consistent with the peace and leisure of mind that is the essence of culture.

It is certainly a shallow philosophy that would make human welfare synonymous with the indiscriminate production and consumption of material goods. If there is one iota of wisdom in all the religions or philosophies that have supported the human race in the past it is that man cannot live by economic goods alone but needs vision and wisdom to determine what things are worth while and what things it would be better to do without. This profound human need of controlling and moderating our consumptive demands cannot be left to those whose dominant interest is to stimulate such demands.

It is characteristic of the low state of our philosophy that the merits of capitalism have been argued by both individualists and socialists exclusively from the point of view of the production and distribution of goods. To the more profound question as to what goods are ultimately worth producing from the point of view of the social effects on the producers and consumers almost no attention is paid. Yet surely this is a matter which requires the guidance of collective wisdom, not one to be left to chance or anarchy.

11 / CHARLES A. REICH

Some thirty years after Cohen's analysis, another American legal scholar has drawn attention to a more recent transformation of the nature of property. Property, which Reich agrees has become essentially a right to a revenue, has become for increasing number of individuals a right conferred by or dependent on government largess and government licence. This he finds is an unexpected, unplanned, and insufficiently noticed effect of the emergence of the welfare and regulatory state, and one which imperils a function of property which he holds to be (and always to have been) of crucial importance, namely, its securing to the individual an area of freedom from domination by society or the state. He shows in convincing detail that the new property, being dependent on government fiat and on executive and judicial interpretations of legislation, does not secure but invades that area of freedom. One may question Reich's apparent assumption that the institution of property did protect that freedom down to the recent emergence of the welfare state: earlier analysts, as far back as Rousseau and Marx, had seen that function of property eroded two or three centuries earlier, when the bulk of the whole working force had ceased to be independent worker-owners. But this does not detract from his perception that something new has happened. At the very least, a new problem about the justification of property has been piled on top of all the earlier problems.

This extract, reprinted by permission of the author and of The Yale Law Journal Company and Fred B. Rothman & Company, comes from the *Yale Law Journal*, vol. 73, pp. 733 and 771-87 (April 1964). Sections I, II, and III of the original article are omitted.

The New Property

The institution called property guards the troubled boundary between individual man and the state. It is not the only guardian; many other institutions, laws, and practices serve as well. But in a society that chiefly values material well-being, the power to control a particular portion of that well-being is the very foundation of individuality.

One of the most important developments in the United States during the past decade has been the emergence of government as a major source of wealth. Government is a gigantic syphon. It draws in revenue and power, and pours forth wealth: money, benefits, services, contracts, franchises, and licenses. Government has always had this function. But while in early times it was minor, today's distribution of largess is on a vast, imperial scale.

The valuables dispensed by government take many forms, but they all share one characteristic. They are steadily taking the place of traditional forms of wealth – forms which are held as private property. Social insurance substitutes for savings; a government contract replaces a businessman's customers and goodwill. The wealth of more and more Americans depends upon a relationship to government. Increasingly, Americans live on government largess – allocated by government on its own terms, and held by recipients subject to conditions which express 'the public interest.'

The growth of government largess, accompanied by a distinctive system of law, is having profound consequences. It affects the underpinnings of individualism and independence. It influences the workings of the Bill of Rights. It has an impact on the power of private interests, in their relation to each other and to government. It is helping to create a new society.

This article is an attempt to explore these changes. It begins with an examination of the nature of government largess. Second, it reviews the system of law, substantive and procedural, that has emerged. Third, it examines some of the consequences, to the individual, to private interests, and to society. Fourth, it considers the functions of property and their relationship to 'the public interest.' Finally, it turns to the future of individualism in the new society that is coming. The object is to present an overview – a way of looking at many seemingly unrelated problems. Inevitably, such an effort must be incomplete and tentative. But it is long past time that we began looking at the transformation taking place around us. ...

IV PROPERTY AND THE PUBLIC INTEREST: AN OLD DEBATE REVISITED

The public interest state ... represents in one sense the triumph of society over private property. This triumph is the end point of a great and necessary movement for reform. But somehow the result is different from what the reformers wanted. Somehow the idealistic concept of the public interest has summoned up a doctrine monstrous and oppressive. It is time to take another look at private property, and at the 'public interest' philosophy that dominates its modern substitute, the largess of government.

A *Property and Liberty*

Property is a legal institution the essence of which is the creation and protection of certain private rights in wealth of any kind. The institution performs many different functions. One of these functions is to draw a boundary between public and private power. Property draws a circle around the activities of each private individual or organization. Within that circle, the owner has a greater degree of freedom than without. Outside, he must justify or explain his actions, and show his authority. Within, he is master, and the state must explain and justify any interference. It is as if property shifted the burden of proof; outside, the individual has the burden; inside, the burden is on government to demonstrate that something the owner wishes to do should not be done.

Thus, property performs the function of maintaining independence, dignity and pluralism in society by creating zones within which the majority has to yield to the owner. Whim, caprice, irrationality and 'antisocial' activities are given the protection of law; the owner may do what all or most of his neighbors decry. The Bill of Rights also serves this function, but while the Bill of Rights comes into play only at extraordinary moments of conflict or crisis, property affords day-to-day protection in the ordinary affairs of life. Indeed, in the final analysis the Bill of Rights depends upon the existence of private property. Political rights presuppose that individuals and private groups have the will and the means to act independently. But so long as individuals are motivated largely by self-interest, their well-being must first be independent. Civil liberties must have a basis in property, or bills of rights will not preserve them.

Property is not a natural right but a deliberate construction by society. If such an institution did not exist, it would be necessary to create it, in order to have the kind of society we wish. The majority cannot be expected, on specific issues, to yield its power to a minority. Only if the minority's will is established as a general principle can it keep the majority at bay in a given instance. Like the Bill of Rights, property represents a general, long range protection of individual and private interests, created by the majority for the ultimate good of all.

Today, however, it is widely thought that property and liberty are separable things; that there may, in fact, be conflicts between 'property rights' and 'personal rights.' Why has this view been accepted? The explanation is found at least partly in the transformations which have taken place in property.

During the industrial revolution, when property was liberated from feudal restraints, philosophers hailed property as the basis of liberty, and argued that it must be free from the demands of government or society.[184] But as private property grew, so did abuses resulting from its use. In a crowded world, a man's use of his property increasingly affected his neighbor, and one man's exercise of a right might seriously impair the rights of others. Property became power over others; the farm landowner, the city landlord, and the working man's boss were able to oppress their tenants or employees. Great aggregations of property resulted in private control of entire industries and basic services capable of affecting a whole area or even a nation. At the same time, much private property lost its individuality and in effect became socialized. Multiple ownership of corporations helped to separate personality from property, and property from power.[185] When the corporations began to stop competing, to merge, agree, and make mutual plans, they became private governments. Finally, they sought the aid and partnership of the state, and thus by their own volition became part of public government.

These changes led to a movement for reform, which sought to limit arbitrary private power and protect the common man. Property rights were considered more the enemy than the friend of liberty. The reformers argued that property must be separated from personality.[186] Walton Hamilton wrote:

184 See generally Philbrick, *Changing Conceptions of Property in Law*, 86 U. Pa. L. Rev. 691 (1938); Hamilton & Till, *Property*, 12 Encyc. Soc. Sci. 528 (1934); Freund, *The Supreme Court of the United States* 31-40 (1961).

185 See generally Berle & Means, *The Modern Corporation and Private Property* (1932); and Berle, *Power Without Property* (1957).

186 Philbrick, *Changing Conceptions of Property in Law*, 86 U. Pa. L. Rev. 691. 732 (1938).

> As late as the turn of the last century justices were not yet distinguishing between liberty and property; in the universes beneath their hats liberty was still the opportunity to acquire property. ...
>
> ... the property of the Reports is not a proprietary thing; it is rather a shibboleth in whose name the domain of business enterprises has enjoyed a limited immunity from the supervision of the state.
>
> In the annals of the law property is still a vestigial expression of personality and owes its current constitutional position to its former association with liberty.[187]

During the first half of the twentieth century, the reformers enacted into law their conviction that private power was a chief enemy of society and of individual liberty. Property was subjected to 'reasonable' limitations in the interests of society. The regulatory agencies, federal and state, were born of the reform. In sustaining these major inroads on private property, the Supreme Court rejected the older idea that property and liberty were one, and wrote a series of classic opinions upholding the power of the people to regulate and limit private rights.

The struggle between abuse and reform made it easy to forget the basic importance of individual private property. The defense of private property was almost entirely a defense of its abuses - an attempt to defend not individual property but arbitrary private power over other human beings. Since this defense was cloaked in a defense of private property, it was natural for the reformers to attack too broadly. Walter Lippmann saw this in 1934:

> But the issue between the giant corporation and the public should not be allowed to obscure the truth that the only dependable foundation of personal liberty is the economic security of private property. ...
>
> For we must not expect to find in ordinary men the stuff of martyrs, and we must, therefore, secure their freedom by their normal motives. There is no surer way to give men the courage to be free than to insure them a competence upon which they can rely.[188]

187 Hamilton, *Property - According to Locke*, 41 Yale L.J. 864, 877-78 (1932); see also Hamilton & Till, *supra* note 184, at 528.

188 Lippmann, *The Method of Freedom* 101 (1934). See also Philbrick, *Changing Conceptions of Property in Law*, 86 U. Pa. L. Rev. 691 (1938) at 726: 'It is not, however, the *use* of ordinary property, nor the property of ordinary or "natural" persons that presents today serious problems of adjusting law to new social conditions. Those problems arise in connection with property for *power*, and therefore primarily in connection with industrial property.'

The reform took away some of the power of the corporations and transferred it to government. In this transfer there was much good, for power was made responsive to the majority rather than to the arbitrary and selfish few. But the reform did not restore the individual to his domain. What the corporation had taken from him, the reform simply handed on to government. And government carried further the powers formerly exercised by the corporation. Government as an employer, or as a dispenser of wealth, has used the theory that it was handing out gratuities to claim a managerial power as great as that which the capitalists claimed. Moreover, the corporations allied themselves with, or actually took over, part of government's system of power. Today it is the combined power of government and the corporations that presses against the individual.

From the individual's point of view, it is not any particular kind of power, but all kinds of power, that are to be feared. This is the lesson of the public interest state. The mere fact that power is derived from the majority does not necessarily make it less oppressive. Liberty is more than the right to do what the majority wants, or to do what is 'reasonable.' Liberty is the right to defy the majority, and to do what is unreasonable. The great error of the public interest state is that it assumes an identity between the public interest and the interest of the majority.

The reform, then, has not done away with the importance of private property. More than ever the individual needs to possess, in whatever form, a small but sovereign island of his own.

B *Largess and the Public Interest*

The fact that the reform tended to make much private wealth subject to 'the public interest' has great significance, but it does not adequately explain the dependent position of the individual and the weakening of civil liberties in the public interest state. The reformers intended to enhance the values of democracy and liberty; their basic concern was the preservation of a free society. But after they established the primacy of 'the public interest,' what meaning was given to that phrase? In particular, what values does it embody as it has been employed to regulate government largess?

Reduced to simplest terms, 'the public interest' has usually meant this: government largess may be denied or taken away if this will serve some legitimate public policy. The policy may be one directly related to the largess itself, or it may be some collateral objective of government. A contract may be denied if this will promote fair labor standards. A television license may be refused if this will promote the policies of the antitrust laws. Veterans benefits may be taken away to promote loyalty to the United States. A liquor license may be revoked to promote civil rights. A franchise for a barber's college may not be given out if it will hurt the local economy, nor a taxi franchise if it will seriously injure the earning capacity of other taxis.

Most of these objectives are laudable, and all are within the power of government. The great difficulty is that they are simplistic. Concentration on a single policy or value obscures other values that may be at stake. Some of these competing values are other public policies; for example, the policy of the best possible television service to the public may compete with observance of the antitrust laws. The legislature is the natural arbiter of such conflicts. But the conflicts may also be more fundamental. In the regulation of government largess, achievement of specific policy goals may undermine the independence of the individual. Where such conflicts exist, a simplistic notion of the public interest may unwittingly destroy some values.

Judges tend to limit their sights to a single issue. In *Nadiak v. CAB*,[189] an airline pilot was grounded for a variety of reasons, some of them admittedly trivial. In upholding the action of the Board, the court said:

The public – including judges who fly – has a vital interest in air safety. Responsibility for air safety has been placed in the administrative hands of those deemed by Congress to have an expert competence. Air safety was of primary importance in the adjudication of this case. The determination was that air safety would be promoted by the certificate revocation.[190]

Barsky v. Board of Regents[191] shows how one-sided the public interest concept may become. New York State suspended a doctor's license because he committed the crime of contempt of Congress. The Supreme Court, upholding this, identified the public interest as the state's 'broad power to establish and enforce standards of conduct relative to the health of everyone there,'[192] and the 'state's legitimate concern for maintaining high standards of professional conduct.'[193] But what about the importance of giving doctors security in their professions? What about the benefits to the state from having physicians who are independent of administrative control? Not only were these ignored by the state and the court; no effort was even made to show how the suspension promoted the one public policy that was named (high professional standards for those concerned with public health). As Justice Frankfurter said,

It is one thing to recognize the freedom which the constitution wisely leaves to the States in regulating the professions. It is quite another thing, however, to sanction a State's deprivation or partial destruction of a man's professional

189 305 F.2d 588 (5th Cir. 1962).
190 *Id.* at 595.
191 Barsky v. Board of Regents, 347 U.S. 442 (1954).
192 *Id.* at 449.
193 *Id.* at 451.

life on grounds having no possible relation to fitness, intellectual or moral, to pursue his profession.[194]

In *Flemming v. Nestor*[195] the concept of the public interest is distorted even more. It was given a meaning injurious to the independence of millions of persons. At stake was the security of the old age Social Security pension system, together with all the social values which might flow from assuring old people a stable, dignified, and independent basis of retirement. Yet Congress and the Supreme Court jeopardized all these values to serve a public policy both trivial and vindictive - the punishment of a few persons for Communist Party membership now long past.

The public interest has also failed to take account of the more specific values of the Bill of Rights. In a case where a radio operator was denied a license for pleading the fifth amendment, the court said:

The Fifth Amendment privilege protects a person who invokes it from self-accusation; but when he seeks a license at the hands of an agency acting under the standard of the public interest, and information substantially relevant to that standard is withheld under the privilege, as may be done, the need for the information and the cooperation of the applicant with respect to it remains. The agency cannot be required to act without the information.[196]

Referring to a law that requires a motorist to submit to a drunkenness test, waiving his state privilege against self-incrimination, or lose his driver's license, the New York Supreme Court said:

Bearing in mind the purpose of the statute and that highway safety is a matter of great concern to the public, it may not be held that it is unreasonable or beyond legislative power to put such a choice to a motorist who is accused upon reasonable grounds of driving while intoxicated.[197]

Another court concluded that a radio operator's freedom of political association could be restricted by FCC action in these words:

Borrow says his First Amendment Rights are being infringed. We cannot agree. ... The public interest must be served. He desires to operate a facility which in the public interest is necessarily licensed by the Government. He has affirma-

194 *Id.* at 470 (dissenting opinion).
195 363 U.S. 603 (1960).
196 Blumenthal v. FCC, 318 F.2d 276, 279 (D.C. Cir. 1963).
197 Schutt v. Macduff, 205 Misc. 43, 48 (Sup. Ct. 1954).

tive standards to meet in order to secure a license, just as do doctors, lawyers, barbers, and lenders of money.[198]

One of the most striking instances of public interest definition in the area of constitutional rights is *Konigsberg v. State Bar.*[199] Konigsberg refused to tell the state bar examiners whether he was or ever had been a member of the Communist Party, arguing that such questions infringed his constitutional rights of free thought, association and expression. Despite substantial evidence of his good character, none of which was rebutted, and despite his uncontradicted statement that he did not believe in violent overthrow of the government, and did not belong to any organization advocating violent overthrow, Konigsberg was refused admission to the bar. The U.S. Supreme Court upheld the refusal. Acknowledging that the questions did involve some deterrence of free speech, the Court said that its decision must depend upon 'an appropriate weighing of the respective interests involved.'[200] It then reached this conclusion:

> [W]e regard the State's interest in having lawyers who are devoted to the law in its broadest sense, including not only its substantive provisions, but also its procedures for orderly change, as clearly sufficient to outweigh the minimal effect upon free association occasioned by compulsory disclosure in the circumstances here presented.[201]

In none of these cases did the courts attempt to assign any weight to the value of unfettered exercise of constitutional rights. Nor did the courts consider what effect their decisions might have on the constitutional rights of motorists, radio operators, businessmen or lawyers generally. Each case was treated as if it existed in isolation – as if each individual's case concerned him alone.

This fundamental fallacy – treating the 'individual interest' as affecting only the party to the case – runs through many of the public interest decisions concerning largess. In a case where the Securities and Exchange Commission suspended a broker-dealer for an alleged violation – without a hearing – the Court of Appeals for the District of Columbia 'balanced' the interests involved as follows: 'protection of the securities-purchasing public' against the individual's 'interest in continuing to issue public offerings of securities.'[202] The court found the 'public's interest' to be the weightier. In deciding whether to revoke a broker-dealer registration for misconduct, another court remarked: 'The bal-

198 Borrow v. FCC, 285 F.2d 666, 670 (D.C. Cir. 1960).
199 366 U.S. 36 (1961).
200 *Id.* at 51.
201 *Id.* at 52.
202 R.A. Holman & Co. v. SEC, 299 F.2d 127, 132 (D.C. Cir. 1962).

ancing of *private detriment* against *public harm* requires the fair and proper exercise by the Commission of its discretionary powers.'[203] In upholding the suspension of a driver's license without a hearing, the Court of Appeals for the First Circuit said:

We have no doubt that these provisions of law are reasonable regulations in the interest of safeguarding lives and property from highway accidents. The incidental hardship upon an individual motorist, in having his license suspended pending investigation and review, must be borne in deference to the greater public interest served by the statutory restriction.[204]

If this is the method of balancing, the result is a foregone conclusion:

We conclude that ... insofar as the circumstances imposed hardship upon the individual, the exigencies of government in the public interest under current conditions must prevail, as they always must where a similar clash arises.[205]

It is not the reformers who must bear the blame for the harmful consequences of the public interest state, but those who are responsible for giving 'the public interest' its present meaning. If 'the public interest' distorts the reformers' high purposes, this is so because the concept has been so gravely misstated. Government largess, like all wealth, must necessarily be regulated in the public interest. But regulation must take account of the dangers of dependence, and the need for a property base for civil liberties. Rightly conceived, the public interest is no justification for the erosion of freedom that has resulted from the present system of government largess.[206]

203 Associated Sec. Corp. v. SEC, 293 F.2d 738, 741 (10th Cir. 1961) (emphasis supplied).

204 Wall v. King, 206 F.2d 878, 883 (1st Cir. 1953). See also Gnecchi v. State, 58 Wash. 2d 467, 364 P.2d 225 (1961), where a dissenting judge said: 'I cannot conceive of a situation where there is a necessity to suspend a license without a hearing if the suspension imposed is for no more than sixty days. What happens to the safety of the public after sixty days? The purpose of such "suspension is primarily punishment, and there is no reason why a hearing should not precede the suspension." ' *Id.* at 477, 364 P.2d at 232.

205 Bailey v. Richardson, 182 F.2d 46, 65 (D.C. Cir. 1950).

206 See generally Gellhorn, *Individual Freedom and Governmental Restraints* 105-57 (1956) (Chapter III, 'The Right to Make a Living'). Although it speaks in different terms, and is limited to occupational licensing Professor Gellhorn's discussion in a most perceptive analysis of the meaning of 'the public interest.' See also Schubert, *The Public Interest* (1960) for an elaborate analysis of differing public interest theories.

V TOWARD INDIVIDUAL STAKES IN THE COMMONWEALTH

Ahead there stretches - to the farthest horizon - the joyless landscape of the public interest state. The life it promises will be comfortable and comforting. It will be well planned - with suitable areas for work and play. But there will be no precincts sacred to the spirit of individual man.

There can be no retreat from the public interest state. It is the inevitable outgrowth of an interdependent world. An effort to return to an earlier economic order would merely transfer power to giant private governments which would rule not in the public interest, but in their own interest. If individualism and pluralism are to be preserved, this must be done not by marching backwards, but by building these values into today's society. If public and private are now blurred, it will be necessary to draw a new zone of privacy. If private property can no longer perform its protective functions, it will be necessary to establish institutions to carry on the work that private property once did but can no longer do.

In these efforts government largess must play a major role. As we move toward a welfare state, largess will be an ever more important form of wealth. And largess is a vital link in the relationship between the government and private sides of society. It is necessary, then, that largess begin to do the work of property.

The chief obstacle to the creation of private rights in largess has been the fact that it is originally public property, comes from the state, and may be withheld completely. But this need not be an obstacle. Traditional property also comes from the state, and in much the same way. Land, for example, traces back to grants from the sovereign. In the United States, some was the gift of the King of England, some that of the King of Spain. The sovereign extinguished Indian title by conquest, became the new owner, and then granted title to a private individual or group.[207] Some land was the gift of the sovereign under laws such as the Homestead and Preemption Acts.[208] Many other natural resources - water, minerals and timber, passed into private ownership under similar grants. In America, land and resources all were originally government largess. In a less obvious sense, personal property also stems from government. Personal property is created by law; it owes its origin and continuance to laws supported by the people as a whole. These laws 'give' the property to one who performs certain actions. Even the man who catches a wild animal 'owns' the animal only as a gift from the sovereign, having fulfilled the terms of an offer to transfer ownership.[209]

207 Johnson v. McIntosh, 21 U.S. (8 Wheat.) 543 (1823).
208 5 Stat. 453, 455 (Sept. 4, 1841), 12 Stat. 392 (May 20, 1862).
209 Pierson v. Post, 3 Cai. R. 175 (1805).

Like largess, real and personal property were also originally dispensed on conditions, and were subject to forfeiture if the conditions failed. The conditions in the sovereign grants, such as colonization, were generally made explicit, and so was the forfeiture resulting from failure to fulfill them. In the case of the Preemption and Homestead Acts, there were also specific conditions.[210] Even now land is subject to forfeiture for neglect; if it is unused it may be deemed abandoned to the state or forfeited to an adverse possessor. In a very similar way, personal property may be forfeited by abandonment or loss.[211] Hence, all property might be described as government largess, given on condition and subject to loss.

If all property is government largess, why is it not regulated to the same degree as present-day largess? Regulation of property has been limited, not because society had no interest in property, but because it was in the interest of society that property be free. Once property is seen not as a natural right but as a construction designed to serve certain functions, then its origin ceases to be decisive in determining how much regulation should be imposed. The conditions that can be attached to receipt, ownership, and use depend not on where property came from, but on what job it should be expected to perform. Thus in the case of government largess, nothing turns on the fact that it originated in government. The real issue is how it functions and how it should function.

To create an institution, or to make an existing institution function in a new way, is an undertaking far too ambitious for the present article. But it is possible to begin a search for guiding principles. Such principles must grow out of what we know about how government largess has functioned up to the present time. And while principles must remain at the level of generality, it should be kept in mind that not every principle is equally applicable to all forms of largess. Our primary focus must be those forms of largess which chiefly control the rights and status of the individual.

A *Constitutional Limits*

The most clearly defined problem posed by government largess is the way it can be used to apply pressure against the exercise of constitutional rights. A first principle should be that government must have no power to 'buy up' rights guaranteed by the Constitution.[212] It should not be able to impose any condition on largess that would be invalid if imposed on something other than

210 The Homestead Act had conditions of age, citizenship, intention to settle was cultivated, and loyalty to the United States. 12 Stat. 392 (1862).

211 Mullett v. Bradley, 24 Misc. 695, 53 N.Y. Supp. 781 (1898); Bridges v. Hawkesworth, 21 L.J. Rep. 75 (Q.B. 1851).

212 Note, *Unconstitutional Conditions*, 73 Harv. L. Rev. 1595, 1599 (1960).

a 'gratuity.'[213] Thus, for example, government should not be able to deny largess because of invocation of the privilege against self-incrimination.[214]

This principle is in a sense a revival of the old but neglected rule against unconstitutional conditions, as enunciated by the Supreme Court:

Broadly stated, the rule is that the right to continue the exercise of a privilege granted by the state cannot be made to depend upon the grantee's submission to a condition prescribed by the state which is hostile to the provisions of the federal constitution.[215] ...

If the state may compel the surrender of one constitutional right as a condition of its favor, it may in like manner, compel a surrender of all. It is inconceivable that guaranties embedded in the Constitution of the United States may thus be manipulated out of existence.[216]

The courts in recent times have gone part of the distance toward this principle. In 1958 the Supreme Court held that California could not use the gratuity theory to deny a tax exemption to persons engaged in certain political activities:

To deny an exemption to claimants who engage in certain forms of speech is in effect to penalize them for such speech. Its deterrent effect is the same as if the state were to fine them for this speech. The appellees are plainly mistaken in their argument that, because a tax exemption is a 'privilege' or a 'bounty,' its denial may not infringe speech.[217]

In 1963 the Court followed this reasoning in the important case of *Sherbert v. Verner.*[218] South Carolina provided unemployment compensation, but re-

213 Compare Calabresi, *Retroactivity: Paramount Powers and Contractual Changes*, 71 Yale L.J. 1191 (1962). In the context of legislation dealing with government obligations, Professor Calabresi argues that certain regulation can only be justified by a 'paramount power of government' (*e.g.*, the commerce power) rather than power incidental to the obligation itself.

214 Judge Curtis Bok wrote: 'We are unwilling to engraft upon our law the notion, nowhere so decided, that unemployment benefits may be denied because of raising the bar of the [Fifth] Amendment against rumor or report of disloyalty or because of refusing to answer such rumor or report. The possible abuses of such a doctrine are shocking to imagine.'
Ault Unemployment Compensation Case, 398 Pa. 250, 259, 157 A.2d 375, 380 (1960).

215 United States v. Chicago, M., St. P. & P.R.R., 282 U.S. 311, 328-29 (1931).

216 Frost & Frost Co. v. Railroad Comm'n, 271 U.S. 583, 594 (1926); Note, *Unconstitutional Conditions*, 73 Harv. L. Rev. 1595 (1960); Hale, *Unconstitutional Conditions and Constitutional Rights*, 35 Colum. L. Rev. 321 (1935). The latter is an elaborate study of the older cases on the Federal conditioning power.

217 Speiser v. Randall, 357 U.S. 513, 518 (1958).

218 374 U.S. 398 (1963).

quired recipients to accept suitable employment when it became available, or lose their benefits. An unemployed woman was offered a job requiring her to work Saturdays, but she refused it because she was a Seventh Day Adventist, to whom Saturday was the Sabbath - a day when work was forbidden. The state thereafter refused to pay her any unemployment benefits. The Supreme Court reversed this action:

The ruling forces her to choose between following the precepts of her religion and forfeiting benefits, on the one hand and abandoning one of the precepts of her religion in order to accept work, on the other hand. Governmental imposition of such a choice puts the same kind of burden upon the free exercise of religion as would a fine imposed against appellant for her Saturday worship.

Nor may the South Carolina Court's construction of the statute be saved from constitutional infirmity on the ground that unemployment compensation benefits are not appellant's 'right' but merely a 'privilege.' It is too late in the day to doubt that the liberties of religion and expression may be infringed by the denial of or placing of conditions upon a benefit or privilege ... [To] condition the availability of benefits upon this appellant's willingness to violate a cardinal principle of her religious faith effectively penalizes the free exercise of her constitutional liberties.[219]

In a somewhat different setting, the District of Columbia Court of Appeals reached an analogous result. The Civil Aeronautics Board attempted to issue a letter of registration to an irregular carrier in terms making the registration subject to suspension without a hearing. The agency claimed that, since it was granting the carrier an exemption from statutory requirements, a form of gratuity, it could provide that suspension might be without a hearing. The court said:

The government cannot make a business dependent upon a permit and make an otherwise unconstitutional requirement a condition to the permit.[220]

On the state level there have been some rather similar decisions.[221]

219 *Id.* at 404-06.

220 Standard Airlines v. CAB, 177 F.2d 18, 20 (D.C. Cir. 1949).

221 In California a political test for use of school auditoriums for holding public meetings was upset: 'Nor can it [the State] make the privilege of holding them dependent on conditions that would deprive any members of the public of their constitutional rights. A state is without power to impose an unconstitutional requirement as a condition for granting a privilege even though the privilege is the use of state property.' Danskin v. San Diego Unified School Dist., 28 Cal. 2d 536, 545-46, 171 P.2d 885 (1946); ACLU v. Board of Educ., 55 Cal. 2d 167, 10 Cal. Rptr. 647, 359 P.2d 45 (1961). See also Syrek v. California Unemployment Ins. Appeals Bd., 2 Cal. Rptr. 40, 47 (Ct. App. 1960), *aff'd*, 54 Cal. 2d 519, 7 Cal. Rptr. 97 (1960).

The problem becomes more complicated when a court attempts, as current doctrine seems to require, to 'balance' the deterrence of a constitutional right against some opposing interest. In any balancing process, no weight should be given to the contention that what is at stake is a mere gratuity. It should be recognized that pressure against constitutional rights from denial of a 'gratuity' may be as great or greater than pressure from criminal punishment. And the concept of the public interest should be given a meaning broad enough to include general injury to independence and constitutional rights.[222] It is not possible to consider detailed problems here. It is enough to say that government should gain no power, as against constitutional limitations, by reason of its role as a dispenser of wealth.

B *Substantive Limits*

Beyond the limits deriving from the Constitution, what limits should be imposed on governmental power over largess? Such limits, whatever they may be, must be largely self-imposed and self-policed by legislatures; the Constitution sets only a bare minimum of limitations on legislative policy. The first type of limit should be on relevance. It has proven possible to argue that practically anything in the way of regulation is relevant to some legitimate legislative purpose. But this does not mean that it is desirable for legislatures to make such use of their powers. As Justice Douglas said in the *Barsky* case:

> So far as I know, nothing in a man's political beliefs disables him from setting broken bones or removing ruptured appendixes, safely and efficiently. A practicing surgeon is unlikely to uncover many state secrets in the course of his professional activities.[223]

222 The approach of the Court of Appeals for the Ninth Circuit in Parker v. Lester, 227 F.2d 708 (9th Cir. 1955) might serve as a model: 'What we must balance in the scales here does not involve a choice between any security screening program and the protection of individual seamen. Rather we must weigh against the rights of the individual to the traditional opportunity for notice and hearing, the public need for a *screening system which denies such right to notice and hearing.* Granted that the Government may adopt appropriate means for excluding security risks from employment on merchant vessels, what is the factor of public interest and necessity which requires that it be done in the manner here adopted?'
Id. at 718.
Later the Court added: 'It is not a simple case of sacrificing the interests of a few to the welfare of the many. In weighing the considerations of which we are mindful here, we must recognize that if these regulations may be sustained, similar regulations may be made effective in respect to other groups as to whom Congress may next choose to express its legislative fears.'
Id. at 721.

223 Barsky v. Board of Regents, 347 U.S. 442, 472, 474 (1954) (Douglas, J., dissenting).

Courts sometimes manage, by statutory construction, to place limits on relevance. One example is the judicial reaction to attempts to ban 'disloyal tenants' from government aided housing projects. The Illinois Court said:

The purpose of the Illinois Housing Authorities Act is to eradicate slums and provide housing for persons of low-income class. ... It is evident that the exclusion of otherwise qualified persons solely because of membership in organizations designated as subversive by the Attorney General has no tendency whatever to further such purpose. ... A construction of section 27 which would enable the housing authority to prescribe conditions of eligibility having no rational connection with the purpose of the act would raise serious constitutional questions.[224]

And the Wisconsin Court said:

Counsel for the defendant Authority have failed to point out to this court how the occupation of any units of a federally aided housing project by tenants who may be members of a subversive organization threatens the successful operation of such housing projects.[225]

It is impossible to confine the concept of relevance. But legislatures should strive for a meaningful, judicious concept of relevance if regulation of largess is not to become a handle for regulating everything else.

Besides relevance, a second important limit on substantive power might be concerned with discretion. To the extent possible, delegated power to make rules ought to be confined within ascertainable limits, and regulating agencies should not be assigned the task of enforcing conflicting policies. Also, agencies should be enjoined to use their powers only for the purposes for which they were designed.[226] In a perhaps naïve attempt to accomplish this, Senator Lausche introduced a bill to prohibit United States government contracting officers from using their contracting authority for purposes of duress. This bill in its own words, would prohibit officials from denying contracts, or the right

224 Chicago Housing Authority v. Blackman, 4 Ill. 2d 319, 326, 122 N.E.2d 522, 526 (1954). See also Housing Authority v. Cordova, 130 Cal. App. 2d 883, 279 P.2d 215 (Super. Ct. 1955).

225 Lawson v. Housing Authority, 270 Wis. 269, 287, 70 N.W.2d 605, 615 (1955).

226 Compare Housing Authority v. Cordova, 130 Cal. App. 2d 883, 889, 279 P.2d 215, 218 (1955):

[W]e fail to find in the act, pursuant to which the plaintiff Housing Authority was created, anything to suggest that it is authorized to use the powers conferred upon it to punish subversives or discourage persons from entertaining subversive ideas by denying to such the right of occupying its facilities. ...

to bid on contracts, with the intent of forcing the would-be contractor to perform or refrain from performing any act which such person had no legal obligation to perform or not perform.[227] Although this bill might not be a very effective piece of legislation, it does suggest a desirable objective.

A final limit on substantive power, one that should be of growing importance, might be a principle that policy making authority ought not to be delegated to essentially private organizations. The increasing practice of giving professional associations and occupational organizations authority in areas of government largess tends to make an individual subject to a guild of his fellows. A guild system, when attached to government largess, adds to the feudal characteristics of the system.

C *Procedural Safeguards*

Because it is so hard to confine relevance and discretion, procedure offers a valuable means for restraining arbitrary action. This was recognized in the strong procedural emphasis of the Bill of Rights, and it is being recognized in the increasingly procedural emphasis of administrative law. The law of government largess has developed with little regard for procedure. Reversal of this trend is long overdue.

The grant, denial, revocation, and administration of all types of government largess should be subject to scrupulous observance of fair procedures. Action should be open to hearing and contest, and based upon a record subject to judicial review. The denial of any form of privilege or benefit on the basis of undisclosed reasons should no longer be tolerated.[228] Nor should the same person sit as legislator, prosecutor, judge and jury, combining all the functions of government in such a way as to make fairness virtually impossible. There is no justification for the survival of arbitrary methods where valuable rights are at stake.

Even higher standards of procedural fairness should apply when government action has all the effects of a penal sanction. In *Milwaukee Social Democratic Publishing Co. v. Burleson*,[229] where the postmaster general revoked the

227 109 Cong. Rec. 3258-59 (daily ed., March 4, 1963). The Senator, while denouncing coercion and government by men rather than laws, failed to discuss the question whether there is any 'right' to a government contract.

228 The Administrative Conference of the United States has recommended 'drastic changes' in the procedures by which persons or firms may be debarred from government contracting. The Conference said that such action should not be taken without prior notice, which includes a statement of reasons, and a trial-type hearing before an impartial trier of facts, all within a framework of procedures. Thus, protections would surround even that form of largess which is closest to being a matter within the managerial function of government. Final Report of the Administrative Conference of the United States, p. 15 and Recommendation 'No. 29' (1962).

229 United States *ex rel.* Milwaukee Social Democratic Publishing Co. v. Burleson, 255 U.S. 407 (1921).

second-class mail privileges of a newspaper because he found its contents in violation of the Espionage Act, Mr. Justice Brandeis wrote a far-seeing dissent on the penal nature of such a denial of government benefits:

... It would in practice deprive many publishers of their property without due process of law. Would it not also violate the Fifth Amendment? It would in practice subject publishers to punishment without a hearing by any court. Would it not also violate Article III of the Constitution? It would in practice subject publishers to severe punishment without trial by jury. Would it not also violate the Sixth Amendment? And the punishment inflicted - denial of a civil right - is certainly unusual. Would it also violate the Eighth Amendment? ...

The actual and intended effect of the order was merely to impose a very heavy fine, possibly $150 a day for supposed transgression in the past. But the trial and punishment of crimes is a function which the Constitution, Article III, 2, cl. 3, entrusts to the judiciary. ...

What is in effect a very heavy fine has been imposed by the Postmaster General. It has been imposed because he finds that the publisher has committed the crime of violating the Espionage Act. And that finding is based in part upon 'representations and complaints from sundry good and loyal citizens' with whom the publisher was not confronted. It may be that the court would hold, in view of Article Six in our Bill of Rights, that Congress is without power to confer upon the Postmaster General, or even upon a court, except upon the verdict of a jury and upon confronting the accused with the witnesses against him, authority to inflict indirectly such a substantial punishment as this.[230]

Today many administrative agencies take action which is penal in all but name. The penal nature of these actions should be recognized by appropriate procedures.[231]

Even if no sanction is involved, the proceedings associated with government largess must not be used to undertake adjudications of facts that normally should be made by a court after a trial. Assuming it is relevant to the grant of a license or benefit to know whether an individual has been guilty of a crime or other violation of law, should violations be determined by the agency? The consequence is an adjudication of guilt without benefit of constitutional criminal proceedings with judge, jury, and the safeguards of the Bill of Rights. In our society it is impossible to 'try' a violation of law for any purpose without

230 *Id.* at 434-35 (dissenting opinion).

231 Recently the Supreme Court, in a case involving revocation of citizenship for evading the draft, held that any action that is in fact punishment cannot be taken 'without a prior criminal trial and all its incidents, including indictment, notice, confrontation, jury trial, assistance of counsel, and compulsory process for obtaining witnesses.' Kennedy v. Mendoza-Martinez, 372 U.S. 144, 167 (1963).

'trying' the whole person of the alleged violator. The very adjudication is punishment, even if no consequences are attached. It may be added that an agency should not find 'guilt' after a court has found innocence. The spirit, if not the letter, of the constitutional ban against double jeopardy should prevent an agency from subjecting anyone to a second trial for the same offense.

D *From Largess to Right*

The proposals discussed above, however salutary, are by themselves far from adequate to assure the status of individual man with respect to largess. The problems go deeper. First, the growth of government power based on the dispensing of wealth must be kept within bounds. Second, there must be a zone of privacy for each individual beyond which neither government nor private power can push – a hiding place from the all-pervasive system of regulation and control. Finally, it must be recognized that we are becoming a society based upon relationship and status – status deriving primarily from source of livelihood. Status is so closely linked to personality that destruction of one may well destroy the other. Status must therefore be surrounded with the kind of safeguards once reserved for personality.

Eventually those forms of largess which are closely linked to status must be deemed to be held as of right. Like property, such largess could be governed by a system of regulation plus civil or criminal sanctions, rather than a system based upon denial, suspension and revocation. As things now stand, violations lead to forfeitures – outright confiscation of wealth and status. But there is surely no need for these drastic results. Confiscation, if used at all, should be the ultimate, not the most common and convenient penalty. The presumption should be that the professional man will keep his license, and the welfare recipient his pension. These interests should be 'vested.' If revocation is necessary, not by reason of the fault of the individual holder, but by reason of overriding demands of public policy, perhaps payment of just compensation would be appropriate. The individual should not bear the entire loss for a remedy primarily intended to benefit the community.

The concept of right is most urgently needed with respect to benefits like unemployment compensation, public assistance, and old age insurance. These benefits are based upon a recognition that misfortune and deprivation are often caused by forces far beyond the control of the individual, such as technological change, variations in demand for goods, depressions, or wars. The aim of these benefits is to preserve the self-sufficiency of the individual, to rehabilitate him where necessary, and to allow him to be a valuable member of a family and a community; in theory they represent part of the individual's rightful share in the commonwealth.[232] Only by making such benefits into rights can

232 The phrase is adapted from Hamilton and Till's definition of the word 'property':

the welfare state achieve its goal of providing a secure minimum basis for individual well-being and dignity in a society where each man cannot be wholly the master of his own destiny.[233]

CONCLUSION

The highly organized, scientifically planned society of the future, governed for the good of its inhabitants, promises the best life that men have ever known. In place of the misery and injustice of the past there can be prosperity, leisure, knowledge, and rich opportunity open to all. In the rush of accomplishment, however, not all values receive equal attention; some are temporarily forgotten while others are pushed ahead. We have made provision for nearly everything, but we have made no adequate provision for individual man.

This article is an attempt to offer perspective on the transformation of society as it bears on the economic basis of individualism. The effort has been to show relationships; to bring together drivers' licenses, unemployment insurance, membership in the bar, permits for using school auditorium, and second class mail privileges, in order to see what we are becoming.

Government largess is only one small corner of a far vaster problem. There are many other new forms of wealth: franchises in private businesses, equities in corporations, the right to receive privately furnished utilities and services, status in private organizations. These too may need added safeguards in the

'a general term for the miscellany of equities that persons hold in the commonwealth.' Hamilton & Till, *Property*, 12 Encyc. Soc. Sci.

233 Experts in the field of social welfare have often argued that benefits should rest on a more secure basis, and that individuals in need should be deemed 'entitled' to benefits. See Ten Broek & Wilson, *Public Assistance and Social Insurance – A Normative Evaluation*, 1 U.C.L.A.L. Rev. 237 (1954); Kieth-Lucas, Decisions about People in Need (1957). The latter author speaks of a 'right to assistance' which is a corollary of the 'right to self-determination' (*id.* at 251) and urges public assistance workers to pledge to respect the rights and dignity of welfare clients (*id.* at 263). See also Wynn, Fatherless Families 78-83, 162-63 (1964). The author proposes a 'fatherless child allowance,' to which every fatherless child would be entitled.

Starting from a quite different frame of reference – the problem of the rule of law in the welfare state – Professor Harry Jones has similarly argued that the welfare state must be regarded as a source of new rights, and that such rights as Social Security must be surrounded by substantial and procedural safeguards comparable to those enjoyed by traditional rights of property. Jones, *The Rule of Law and the Welfare State*, 58 Colum. L. Rev. 143, 154-55 (1958). See also Note, *Charity Versus Social Insurance In Unemployment Compensation Laws*, 73 Yale L.J. 357 (1963).

A group called the Ad Hoc Committee on the Triple Revolution recently urged that, in view of the conditions created by the 'cybernation revolution' in the United States, every American should be guaranteed an adequate income as a matter of right whether or not he works. N.Y. Times, March 23, 1964, p. 1, cols. 2-3.

future. Similarly, there are many sources of expanded governmental power aside from largess. By themselves, proposals concerning government largess would be far from accomplishing any fundamental reforms. But, somehow, we must begin.

At the very least, it is time to reconsider the theories under which new forms of wealth are regulated, and by which governmental power over them is measured. It is time to recognize that 'the public interest' is all too often a reassuring platitude that covers up sharp clashes of conflicting values, and hides fundamental choices. It is time to see that the 'privilege' or 'gratuity' concept, as applied to wealth dispensed by government, is not much different from the absolute right of ownership that private capital once invoked to justify arbitrary power over employees and the public.

Above all, the time has come for us to remember what the framers of the Constitution knew so well – that 'a power over a man's subsistence amounts to a power over his will.' We cannot safely entrust our livelihoods and our rights to the discretion of authorities, examiners, boards of control, character committees, regents, or license commissioners. We cannot permit any official or agency to pretend to sole knowledge of the public good. We cannot put the independence of any man – least of all our Barskys and our Anastaplos – wholly in the power of other men.

If the individual is to survive in a collective society, he must have protection against its ruthless pressures. There must be sanctuaries or enclaves where no majority can reach. To shelter the solitary human spirit does not merely make possible the fulfillment of individuals; it also gives society the power to change, to grow, and to regenerate, and hence to endure. These were the objects which property sought to achieve, and can no longer achieve. The challenge of the future will be to construct, for the society that is coming, institutions and laws to carry on this work. Just as the Homestead Act was a deliberate effort to foster individual values at an earlier time, so we must try to build an economic basis for liberty today – a Homestead Act for rootless twentieth century man. We must create a new property.

12 / Liberal-Democracy and Property*

1

Property has always been a central concern of political theory, and of none more so than liberal theory. And nothing has given more trouble in liberal-democratic theory than the liberal property right. I shall suggest that the trouble it has given, both to liberal-democrats and to most of their critics (at least those critics who want to retain the ethical values of liberalism), is due to all of them having stayed within a historically understandable but unnecessarily narrow concept of property. I shall argue that a change in the prevailing concept of property would help to get liberal theory out of its main difficulties; that the change which I shall suggest is legitimate; and that it leaves a theory which can still properly be called liberal. I shall be speaking mainly of post-Millian liberalism, the liberalism of the twentieth century: to emphasize this I shall generally call its theory 'liberal-democratic theory,' which I take to have reached its first positive ethical formulation in the work of John Stuart Mill and T.H. Green (although a purely negative case for liberal-democracy was made a generation earlier by Bentham and James Mill[1]).

The central problem of liberal-democratic theory may be stated as the difficulty of reconciling the liberal property right with that equal effective right of all individuals to use and develop their capacities which is the essential ethical principle of liberal democracy. The difficulty is great. For when the liberal property right is written into law as an individual right to the exclusive use and disposal of parcels of the resources provided by nature and of parcels of the

* An earlier version of this article appeared in *Domination*, edited by Alkis Kontos (University of Toronto Press, 1975).

1 Cf. my *The Life and Times of Liberal Democracy* (Oxford University Press, 1977).

capital created by past work on them, and when it is combined with the liberal system of market incentives and rights of free contract, it leads to and supports a concentration of ownership and a system of power relations between individuals and classes which negates the ethical goal of free and independent individual development. There thus appears to be an insoluble difficulty within the liberal-democratic theory. If, as liberal theory asserts, an individual property right is required by the very necessities of man's nature and condition, it ought not to be infringed or denied. But unless it is seriously infringed or denied, it leads to an effective denial of the equal possibility of individual human fulfilment.

The difficulty was inherent in the liberal theory at least as soon as it had any concern about equality. One way out was proposed by Rousseau, who argued that the property right that is required to permit the realization of the human essence is not the right of unlimited individual appropriation, but a limited right to as much as a man needs to work on. The essentially human property right, being thus limited, would not contradict the equal right: everyone could have it. But Rousseau's (and Jefferson's) way out was no way out. For the capitalist market society, to operate by free contract, required a right of individual appropriation in amounts beyond that limit. And by the nineteenth century the possibility of a society consisting entirely of worker-owners could no longer be seriously entertained. A proletariat existed, as Mill and Green saw. It was the fact that it did exist, and that its condition of life was a denial of humanity, that made sensitive liberals, beginning with Mill and Green, seek some other way out. They did not find one, nor could they have done so from their postulates. For they assumed the need for an unlimited exclusive individual property right, and equated it with the property right which is essential to the very nature and condition of man. So they were back with the basic contradiction.

Liberal-democratic theory has not yet found a way out of this difficulty. I have argued elsewhere[2] that the difficulty could be traced to the deep-rootedness of what I called the possessive individualism of the liberal theory, a set of assumptions about man and society which proved incompatible with democratic aspirations but which could not be given up as long as society was to rely on market incentives and institutions. Alternatively, I have suggested[3] that the difficulty could be stated as an incompatibility between two concepts of the human essence both of which are present within liberal-democratic theory – a concept of man as consumer, desirer, maximizer of utilities, and a concept of man as doer, as exerter and developer of his uniquely human attributes. I do not wish to retract or abandon either of these analyses, but I want now to

2 *The Political Theory of Possessive Individualism: Hobbes to Locke* (Oxford University Press, 1962)

3 'Democratic Theory: Ontology and Technology,' in *Democratic Theory: Essays in Retrieval* (Oxford University Press, 1973).

propose a theoretically simpler statement of the central difficulty, which may point the way to a simpler resolution of it.

The difficulty, I suggest, is not that a liberal-democratic society, in order to have any prospect of achieving its ethical goals, must infringe and thus narrow an individual property right which is derived from the very nature of man. On the contrary, the difficulty is that the individual property right which liberal theory has inferred from the nature of man is already too narrow. What is needed is to broaden it. When this is seen, the old difficulty disappears. I shall argue that we have all been misled by accepting an unnecessarily narrow concept of property, a concept within which it is impossible to resolve the difficulties of any liberal theory. We have treated as the very paradigm of property what is really only a special case. It is time for a new paradigm, within which we may hope to resolve difficulties that could not be resolved within the old.

As I have already shown, property, although it must always be an individual right, need not be confined, as liberal theory has confined it, to a right to exclude others from the use or benefit of some thing, but may equally be an individual right not to be excluded by others from the use or benefit of some thing.[4] When property is so understood, the problem of liberal-democratic theory is no longer a problem of putting limits on the property right, but of supplementing the individual right to exclude others by the individual right not to be excluded by others. The latter right may be held to be the one that is most required by the liberal-democratic ethic, and most implied in a liberal concept of the human essence. The right not to be excluded by others may provisionally be stated as the individual right to equal access to the means of labour and/or the means of life.

2

Let me argue first that there is no logical difficulty about broadening the concept.

The concept of property, like all concepts, has been shaped by theorists. Political concepts are generally shaped by theorists who are not simply grammarians or logicians but who are seeking to justify something. The most solid basis on which to justify an institution or a right is to derive it from the supposed essential nature and needs of man – to show that the human being, to be fully human, requires that institution or that right. The theorists who have shaped the concept of property have generally done this. And no matter how much they might insist that man was a social animal, in the end they had to come down to the individual human being. So the concept of property had to

4 Above, chapter 1, pp. 4-6.

be based on the individual: property could only be seen as a right of an individual, a right derivable from his human essence, a right to some use or benefit of something without the use or benefit of which he could not be fully human. The very idea of property, therefore, is the idea of an individual right.

A second general proposition, which would scarcely have to be stated here were it not for the fact that current common usage appears to contradict it, is that property is a right, not a thing. It is an enforceable claim to some use or benefit of something (and sometimes, but not always, to its disposal): it is not the thing itself.[5]

A third proposition may also be asserted. Inasmuch as the concept of property is the concept of an enforceable claim – an individual claim that will be enforced by society – property is the creation of society, i.e., in modern times, the creation of the state. Property is, as Bentham said, entirely the work of law.

These three propositions are, I think, all that can be asserted of property as such. Property is a right, not a thing. It is an individual right. It is an enforceable claim created by the state.

What I would now point out is that none of these propositions, nor all of them together, require that property be only an individual right to exclude others from the use or benefit of something. Property as an individual right not to be excluded from the use or benefit of something meets these stipulations equally well. Exclusiveness is not logically entailed in the concept of property as an individual right needed to enable men to realize their human essence as moral or rational beings: a right not to be excluded from something is as much an individual right as is the right to exclude others. Both kinds may be created by society or the state, and neither can be created otherwise. Both meet the essential requisites of property, in that both are enforceable claims of individuals to some use or benefit of something. An individual right not to be excluded from something held in common is as much an individual property as is the right to exclude.

How, then, did the idea that property is an exclusive right get so firmly embedded as it has done in the very concept of property? It goes back a long way, although it was not so firmly established in pre-liberal theory as it was from Locke on. From Plato to Bodin, theorists could talk about common property as well as private. But most of the concern was about property as an individual exclusive right. Whether the theorist opposed it, as Plato did for his guardian class, or supported it, as Aristotle and the medieval theorists did within limits, it was property as *meum* and *tuum*, my right to exclude you, that they were mainly concerned with.

Why should these early theorists, who were familiar enough with common

5 Above, chapter 1, pp. 3-4.

property not to think it a contradiction in terms, nevertheless generally have taken property to mean an exclusive right? When we recall that they were deriving property from human needs and the human condition it is not difficult to see a reason for their treating property as an exclusive right. Given their postulate about human inequality they needed to do so. Slaves and serfs they regarded as not fully human, not naturally capable of a fully moral or rational life. These lower ranks therefore did not need, and were not entitled to, a property right, exclusive or otherwise. But citizens, freemen, those above the level of slave or serf, those who were capable of a fully human life, did need a property right which would exclude those others. They had to have an exclusive right. And since they were the only ones who needed a property right at all, the property right as such was taken to be the exclusive right. Strictly, of course, the exclusion of the lower orders did not require that property be taken as the right of each individual to exclude every other individual within as well as beyond the propertied upper orders. But it did require that property be a right to exclude, and this was very easily generalized into an individual right to exclude all others.

This derivation of an exclusive right from the nature of rational man obviously ceases to be valid when all men are asserted to be naturally equally capable of a fully human rational life. And this is the assertion made by liberal theory, from at least Locke on (though Locke was ambiguous about this, as about much else). How, then, could the liberal theorists still see property as only an exclusive right? They could, of course, assert intelligibly enough that each individual needed an exclusive right to a flow of consumable things which would enable him to live. But it had never been merely a property in consumable things that theorists of property had sought to justify by derivation from human needs. The theory of property had always been a theory of rights in land and capital.

Once the natural equal humanity of all men was asserted, the derivation, from human needs, of an exclusive right in land and capital required another postulate. The additional postulate was found by the first generation of liberal theorists, in the seventeenth century: it was the postulate that a man's labour is his own. On this postulate the labour justification of property was built, and it had the effect of reinforcing the concept of exclusiveness. The labour of a man's body, the work of his hands, was seen as peculiarly, exclusively, his. So the right to that with which he has mixed his labour is an exclusive right. This was the principle which Locke made central to the liberal concept of property.

The labour justification of individual property was carried down unquestioned in the liberal theory. Even Bentham, scorning natural rights and claiming to have replaced them by utility, rested the property right on labour. Security of enjoyment of the fruits of one's labour was the reason for property: without a property in the fruits and in the means of labour no one would have an incentive to labour, and utility could not be maximized. Mill and Green also held to the labour justification. 'The institution of property,' Mill wrote, 'when limited to its essential elements, consists in the recognition, in each person, of a right to the exclusive disposal of what he or she have produced by their own exertions, or received either by gift or by fair agreement, without force or fraud, from those who produced it. The foundation of the whole is the right of producers to what they themselves have produced.'[6] Similarly Green: 'The rationale of property, in short, requires that everyone who will conform to the positive condition of possessing it, viz. labour, and the negative condition, viz. respect for it as possessed by others, should, so far as social arrangements can make him so, be a possesser of property himself, and of such property as will at least enable him to develope a sense of responsibility, as distinct from mere property in the immediate necessaries of life.'[7] So the derivation of property in things from the property in one's labour stamped property as an exclusive right from the beginning of the liberal tradition.

Our question – how could liberal theorists regard property as only an exclusive right? – is now answered: they did so by deducing property in things from the property in one's labour. In doing so, they created a new difficulty. For the derivation of the property right from labour was added to, it did not replace, the derivation from the needs of man. It was still, for Locke, the individual right to life that made property necessary; the labour expended merely justified particular appropriations. And for Green it was man's essence as a moral being that required that each should have the property without which he could not fulfil his moral vocation: labour expended was simply an additional requirement. Unfortunately, the added derivation of property from labour conflicted with the more basic and continuing derivation from the human essence.

The derivation from labour, as we have seen, was only needed when, and because, the liberal postulate of natural equality displaced the pre-liberal postulate of natural inequality. But we have also to notice that it was only needed when and because a moral case had to be made for putting every individual on his own in a market society, for letting the allocation of incomes and wealth be done by the market rather than by a political authority. If the market was to do the job of inducing people to work and of allocating the whole product, men had to be given the right to alienate the use of their labour. A man's labour, his own exclusive property, had to be made an alienable property: the right to its exclusive use had to be made something he could sell. And whenever there was not enough free land for everyone, the man who had none had to sell the use of his labour. Those who had no land lost the right to the pro-

6 Above, p. 85.
7 Above, pp. 110-111.

duct of their labour. They lost also the possibility of their labour entitling them to a property in what they had mixed their labour with. They lost, therefore, the effective right to that which they needed in order to be fully human.

In short, in the circumstances in which the labour derivation of the property right was developed, the exclusive property right derived from labour became a denial, for many, of the property right derived from their essential human needs. As soon as a property in things is derived from an exclusive right which is at the same time an alienable right, i.e., the right to or property in one's labour, the damage is done: property as a right needed by all to enable them to express their human essence is denied to many.

3

I have argued that the narrow concept of property as an individual right to exclude others from the use or benefit of something became the paradigm of property for historical rather than logical reasons: in the pre-liberal era it was the postulate of natural human inequality that required exclusiveness; in the liberal era it has been the postulate that a man's labour is his own. Each postulate was, in its time, needed to justify and support the prevailing or desired system of productive relations – slavery or serfdom in the earlier period, the free competitive market system in the later. But, by whichever postulate the narrow paradigm was reached, it led to a denial of property as a right to what is needed to be human.

What are the prospects that liberal-democratic theory may now move beyond the narrow paradigm? The market system is no longer freely competitive, and it is acknowledged not to be an adequate *system*, as witness the myriad government interferences with it and partial take-overs of it that all liberal-democratic societies have deemed necessary. But the monopolistic corporate structure, with government patchwork, which has become the twentieth century version of the market system, is still supported by the supposed sacredness of the exclusive individual property right. And its sacredness rests on no firmer basis than the acceptance of the narrow paradigm of property, that is, on the equation of individual property with exclusive property, an equation which never had any logical standing (except as applied to consumables).

It is surely now time to recognize that the concept of property as the right to exclude others is unnecessarily narrow; that its acceptance as the paradigm of property stands in the way of any rethinking of liberal-democratic problems; and that the assertion of the need for the exclusive right now works against the realization of liberal-democratic goals. If liberal-democratic societies are to be the guarantors of rights essential to the equal possibility of individual members using and developing their human capacities, the individual property right that is needed is not the exclusive right but the right not to be excluded from the use or benefit of those things (including society's productive powers) which are the achievements of the whole society. And the latter right does not contradict, but includes part of, the former, as will be shown in a moment.

Property, as the individual right not to be excluded from the use or benefit of the achievements of the whole society, may take either or both of two forms: (*a*) an equal right of access to the accumulated means of labour, i.e., the accumulated capital of society and its natural resources (with a consequent right to an income from one's work on them); or (*b*) a right to an income from the whole produce of the society, an income related not to work but to what is needed for a fully human life.

Some questions arise when this new paradigm of property, as the individual right not to be excluded, is proposed.

First, is such a new concept of property legitimate, or is it so contradictory of everything property has always meant as to be an improper forcing of the very concept of property? I suggest that it is legitimate, on two grounds. (i) As already noticed, from Plato to Bodin 'property' was not confined to an exclusive individual right: that confinement is a modern phenomenon - an invention of the liberal seventeenth century. (ii) The new paradigm of property, now proposed, is not wholly contrary to the confined liberal concept of property as an exclusive individual right. It does not contradict, but subsumes, as much of that exclusive right as is consistent with the liberal-democratic ethic. For it does include an individual exclusive right to consumables (though not an individual exclusive right to accumulated social capital and parcels of natural resources). This is evident from the definition of property as the right not to be excluded. For that right consists, as we have seen, in either or both a right of access to the means of labour (and consequently a right to an income from work on those), or a right to an income unrelated to work. In either case there is a right to an income, that is, a right to a flow of consumables, and it is assumed that this includes consumables which can be enjoyed only as exclusive property.

A second question arises: is the acceptance of this new paradigm of property consistent with twentieth century liberal-democracy? There are already some indications that it is: that liberal-democratic societies are moving away from the concept of property as exclusion. Practice is moving faster than theory. The theorist may not have seen it yet, but the businessman is perfectly accustomed to looking at property as the right to an income not necessarily related to work, i.e., not derived from one's own exclusive labour. And the politician is coming to see that the right to an income has to be regarded as a right to a share in the annual produce which is increasingly the creation of technology rather than of current labour.

It is true that all the operations of the welfare state, and all the talk of a guaranteed annual income unrelated to work, amount at most to a right to some minimum share in the means of life. They do not amount to a concept of property as a non-exclusive right of access to the means of labour. That concept of property is only clearly consistent with a socialist society. But the individual right of access to the means of labour becomes less important as the need for productive labour decreases. At the theoretical extreme of a fully automated productive system powered by non-human energy there would be no problem about access to the means of labour, for there would be no need for labour (in the sense of productive work that has to be induced). Every move towards that limit reduces the importance of access to the means of labour.

That is not to say that there will be no political problem left as the need for induced labour diminishes. On the contrary, it is to say that the economic problem which has been central to the liberal tradition will become purely a political problem, a problem of democratic control over the uses to which the amassed capital of a society is put. That is a problem that can be tackled with the concept of property as a right not to be excluded, but cannot be handled with the narrower concept of property as an exclusive right.

A third question remains: would a liberal-democratic theory which embodied the new concept of property still be in any significant sense a liberal theory? That depends, of course, on what you put into liberalism. If you insist that it must mean all the market freedoms - not just consumers' choice, and the freedom of the independent producer, but freedom of capitalist appropriation (with which liberalism was largely identified in the eighteenth and nineteenth centuries) - then clearly a political theory built around the new concept of property could not be called liberal. But if you take liberalism to be essentially an assertion of the right of all to full human development (as Mill and Green tried to make it), then a political theory built around the new concept of property is eminently qualified as a liberal theory. I argue simply that a new, less historically inhibited, paradigm of property would not destroy but would liberate the essential liberal-democratic theory.